Harness the
Power of Big Data

About the Authors

Paul C. Zikopoulos, B.A., M.B.A., is the Director of Technical Professionals for IBM Software Group's Information Management division and additionally leads the World-Wide Competitive Database and Big Data Technical Sales Acceleration teams. Paul is an award-winning writer and speaker with over 19 years of experience in Information Management. In 2012, Paul was chosen by SAP as one of its Top 50 Big Data Twitter influencers (@BigData_paulz). Paul has written more than 350 magazine articles and 16 books, including *Understanding Big Data: Analytics for Enterprise Class Hadoop and Streaming Data*; *Warp Speed, Time Travel, Big Data, and More: DB2 10 New Features*; *DB2 pureScale: Risk Free Agile Scaling*; *DB2 Certification for Dummies*; and *DB2 for Dummies*. In his spare time, Paul enjoys all sorts of sporting activities, including running with his dog Chachi, avoiding punches in his MMA training, and trying to figure out the world according to Chloë—his daughter. You can reach him at: paulz_ibm@msn.com.

Dirk deRoos, B.Sc., B.A., is IBM's World-Wide Technical Sales Leader for IBM InfoSphere BigInsights. Dirk spent the past two years helping customers with BigInsights and Apache Hadoop, identifying architecture fit, and advising early stage projects in dozens of customer engagements. Dirk recently coauthored a book on this subject area, *Understanding Big Data: Analytics for Enterprise Class Hadoop and Streaming Data* (McGraw-Hill Professional, 2012). Prior to this, Dirk worked in the IBM Toronto Software Development Lab on the DB2 database development team where he was the Information Architect for all of the DB2 product documentation. Dirk has earned two degrees from the University of New Brunswick in Canada: a Bachelor of Computer Science, and a Bachelor of Arts (Honors English). You can reach him at: dirk .ibm@gmail.com or on Twitter at @Dirk_deRoos.

Krishnan Parasuraman, B.Sc., M.Sc., is part of IBM's Big Data industry solutions team and serves as the CTO for Digital Media. In his role, Krishnan works very closely with customers in an advisory capacity, driving Big Data solution architectures and best practices for the management of Internet-scale analytics. He is an authority on the use of Big Data technologies, such as Hadoop and MPP data warehousing platforms, for solving analytical problems in the online digital advertising, customer intelligence, and real-time marketing space. He speaks regularly at industry events and writes for trade publications and blogs. Prior to his current role, Krishnan worked in research, product development, consulting, and technology marketing across multiple disciplines within information management. Krishnan has enabled data warehousing and customer analytics solutions for large media and consumer electronics organizations, such as Apple, Microsoft, and Kodak. He holds an M.Sc. degree in computer science from the University of Georgia. You can keep up with his musings on Twitter @kparasuraman.

Thomas Deutsch, B.A, M.B.A., is a Program Director for IBM's Big Data team. Tom played a formative role in the transition of Hadoop-based technology from IBM Research to IBM Software Group and continues to be involved with IBM Research around Big Data. Tom has spent several years helping customers, identifying architecture fit, developing business strategies, and managing early stage projects across more than 300 customer engagements with technologies such as Apache Hadoop, InfoSphere BigInsights (IBM's Hadoop distribution), InfoSphere Streams, Cassandra, and other emerging NoSQL technologies. Tom has coauthored a book and multiple thought papers about Big Data, and is a columnist for *IBM Data Management* magazine. He's a frequent speaker at industry conferences and a member of the IBM Academy of Technology. Prior to this, Tom worked in the Information Management CTO's office, focused on emerging technologies; he came to IBM through the FileNet acquisition, where he was its flagship product's lead product manager. With more than 20 years in the industry, and as a veteran of two startups, Tom is an expert on the technical, strategic, and business information management issues facing the enterprise today. Tom earned a B.A. degree from Fordham University in New York and an M.B.A. degree from the University of Maryland University College.

David Corrigan, B.A., M.B.A., is currently the Director of Product Marketing for IBM's InfoSphere portfolio, which is focused on managing trusted information. His primary focus is driving the messaging and strategy for the InfoSphere portfolio of information integration, data quality, master data management (MDM), data lifecycle management, and data privacy and security. Prior to his current role, David led the product management and product marketing teams for IBM's MDM portfolio, and has worked in the Information Management space for over 12 years. David holds an M.B.A.

degree from York University's Schulich School of Business, and an undergraduate degree from the University of Toronto.

James Giles, BSEE, B.Math, MSEE, Ph.D., is an IBM Distinguished Engineer and currently a Senior Development Manager for the IBM InfoSphere BigInsights and IBM InfoSphere Streams Big Data products. Previously, Jim managed the Advanced Platform Services group at the IBM T. J. Watson Research Center, where Jim and his team developed the technology for the System S stream-processing prototype, which is now the basis for InfoSphere Streams. Jim joined IBM in 2000 as a Research Staff Member and led research and development in content distribution, policy management, autonomic computing, and security. He received his Ph.D. in electrical and computer engineering from the University of Illinois at Urbana-Champaign, where he studied covert communications in data networks. Jim has several patents and is the recipient of an IBM Corporate Award for his work on stream computing.

About the Technical Editor
Roman B. Melnyk, B.A., M.A., Ph.D., is a senior member of the DB2 Information Development team. During more than 18 years at IBM, Roman has written numerous books, articles, and other related materials about DB2. Roman coauthored *DB2 Version 8: The Official Guide*; *DB2: The Complete Reference*; *DB2 Fundamentals Certification for Dummies*; and *DB2 for Dummies*.

Harness the Power of Big Data

The IBM Big Data Platform

Paul C. Zikopoulos
Dirk deRoos
Krishnan Parasuraman
Thomas Deutsch
David Corrigan
James Giles

New York   Chicago   San Francisco
Lisbon   London   Madrid   Mexico City
Milan   New Delhi   San Juan
Seoul   Singapore   Sydney   Toronto

The **McGraw·Hill** Companies

Cataloging-in-Publication Data is on file with the Library of Congress

McGraw-Hill books are available at special quantity discounts to use as premiums and sales promotions, or for use in corporate training programs. To contact a representative, please e-mail us at bulksales@mcgraw-hill.com.

Harness the Power of Big Data: The IBM Big Data Platform

The contents of this book represent those features that may or may not be available in the current release of any products mentioned within this book despite what the book may say. IBM reserves the right to include or exclude any functionality mentioned in this book for the current or subsequent releases of InfoSphere Streams, InfoSphere BigInsights, the family of IBM PureData Systems, or any other IBM products mentioned in this book. Decisions to purchase any IBM software should not be made based on the features said to be available in this book. In addition, any performance claims made in this book aren't official communications by IBM; rather, they are the results observed by the authors in unaudited testing. The views expressed in this book are also those of the authors and not necessarily those of IBM Corporation.

34567890   DOC DOC   109876543

ISBN   978-0-07-180817-0
MHID   0-07-180817-5

Sponsoring Editor	Acquisitions Coordinator	Production Supervisor
Paul Carlstroem	Ryan Willard	Jean Bodeaux
Editorial Supervisor	**Technical Editor**	**Composition**
Janet Walden	Roman B. Melnyk	Cenveo Publisher Services
Project Manager	**Copy Editor**	**Illustration**
Harleen Chopra, Cenveo Publisher Services	Margaret Berson	Cenveo Publisher Services
	Proofreader	**Art Director, Cover**
	Emilia Thiuri	Jeff Weeks

My sixteenth book in my nineteenth year at IBM. Looking back, as this collection of books literally occupies an entire shelf, one thing strikes me: the caliber of people I work with. From this authoring team (some of whom are newfound friends), to past ones, I'm luckily surrounded by some of the smartest and most passionate professionals in the world: IBMers—and it's an honor to learn from you all.

To the people who have created an environment in which I never want to slow down (Martin Wildberger, Bob Picciano, Dale Rebhorn, and Alyse Passarelli), thanks for your mentorship and belief in me, but also your patience with some of those 2 A.M. run-on notes with the red markup.

It's interesting the toll that writing a book takes on your life. For example, I found that my golf handicap experienced double-digit percentage growth after I started to write this one, leaving my retirement portfolio green with envy. (I'd be remiss if I didn't thank Durham Driving Range's Dave Dupuis for always greeting me with a smile and listening to me complain as he watches the odd—perhaps more than odd—ball shank hard right.) Although that stuff doesn't matter, the personal impact and trade-offs you have to make to write a book lead me to my most important thank-you I've got to give: to my family, Chloë, Kelly, and the spirit of Grace. You gals keep me strong and in overdrive.

—Paul Zikopoulos

To Sandra, Erik, and Anna: the truly wonderful people I have in my life. Thanks for giving me the time to help make this happen and for your patience with me! I would also like to dedicate my work on this book to my beloved Netherlands national football team, who, yet again, broke my heart this year. May the collaboration of the many authors on this book be an example to you of what teamwork looks like! (Mental note: Never work on a book with a fellow Dutchman.)

—Dirk deRoos

I would like to thank the Netezza team for all the fond memories and good times; and to Brad Terrell…for being my Force Field.

—Krishnan Parasuraman

I would like to thank (again) my slightly less patient (from last year when I thanked them) family for their patience during this process. I would also like to thank Paul Zikopoulos; I've lost count of the number of drinks I owe him. Finally, thanks to Nagui Halim, John McPherson, Hamid Pirahesh, and Neil Isford for being such good dance partners in emerging compute spaces.

—Thomas Deutsch

I'd like to thank Karen, Kaitlyn, and Alex for all of their love and support. I'd also like to thank all of my integration and governance colleagues for continuing to drive a strategy that makes this a market-leading platform and a very interesting place to work.

—David Corrigan

I would like to dedicate this book to the tireless IBM Big Data development and research teams worldwide. This book would not be possible without the countless innovations and commitment to building great technology for the enterprise. Thank you all!

—James Giles

CONTENTS

Part I
The Big Deal About Big Data

Part II
Analytics for Big Data at Rest

Part III
Analytics for Big Data in Motion

Part IV
Unlocking Big Data

Part V
Big Data Analytic Accelerators

Part VI
Integration and Governance in a Big Data World

FOREWORD

"Big Data" is a curious phrase. Since I first encountered it some three-and-a-half years ago, it has come to be one of the IT industry's dominant trends, and yet I don't believe I have come across a single person in that time who will admit to liking the term.

Attend any data management conference or webinar and you'll hear the same thing: vendors, practitioners, commentators, and analysts describing how unsuitable the term Big Data is, before launching into an explanation of how important Big Data is to their business, or the reverse. Unlike many other industry buzzwords, the origins of Big Data cannot be traced back to a specific vendor or individual. It is not uncommon, therefore, to hear those vendors, practitioners, commentators, and analysts complaining about the lack of definition before introducing their own description of what Big Data means to them.

There is very rarely a significant difference from one definition to the next, however. While the term Big Data might be almost universally unloved, it is also now almost universally understood to refer to the realization of greater business intelligence by storing, processing, and analyzing data that was previously ignored due to the limitations of traditional data management technologies.

Those limitations have come to be defined by a combination of words beginning with the letter "V": typically volume, variety, and velocity, but with others increasingly added to the mix (more about this in a moment).

The increased use of interactive applications and websites—as well as sensors, meters, and other data-generating machines—means that an increasing volume of data is being produced. At the same time, the cost of storage, processing, and bandwidth has dropped enormously, while network access has increased significantly.

The result is that it is now more economically feasible to store, process, and analyze data that was previously ignored or under-utilized—such as web and network log data, or social media content—to ensure that the business is performing adequately and efficiently, and to track customer sentiment and generate new revenue-generation opportunities.

Much of the data that is being produced by these interactive applications and data-generating machines lacks the structure to make it suitable for storage and analysis in traditional relational databases and data warehouses. In addition to this variety, the data is also being produced at a velocity that is often beyond the performance limits of traditional systems.

It is interesting to note that since the first edition of this book, the authors have added a fourth "V": veracity. This succinctly highlights the fact that tried and tested data management principles—data quality, data cleansing, master data management, and data governance—are not completely redundant in a world of Big Data. In fact, they are increasingly being seen as critical factors in the ability of users to ensure they can create another "V"—value—from this increased volume, variety, and velocity of data.

The ongoing importance of existing data management techniques also illustrates another important point about Big Data: that new data management and analytic technologies are being implemented to complement rather than replace traditional approaches to data management and analytics.

Thus Apache Hadoop does not replace the data warehouse and NoSQL databases do not replace transactional relational databases, while neither MapReduce nor streaming analytics approaches replace existing SQL-based reporting and analytics tools. As stated earlier, Big Data is about adopting new technologies that enable the storage, processing, and analysis of data that was previously ignored.

It is also about the adoption of new business processes and analytics approaches that take advantage of that data. As an industry analyst company focused on innovation and the development and adoption of new technologies, 451 Research has observed that the adoption of nontraditional data management technologies is being driven not just by the volume, variety, velocity, and veracity of data, but also by changes in the manner in which users want to interact with their data.

451 Research uses the term "Total Data" to describe the management approach being embraced by early adopters to process and explore Big Data using the range of new technologies available. "Total Data" is not an alternative to "Big Data." We believe that if your data is "big," the way you manage it should be "total."

Specifically, we look at three key aspects of the way in which users want to interact with their data: totality, exploration, and frequency. *Totality* refers to the increased desire to process and analyze all available data, rather than analyzing a sample of data and extrapolating the results; *exploration* relates to analytic approaches in which the schema is defined in response to the nature of the query; and *frequency* refers to the desire to increase the rate of analysis in order to generate more accurate and timely business intelligence.

Since it is important to consider the ongoing importance of existing data management, processing, and analytic approaches, we add a fourth factor: dependency, which relates to the need to balance investment in existing technologies and skills with the adoption of new techniques.

While the authors of this book may not use the term "Total Data," we see evidence of these four factors influencing the technology and business process choices being made by businesses in the numerous Big Data success stories contained within these pages, as well as the portfolio of technologies being assembled by IBM to address its customers' Big Data needs.

This brings us back to definitions, and the futility of getting hung up on the meaning of Big Data rather than embracing the associated new data management technologies and approaches. IBM's research has highlighted that companies that invest in analytics and understanding their business and their customers are significantly more likely to achieve competitive advantage over their rivals.

Whatever you might think of the term Big Data, the adoption of new data processing technologies and techniques that complement established analytics approaches promises to deliver new levels of business intelligence, customer service, and revenue opportunities. Many companies are finding that is not something they can afford to ignore.

M. Aslett

Matt Aslett
Research Manager, Data Management and Analytics, 451 Research

PREFACE

Executive Letter from Bob Picciano

When the technology market shifts, big things happen. Opportunities arise and risks are confronted. Organizations and practitioners need to understand and prepare for such change. Part of this process includes being on the lookout for the emerging "factoids" that tell us in advance that we're approaching a shift, lift, rift, or cliff. But even more interesting is that emotional sense of promise for what a new space might bring. In our industry, we often see the predictive data, and we're told about the perils in failing to act. But rarely do we also get that sense of pure excitement about a whole new frontier that is being invented, discovered, forged, and fostered. When both elements are present simultaneously, really interesting things start to happen. Think about it for a moment…when was the last time you had the opportunity to be part of an inflection point? Big Data is one of those rare opportunities.

Studies strongly indicate marked performance differences in those organizations that embrace the opportunities around the broad space of analytics. Our own study, conducted jointly by IBM and MIT, showed that organizations that focus on analytics significantly outperform their segment peers on the key business metrics of growth, earnings, and performance. Consider the emotional side of this. For years, so many of us in the field of analytics and information management have worked to rapidly turn any type of structured or unstructured data into useful insights to differentiate performance. Now, with the emergence of Big Data, for the first time we can really get a sense that the hurdles of volume, variety, velocity, and veracity can be tackled and overcome.

Big Data represents a huge opportunity for businesses across many problem domains. As a new wave of technology emerges to help realize the promise, there also comes a set of challenges. There is a need for new skills; a need to handle larger data volumes, strains on data quality, and countless evolutions of data types, among a host of other challenges. Very few companies can afford to hire and train thousands of new workers just to address this new challenge as a sideline. Our clients demand a short time to value for their Big Data investments because they seek leadership in their respective marketplaces. One of the most compelling ways to do that is through a platform with a maniacal focus on consumability, instantiated by a well thought out and planned tools ecosystem, declarative languages, and techniques that accelerate the ability to quickly drive results. This is *exactly* what IBM is focusing on and delivering to our clients and partners…today.

Some aspects of the traditional ways in which data is structured and managed also apply in the Big Data arena. But new demands will be placed on areas like data governance, the integration of traditional sources, and security. IBM is focused on delivering in these domain areas, in addition to the mainstream Big Data areas.

IBM has long believed in "workload optimized systems." You see this manifested today in our IBM PureSystems and IBM PureData Systems family, which delivers extraordinary economies of scale while reducing labor impact and increasing compute density. The same dynamics are needed in the world of Big Data. There are different tasks to perform, and we have a set of finely tuned, highly consumable engines for them. We have a non-forked version of Hadoop (InfoSphere BigInsights), so the implementation remains pure, with a number of committers contributing assets across the entire Apache Hadoop ecosystem. Looking at our one hundred plus years of history, it's evident that IBM is also committed to providing the most open systems possible, and it's key for us to contribute to the Big Data open source movement. Besides Hadoop, IBM's open source contributions include Apache Derby, Lucene, Jakarta, Geronimo, Eclipse, DRDA, Xerces, parts of Linux, and much more. In fact, many of the open source contributions, along with IBM differentiating technologies, were showcased in unison by the famous Watson win on the popular game show *Jeopardy!* Quite simply, we believe that strong partnership with the open source community helps the entire domain innovate at a more rapid rate, in service of what our clients need to solve the more challenging business problems that they face.

IBM has workload-optimized systems for deep analytics and operational analytics. And if you want to apply analytics to data in motion, we have that too (InfoSphere Streams), because one of the most important opportunities resides within the emerging field of in-motion analytics. Today, most implementations that we see are in the area of at-rest analytics. While IBM is a leader in that space; showcased by the family of analytics-based IBM Pure-Data Systems (which incorporate Netezza and DB2 technologies), InfoSphere BigInsights, and more. But the analytics of data in motion will also drive more valuable insight and decision making for front office systems of engagement, where seconds—even micro-seconds—can matter. IBM is perhaps the only innovator combining in-motion and at-rest analytics in one platform.

Finally, organizations seem to really struggle in trying to get their hands around the data assets that they already own, and are often guilty of not knowing what they could already know. Enterprise discovery and search services are needed, and they have to be built from the ground up for Big Data. InfoSphere Data Explorer (technology acquired through IBM's Vivisimo acquisition) has specialized indexing techniques and social algorithms that provide exactly this.

Big Data is flowing like an enormous river, a huge, nearly untapped, resource. What are you doing to tap that stream and make Big Data work for you? You have to decide how you will improve your skills, capabilities, and involvement to take advantage of all that Big Data has to offer. This book is an excellent way to start your journey.

I would like to thank Paul, Dirk, Krishnan, Tom, David, and James for writing this book. They are an outstanding group whose dedication to our clients and to their fellow IBMers is unmatched. Behind them is a large eco-system of IBMers that make the IBM Big Data platform possible. It's a privilege, not a right, to work with good people. The team behind the IBM Big Data platform is an outstanding group of people who are passionate about our customers' success, dedicated to their work, and continually innovate. Thank you, and enjoy the book.

Bob Picciano
IBM, General Manager, Software Sales

ACKNOWLEDGMENTS

Collectively, we want to thank the following people, without whom this book would not have been possible: John Choi, Nancy Kopp, Phil Francisco, Shivakumar (Shiv) Vaithyanathan, Roger Rea, Robert Uleman, Tina Chen, Bert Van der Linden, Hui Liao, Klaus Roder, Kevin Foster, Nagui Halim, Cindy Saracco, Vijay R. Bommireddipalli, Tony Curcio, Mike Spicer, Mike Koranda, Stewart Tate, Gary Robinson, Kayla Martell, Bill O'Connell, Anshul Dawra, Andrey Balmin, Manny Corniel, our Research and Development teams, and all the others in our business who make personal sacrifices day in and day out to bring you the IBM Big Data platform. We also want to thank Dan Wolfson, Jeff Pollock, Rick Clements, Paula Sigmon, Aarti Borkar, and the entire InfoSphere Information Integration and Governance team for their help as well.

Tracey Mustacchio, Jerome Pesenti, and Mark Myers joined IBM as part of the Vivisimo acquisition and helped us with this information—welcome and thanks! There's a special team of Big Data superstars at our disposal, we use and abuse them, and they seem to love it. So we wanted to thank Stephen Brodsky, Anjul Bhambhri, Shankar Venkataraman, and Rafael Coss too.

Jeff Jonas deserves a special thanks for his puzzle inspiration; if you ever get a chance to see this guy speak, don't miss it: you'll be wildly entertained and begin to think differently about certain things—albeit not just technology.

A special thanks to Linda Snow and Lauri Saft, for their passion and for being our pro-bono (we forgot to tell them that ahead of time) side-reviewers. We also want to specifically thank Chris Eaton, Steven Sit, and George Lapis for working with some of us on the last book; some of that effort can be found in this one.

To our technical editor, Roman Melnyk; he's like the Betamax of technical editors, they just don't make them like that anymore, and we thank you for your dedication to our project. We don't pay you nearly enough (and we don't have the money to pay more, so don't even ask); we'll pay you back with our tax-exempt words of thanks.

Finally, we want to thank (although at times we cursed) Susan Visser, Steve Miller, and Linda Currie for getting the book in place; an idea is an idea, but it takes people like this to help get an idea off a Buffalo wings–stained napkin and into your hands without the mess. Our editing and production team—Harleen Chopra, Jean Bodeaux, Janet Walden, Margaret Berson, and Emilia Thiuri—all played a key role behind the scenes and we want to extend our thanks for that. Our thanks isn't enough—when they had to deal with unfair requests in the moments before print, these ladies put it into overdrive to get this book in the hands of our clients sooner than later. It means a lot to work with such success-oriented professionals. And, of course, to our McGraw-Hill guru, Paul Carlstroem—there's a reason why we specifically wanted to work with you: passion, credibility, and knowing when to push and pull (by the way, that extra week came in handy!).

ABOUT THIS BOOK

This book provides an overview of the IBM Information Management Big Data platform. It's intended for a broad audience, ranging from those who are brand new to Big Data, to those on the business and management side, to architects, and to developers who want a glimpse into the technical details that underpin this platform. That said, we couldn't cover everything in this book. *Harness the Power of Big Data: The IBM Big Data Platform* is meant to be a jumping-off point, igniting a desire to explore more of this platform and leave you with a strong understanding of what makes it so different. You don't have to read this book from front to back, because it's organized into six parts that enable you to jump into the specific topics in which you're interested. That said, we do reference other parts of the book, so you will benefit the most if you read it from front to back.

The chapters in Part I, "The Big Deal About Big Data," show you how to identify and define what Big Data is (Chapter 1), apply usage patterns to business scenarios to avoid the doomsday Big Data "science project" (Chapter 2), and articulate the key components that make up the IBM Big Data platform (Chapter 3). Having a strong understanding of the IBM Big Data platform capabilities gives you some insight into how and why we built it the way we did (integrated, governed, well tooled, accelerated, consumable, and capable). That said, even if you don't make IBM a partner on your Big Data journey, you're going to discover the right questions to ask whatever partner you choose. (We think when you ask these question to other vendors, you'll start to really appreciate what IBM has to offer in this space.) Unfortunately, some folks believe that Big Data is just Hadoop; after reading Chapter 3, we think that you'll be able to articulate why Hadoop is critical to a Big Data platform, but only as part of a much broader ecosystem that includes many Big Data capabilities, such as analytics, visualization, search, and more.

In Part II, "Analytics for Big Data at Rest," we cover the optimized IBM Big Data platform repositories for data at rest. Chapter 4 describes the IBM

PureData System for Analytics (formerly known as Netezza) and some light references to the IBM PureData System for Operational Analytics (formerly known as the IBM Smart Analytics System). The family of IBM PureData Systems represents the culmination of years of learned expertise and deployment patterns, packaged together as an expertly integrated system with an optimized and balanced runtime engine for any Big Data tasks at hand. Chapter 5 describes Hadoop. You'll learn about IBM's commitment to Hadoop, IBM's Hadoop distribution (called IBM InfoSphere BigInsights), enterprise hardening features that IBM delivers for Hadoop (some of which can be run on Cloudera's Hadoop distribution), and more.

"Analytics for Big Data in Motion" is the title of Part III, and it's an area in which IBM has differentiated itself from any other vendor in the marketplace. In fact, few Big Data vendors even talk about it. IBM is well travelled in this area, with a high-velocity Big Data engine, called InfoSphere Streams, which we cover in Chapter 6. We show you how it integrates with at-rest repositories, enabling you to move harvested at-rest analytic artifacts from the interior of the business to the frontier, thereby transforming your analysis from a forecast model to a *nowcast* model.

Part IV, "Unlocking Big Data," details the components of the IBM Big Data platform that come from the Vivisimo acquisition earlier in 2012. InfoSphere Data Discovery (Data Discovery) is the IBM name for this suite of technologies that includes industry-leading enterprise search, security considerations, a front-end tooling framework for customization of personalized push/pull search, and more. Data Discovery presents an interesting opportunity for many companies to get started with Big Data; after all, shouldn't you have a crisp understanding of what Big Data assets you already have before starting a new Big Data project? The Vivisimo technology literally took the enterprise landscape by storm with its uncanny ability to find data assets of different variety, size, and shape. We talk about this technology in Chapter 7, as well as highlighting a number of very compelling client success stories. After reading this chapter, we think you'll agree that the word *Vivisimo!* could replace Eureka! (for "I found it!").

We cover many of the things that IBM has put in place to make the IBM Big Data platform *consumable*. We highlight that term because it's core to our platform. Quite simply, our clients don't have unlimited pools of resources to get Big Data solutions working for them. For that reason, the IBM Big Data platform comes with a rich set of toolkits and accelerators for text analytics and machine learning (among others), a vast array of samples, enriched tooling environments, and declarative languages that are purpose-built and optimized for specific Big Data tasks at hand. Collectively, these efforts flatten the time to analytics, enabling our clients to monetize their data with unprecedented speed and agility—showcasing some of these IBM Big Data platform characteristics is the focus of Part V.

Chapter 8 provides details about the Advanced Text Analytics Toolkit. Text analytics requires a different set of optimization choices than a Big Data workload that crunches through millions of files. In the Hadoop benchmark world, you see many references to `grep` or `terasort`, which stress the I/O characteristics of the cluster. However, text analytics is heavily dependent on CPU. The IBM Big Data platform has a declarative language called Annotated Query Language (AQL), which is part of this toolkit. Writing AQL programs is facilitated by an Eclipse plug-in that provides design-time assistance, context-sensitive help, and other rapid application development features that are associated with a typical IDE. The toolkit includes a cost-based optimizer that understands the resource requirements of text analysis and optimizes the execution plan with this consideration (IBM, the company that invented SQL and its associated cost-based optimization processing engines is doing the same for AQL).

You'll build your analytical text-based Big Data applications 50 percent faster than using alternative approaches, they will run up to ten times faster (that's what we found when we compared it to some alternatives), and the results you get will be more precise and complete (read Chapter 8 for more details).

Chapter 9 describes the three accelerators that IBM has delivered for specific Big Data usage patterns: machine data, social media, and call detail records (CDRs). These accelerators reflect years of client interaction and are packaged together for quick deployment. What's more, they showcase the component integration of the IBM Big Data platform, combining text analytics, Streams, and BigInsights.

The book finishes with Part VI, "Integration and Governance in a Big Data World." What's true in the relational world applies to the Big Data world as well. Chapter 10 provides a brief overview of Big Data governance, from reducing the surface area security profile of data at rest, to archiving, to trusting the lineage of that data, and more. Chapter 11 highlights the various integration components within the IBM Big Data platform itself, and across other IBM and non-IBM products.

We recognize that your time is precious and we thank you for the time that you're about to invest in reading this book. We hope that we've provided technical readers with enough information to understand the capabilities of the IBM Big Data platform, and business readers with sufficient high-level strategic information. We believe that by the time you've read this book, you'll not only be well versed in Big Data, its usage patterns, and the technology criteria that should be applied to the platform of choice, but you'll have the knowledge and confidence to contribute to your company's Big Data strategy. In short, you'll THINK BIGger!

Part I

The Big Deal About Big Data

1

What Is Big Data?

The term *Big Data* is a bit of a misnomer. Truth be told, we're not even big fans of the term—despite the fact that it's so prominently displayed on the cover of this book—because it implies that other data is somehow small (it might be) or that this particular type of data is large in size (it can be, but doesn't have to be). For this reason, we think it's best to devote an entire chapter to the task of explaining exactly what Big Data is.

Why Is Big Data Important?

Before you try to understand what Big Data is, you should know why Big Data matters to business. In a nutshell, the quest for Big Data is directly attributable to analytics, which has evolved from being a business *initiative* to a business *imperative*.

In fact, we'd say that analytics has caused a bifurcation of industry participants: some are leaders and some are followers. It's hard to overlook the impact that analytics has had on organizations during the last decade or so. IBM's Institute of Business Value, in partnership with MIT's *Sloan Management Review*, published the results of a study in a paper called *The New Intelligent Enterprise*. This paper concluded that organizations that achieve a competitive advantage with analytics are over two times more likely to substantially outperform their industry peers. Think about that for a moment: Analytics (specifically, analytics enriched with Big Data) will help you to outperform your competitors, so if your business is simply curious about Big Data, and your competitors are more than curious—well, you get the point.

Big Data is all about better analytics on a broader spectrum of data, and therefore represents an opportunity to create even more differentiation among industry peers. This is a key point that's often overlooked: no one has ever delivered a single penny of value out of storing data. Many vendors are talking about Big Data, but we're not seeing much more than the ability to store large volumes of data, leaving the organization to "roll their own" applications without much help to make sense of it all. Real value can only emerge from a consumable analytics platform that saves you from having to build applications from scratch—one that effectively flattens the time-to-insight curve. Big Data is truly all about analytics.

The joint IBM/MIT study described in *The New Intelligent Enterprise* also found that the number of enterprises using analytics in an attempt to create a competitive advantage had jumped by almost 60 percent since its previous iteration, which was conducted one year earlier. The study concludes with the observation that nearly six out of ten organizations are now differentiating through analytics.

Quite simply, early analytics adopters are extending their leadership. If you want to lead, you have to know analytics, and if you want to be on the forefront of analytics, you have to put your arms around Big Data.

Now, the "What Is Big Data?" Part

A number of years ago, IBM introduced its Smarter Planet campaign ("Instrumented, Interconnected, and Intelligent"), which foreshadowed the Big Data craze that hit the IT landscape just a few short years later.

We think that Walmart's push to use radio frequency identification (RFID) tags for supply chain optimization is a great story that illustrates the dawn of the Big Data era. RFID is a great example of machine-speed-generated data that could be collected and analyzed. Today, the world has become much more instrumented and interconnected thanks to many technologies, including RFID tagging. Examples of RFID technology today include tracking products at the skid level or the stock-keeping unit (SKU) level; tracking livestock; using badges to track conference attendees; monitoring the temperature of food in transit; tracking luggage (from our experience as frequent travelers, there's lots of room for improvement here); monitoring the health of a bridge's concrete structure; and monitoring the heat-related expansion of railroad tracks for speed regulation, among thousands of other use cases.

If you would like the opportunity to work with IBM's Software architects, Research Scientists or Problem Solvers to discuss ideas you are exploring, challenges you might be facing or to simply help you think through a problem, please provide a brief description of your problem, challenge or idea, fill in your information below and submit today. IBM will assemble a team for your THINK Workshop and contact you for your availability to **THINK** with IBM.

Connect with me @www.linkedin.com/pub/jane-washington/24/a20/787/

Follow me @janemwashington

washing@us.ibm.com

914.299.1566

Name: _____

Consumer _____ VES _____ Wireless _____ Corporate _____ Network _____ Other: _____

Dept Name: _____ Title: _____

Email: _____ Phone: _____

Description of your **THINK** Workshop Request: _____

THINK

A Forum on the Future of Leadership

Presented by **IBM**

In 2005, there were an estimated 1.3 billion RFID tags in circulation; by the end of 2011, this number had risen to 30 billion! Now consider that RFID price points are expected to drop below 1 US cent by 2015, and that there are all kinds of other sensory and measurement technologies already available; in fact, we'd argue at this point, the world can pretty much measure almost anything it wants.

From an instrumentation perspective, what doesn't have some amount of coding in it today? Just look at your car: you can't diagnose a problem these days without hooking a computer up to it. Today's hardware network switches have more software code than components in them. The latest passenger airplanes are instrumented with over one billion lines of code that generates about 10 terabytes (TB) of data, per engine, during every half hour of operation. Let's put that in perspective: A single flight from London's Heathrow Airport to John F. Kennedy in New York would generate about 650TB of data! That's likely more data than what you have sitting in your warehouse today. Most of this data is likely never looked at, unless disaster strikes. Imagine the efficiencies, potential disaster prevention, insights, and other optimization opportunities if all of the data were cost-effectively analyzed.

One important enterprise differentiator is the ability to capture data that's getting "dropped to the floor"; this type of data can yield incredible insights and results, because it enriches the analytics initiatives going on in your organization today. *Data exhaust* is the term we like to use for this kind of data: it's generated in huge amounts (often terabytes per day) but typically isn't tapped for business insight. Online storefronts fail to capture terabytes of generated clickstreams to perform web sessionization, optimize the "last mile" shopping experience, and perhaps understand why online shopping baskets are getting abandoned. Mountains of data could be collected and analyzed to judge the health of an oil rig. Log files for your most important networks could be analyzed for trends when nothing obvious has gone wrong to find the "needle in the stack of needles" that potentially indicates downstream problems. There's an *"if"* here that tightly correlates with the promise of Big Data: *"If* you could collect and analyze all the data…" We like to refer to the capability to analyze all the data as *whole population analytics*. It's one of the value propositions of Big Data. It's a consideration on the kind of predictions and insights your analytic programs could make if they weren't restricted to samples and subsets of the data.

Today, many utilities are moving to smart meters and grids as part of long-range plans to ensure a reliable energy supply, incorporate distributed generation resources, and enable customers to have more control over their energy use. Many are deploying smart meter systems as a first step, which presents an immediate technical challenge: Going from one meter reading a month to smart meter readings every 15 minutes works out to 96 million reads per day for every million meters: a 3,000-fold increase in data collection rates! As you can imagine, such rates could be crippling if not properly managed.

There's an upside, of course. The additional data opens up new opportunities, enabling energy companies to do things they never could do before. Data gathered from smart meters can provide a better understanding of customer segmentation and behavior, and of how pricing influences usage—but only *if* companies have the ability to use such data. For example, time-of-use pricing encourages cost-savvy energy consumers to run their laundry facilities, air conditioners, and dishwashers at off-peak times. But the opportunities don't end there. With the additional information that's available from smart meters and smart grids, it's possible to transform and dramatically improve the efficiency of electrical generation and scheduling.

Smart meters are smart because they can communicate, not only with the consumer about electricity usage and pricing, but also with the utility provider about fluctuations in power or the precise location of outages. Smart meters are generating a wealth of new information that's fundamentally changing the way that utility companies interact with their customers.

What about the advent of the *prosumer*, a new consumer class that's also a producer. Prosumers generate power through solar panels and sell it back to the grid; this too has ripple effects across the supply chain. Using predictive analytics on their data, companies can make a wide range of forecasts, such as excess energy calculations with sell and transmittal considerations, typical failure points and grid downtime locations, and which clients are likely to feed energy back to the grid and when they are likely to do so.

Now consider the additional impact of social media. A social layer on top of an instrumented and interconnected world generates a massive amount of data too. This data is more complex, because most of it is unstructured (images, Twitter tweets, Facebook posts, micro-blog commentaries, and so on). If you eat Frito-Lay SunChips, you might remember its move to the world's first biodegradable environmentally friendly chip bag; you might also remember how loud the packaging was. Customers created thousands of YouTube videos showing how noisy the environmentally friendly bag was. A "Sorry, but I can't hear you over this SunChips bag" Facebook page had over 50,000 likes, and bloggers let their feelings be known. In the end, Frito-Lay introduced a new quieter SunChips bag, demonstrating the power and importance of social media.

For a number of years, Facebook was adding a new user every three seconds; today these users collectively generate double-digit terabytes of data every day. In fact, in a typical day, Facebook experiences over 2.5 billion likes and 300 million photo uploads. The format of a Facebook post is indeed structured data; it's marked up in the JavaScript Object Notation (JSON) format:

```
{
"data": [
    { "id": "53423432999_23423423_19898799",
    "from": { "name": "Paul Zikopoulos", "id": "Z12" },
    "message": "Thinking of surprising my wife with a quality time gift that
    lets her know she's special, any ideas? I thought about taking her to
    the driving range, perhaps play a round and caddie my game.",
    "created_time": "2012-08-02T21:27:44+0000", "likes: 5,"

    "comments": { "data": [ { "id": 2847923942_723423423",
    "from": { "name": "MaryAnne Infanti", "id": "948574763" },
    "message": "Paul! Purses and gold! Costco's got a great Kate Spade purse
    on sale this week that says I love you without having to lift a pen.
    If you go with your idea, the only thing driving will be you: alone! ",
    "created_time 2012-00-02T11:27:44+0000", "likes: 64 }        }
```

Although there is no doubt that this Facebook posting is structured, it's the *unstructured* part that has even more potential value; it holds the intent of a bad plan and commentary that strongly suggests what a better plan might be. The structured data is easy to store and analyze; however, analyzing its unstructured components for intent, sentiment, and so on is very hard, but it's got the potential to be very rewarding, *if...*

Twitter is another phenomenon. The world has taken to generating double-digit terabytes of short opinions (140 characters or less) and commentary (often unfiltered) about sporting events, sales, images, politics, and more. Twitter is yet another medium that provides enormous amounts of data that's structured in format, but it's the unstructured part within the structure that holds most of the untapped value. Consider that Noah Kravitz (@noahkravitz), prior to leaving his company for a competitor, had over 25,000 followers when he worked for a certain company. When he resigned, that former employer sued him, claiming that Mr. Kravitz's Twitter followers represented a client list belonging to the employer (imagine your own name the subject of a court case). This case is before the courts today and will certainly set a precedent, but it illustrates that there is at least perceived, if not factual, value (we think it's the latter) embodied within the Twitter ecosystem.

Most of today's collected data is also temporally and spatially enriched. For example, we know where one of the stars of the television show *Myth Busters* lives—not because he told us, but because he tweeted a picture of his car with location-based services (LBS) enabled on his smart device and ended up sharing his home's geographic (LAT/LONG) coordinates with over 650,000 of his closest friends! Most people don't know what LBS is, but they have it turned on because they're using some mobile mapping application. These days, folks just let you know when they've checked in at the gym or what restaurant they're in through social apps that just convert geographic coordinates into easily identifiable places. Such data often has built-in location awareness, which represents another tremendous opportunity for finer granularities of personalization or profiled risk assessment, *if...* Today, a number of major credit card companies have programs based on this approach that you can join; for example, if you purchase a coffee using your credit card, they will profile your location (via LBS), your purchase history, and make an offer that is tailored to you from a retailer in the proximity of your current location.

Time stamps are ubiquitous, and include, among others, the autodating metadata on the pictures that were taken with your camera or smart phone, the time of your Facebook posts, and the times when you turn on your smart phone or watch your favorite show, and so on; in fact, it's getting kind of easy to construct a timeline of your life. If you consider that, on average, commuters in London, England will have their picture taken over 150 times a day as they make their way home from London's downtown core, and then add that to the variety of sentiment, temporal, and spatial data that's generated during that time frame, you've got a lot of information—Big Data information—at your disposal.

Brought to You by the Letter V: How We Define Big Data

To keep things simple, we typically define Big Data using four Vs; namely, *volume*, *variety*, *velocity*, and *veracity*. We added the veracity characteristic recently in response to the quality and source issues our clients began facing with their Big Data initiatives. Some analysts include other V-based descriptors, such as variability and visibility, but we'll leave those out of this discussion.

No Question About It: Data Volumes Are on the Rise

Volume is the obvious Big Data trait. At the start of this chapter we rhymed off all kinds of voluminous statistics that do two things: go out of date the moment they are quoted and grow bigger! We can all relate to the cost of home storage; we can remember geeking out and bragging to our friends about our new 1TB drive we bought for $500; it's now about $60; in a couple of years, a consumer version will fit on your fingernail.

The thing about Big Data and data *volumes* is that the language has changed. Aggregation that used to be measured in petabytes (PB) is now referenced by a term that sounds as if it's from a Star Wars movie: *zettabytes* (ZB). A zettabyte is a trillion gigabytes (GB), or a billion terabytes!

Since we've already given you some great examples of the volume of data in the previous section, we'll keep this section short and conclude by referencing the world's aggregate digital data growth rate. In 2009, the world had about 0.8ZB of data; in 2010, we crossed the 1ZB marker, and at the end of 2011 that number was estimated to be 1.8ZB (we think 80 percent is quite the significant growth rate). Six or seven years from now, the number is estimated (and note that any future estimates in this book are out of date the moment we saved the draft, and on the low side for that matter) to be around 35ZB, equivalent to about four trillion 8GB iPods! That number is astonishing considering it's a low-sided estimate. Just as astounding are the challenges and opportunities that are associated with this amount of data.

Variety Is the Spice of Life

The *variety* characteristic of Big Data is really about trying to capture all of the data that pertains to our decision-making process. Making sense out of unstructured data, such as opinion and intent musings on Facebook, or analyzing images, isn't something that comes naturally for computers. However, this kind of data complements the data that we use to drive decisions today. Most of the data out there is semistructured or unstructured. (To clarify, all data has some structure; when we refer to *unstructured data*, we are referring to the sub-components that don't have structure, such as the freeform text in a comments field or the image in an auto-dated picture.)

Consider a customer call center; imagine being able to detect the change in tone of a frustrated client who raises his voice to say, "This is the third outage I've had in one week!" A Big Data solution would not only identify the terms "third" and "outage" as negative polarity trending to consumer vulnerability, but also the tonal change as another indicator that a customer churn incident is trending to happen. All of this insight can be gleaned from unstructured data. Now combine this unstructured data with the customer's record data and transaction history (the structured data with which we're familiar), and you've got a very personalized model of this consumer: his value, how brittle he's become as your customer, and much more. (You could start this usage pattern by attempting to analyze recorded calls not in real time, and mature the solution over time to one that analyzes the spoken word in real time.)

An IBM business partner, TerraEchos, has developed one of the most sophisticated sound classification systems in the world. This system is used for real-time perimeter security control; a thousand sensors are buried under-ground to collect and classify detected sounds so that appropriate action can be taken (dispatch personnel, dispatch aerial surveillance, and so on) depend-ing on the classification. Consider the problem of securing the perimeter of a nuclear reactor that's surrounded by parkland. The TerraEchos system can near-instantaneously differentiate the whisper of the wind from a human voice, or the sound of a human footstep from the sound of a running deer. In fact, if a tree were to fall in one of its protected forests, TerraEchos can affirm that it makes a sound even if no one is around to hear it. Sound classification is a great example of the variety characteristic of Big Data.

How Fast Can You Analyze? The Velocity of Your Data

One of our favorite but least understood characteristics of Big Data is *velocity*. We define velocity as the rate at which data arrives at the enterprise and is processed or well understood. In fact, we challenge our clients to ask them-selves, once data arrives at their enterprise's doorstep: "How long does it take you to do something about it or know it has even arrived?"

Think about it for a moment. The opportunity cost clock on your data starts ticking the moment the data hits the wire. As organizations, we're taking far too long to spot trends or pick up valuable insights. It doesn't matter what industry you're in; being able to more swiftly understand and respond to data signals puts you in a position of power. Whether you're trying to understand the health of a traffic system, the health of a patient, or the health of a loan portfolio, reacting faster gives you an advantage. Velocity is perhaps one of the most overlooked areas in the Big Data craze, and one in which we believe that IBM is unequalled in the capabilities and sophistication that it provides.

In the Big Data craze that has taken the marketplace by storm, everyone is fixated on at-rest analytics, using optimized engines such the Netezza technology behind the IBM PureData System for Analytics or Hadoop to perform analysis that was never before possible, at least not at such a large scale. Although this is vitally important, we must nevertheless ask: "How do you analyze data in motion?" This capability has the potential to provide businesses with the highest level of differentiation, yet it seems to be somewhat overlooked. The IBM InfoSphere Streams (Streams) part of the IBM Big Data platform provides a real-time streaming data analytics engine. Streams is a platform that provides fast, flexible, and scalable processing of continuous streams of time-sequenced data packets. We'll delve into the details and capabilities of Streams in Part III, "Analytics for Big Data in Motion."

You might be thinking that velocity can be handled by Complex Event Processing (CEP) systems, and although they might seem applicable on the surface, in the Big Data world, they fall very short. Stream processing enables advanced analysis across diverse data types with very high messaging data rates and very low latency (μs to s). For example, one financial services sector (FSS) client analyzes and correlates over five million market messages/second to execute algorithmic option trades with an average latency of 30 microseconds. Another client analyzes over 500,000 Internet protocol detail records (IPDRs) per second, more than 6 billion IPDRs per day, on more than 4PB of data per year, to understand the trending and current-state health of their network. Consider an enterprise network security problem. In this domain, threats come in microseconds so you need technology that can respond and keep pace. However you also need something that can capture lots of data quickly, and analyze it to identify emerging signatures and patterns on the network packets as they flow across the network infrastructure.

Finally, from a governance perspective, consider the added benefit of a Big Data analytics velocity engine: If you have a powerful analytics engine that can apply very complex analytics to data as it flows across the wire, and you can glean insight from that data without having to store it, you might not have to subject this data to retention policies, and that can result in huge savings for your IT department.

Today's CEP solutions are targeted to approximately tens of thousands of messages/second at best, with seconds-to-minutes latency. Moreover, the analytics are mostly rules-based and applicable only to traditional data types (as opposed to the TerraEchos example earlier). Don't get us wrong; CEP has its place, but it has fundamentally different design points. CEP is a non-programmer-oriented solution for the application of simple rules to discrete, "complex" events.

Note that not a lot of people are talking about Big Data velocity, because there aren't a lot of vendors that can do it, let alone integrate at-rest technologies with velocity to deliver economies of scale for an enterprise's current investment. Take a moment to consider the competitive advantage that your company would have with an in-motion, at-rest Big Data analytics platform, by looking at Figure 1-1 (the IBM Big Data platform is covered in detail in Chapter 3).

You can see how Big Data streams into the enterprise; note the point at which the opportunity cost clock starts ticking on the left. The more time that passes, the less the potential competitive advantage you have, and the less return on data (ROD) you're going to experience. We feel this ROD metric will be one that will dominate the future IT landscape in a Big Data world: we're used to talking about return on investment (ROI), which talks about the entire solution investment; however, in a Big Data world, ROD is a finer granularization that helps fuel future Big Data investments. Traditionally, we've used at-rest solutions (traditional data warehouses, Hadoop, graph stores, and so on). The T box on the right in Figure 1-1 represents the analytics that you discover and harvest at rest (in this case, it's text-based sentiment analysis). Unfortunately, this is where many

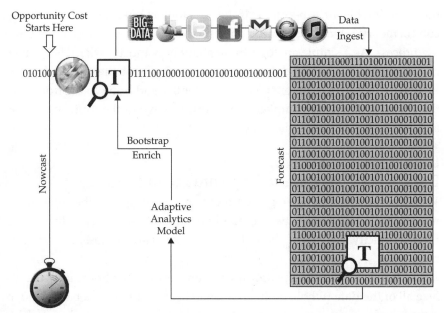

Figure 1-1   *A real-time analytics-processing (RTAP) ecosystem*

vendors' Big Data talk ends. The truth is that many vendors can't help you build the analytics; they can only help you to execute it. This is a key differentiator that you'll find in the IBM Big Data platform. Imagine being able to seamlessly move the analytic artifacts that you harvest at rest and apply that insight to the data as it happens in motion (the T box by the lightning bolt on the left). This changes the game. It makes the analytic model adaptive, a living and breathing entity that gets smarter day by day and applies learned intelligence to the data as it hits your organization's doorstep. This model is cyclical, and we often refer to this as adaptive analytics because of the real-time and closed-loop mechanism of this architecture.

The ability to have seamless analytics for both at-rest and in-motion data moves you from the *forecast* model that's so tightly aligned with traditional warehousing (on the right) and energizes the business with a *nowcast* model. The whole point is getting the insight you learn at rest to the frontier of the business so it can be optimized and understood as it happens. Ironically, the more times the enterprise goes through this adaptive analytics cycle, the more intelligent it becomes. If you're familiar with control systems or control theory, which adapt based on observations, it's a similar kind of looping process. As a simple analogy, think about how much easier it is to finish a puzzle when it's almost done, or even when you have the outside framed. In an RTAP system, the more pieces you identify and bring to the frontier of the business, the more complete a picture you have of the topic of interest, and you have it earlier in the cycle.

Data Here, Data There, Data, Data Everywhere: The Veracity of Data

Veracity is a term that's being used more and more to describe Big Data; it refers to the quality or trustworthiness of the data. Tools that help handle Big Data's veracity transform the data into trustworthy insights and discard noise.

Collectively, a Big Data platform gives businesses the opportunity to analyze all of the data (whole population analytics), and to gain a better understanding of your business, your customers, the marketplace, and so on. This opportunity leads to the Big Data conundrum: although the economics of deletion have caused a massive spike in the data that's available to an organization, the percentage of the data that an enterprise can understand is on the decline. A further complication is that the data that the enterprise is trying to understand is saturated with both useful signals and lots of noise (data that can't be trusted, or isn't useful to the business problem at hand), as shown in Figure 1-2.

We all have firsthand experience with this; Twitter is full of examples of spambots and directed tweets, which is untrustworthy data. The

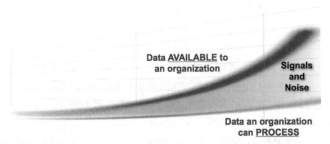

Figure 1-2   *As the amount of data that is available to an organization increases, the relative amount of data that it can process decreases.*

2012 presidential election in Mexico turned into a Twitter veracity example with fake accounts, which polluted political discussion, introduced derogatory hash tags, and more. Spam is nothing new to folks in IT, but you need to be aware that in the Big Data world, there is also Big Spam potential, and you need a way to sift through it and figure out what data can and can't be trusted. Of course, there are words that need to be understood in context, jargon, and more (we cover this in Chapter 8).

As previously noted, embedded within all of this noise are useful signals: the person who professes a profound disdain for her current smartphone manufacturer and starts a soliloquy about the need for a new one is expressing monetizable intent. Big Data is so vast that quality issues are a reality, and veracity is what we generally use to refer to this problem domain. The fact that one in three business leaders don't trust the information that they use to make decisions is a strong indicator that a good Big Data platform needs to address veracity.

What About My Data Warehouse in a Big Data World?

There are pundits who insist that the traditional method of doing analytics is over. Sometimes these NoSQL (which really means Not Only SQL) pundits suggest that all warehouses will go the way of the dinosaur—ironic, considering a lot of focus surrounding NoSQL databases is about bringing SQL interfaces to the runtime. Nothing could be further from the truth. We see a number of purpose-built engines and programming models that are well suited for certain kinds of analytics. For example, Hadoop's MapReduce programming model is better suited for some kinds of data than traditional warehouses. For this reason, as you will learn in Chapter 3, the IBM Big Data platform includes a Hadoop engine (and support for other Hadoop engines as well, such as Cloudera). What's more, IBM recognizes the flexibility of the programming model, so the IBM PureData System for Analytics (formerly known as Netezza) can execute MapReduce programs within a database. It's really important in the Big Data era that you choose a platform that provides the flexibility of a purpose-built engine that's well suited for the task at hand (the kind of analytics you are doing, the type of data you are doing it on, and so on). This platform must also allow you to seamlessly move programming skills, APIs, and assets across the platform so that the analytics can be applied to an engine that's optimized for the data at hand. For example, the IBM Big Data platform lets you take text analytics that are built via its Annotated Query Language (AQL) and seamlessly deploy them from an at-rest Hadoop engine into its Streams Big Data velocity engine. Most of the MapReduce programs that you code in Hadoop can be run in the IBM PureData System for Analytics; the SQL reports that you generate on IBM pureSystems for Operational Analytics (formerly known as the IBM Smart Analytics System) can pretty much be deployed without change on DB2 for z/OS.

When you consider where data should be stored, it's best to first understand how data is stored today and what features characterize your persistence options. Data that's stored in a traditional data warehouse goes through a lot of processing before making it into the warehouse. The data is expected to be of high quality once it lands in the warehouse, and so it's cleaned up through enrichment, matching, glossaries, metadata, master data management, modeling, and other quality services that are attached to the data *before* it's ready for analysis. Obviously, this can be an expensive process, and the data that lands in a warehouse is viewed as having both high value and broad purpose: it's going places and will appear in reports and dashboards where accuracy is key.

In contrast, data in some of the newer Big Data repositories rarely undergoes (at least initially) such rigorous preprocessing because that would be cost-prohibitive, and the work in these repositories is subject to more discovery than known value. What's more, each repository has different characteristics with different tradeoffs. One might prioritize on the application of ACID (atomicity, consistency, isolation, and durability) properties, and another might operate in a relaxed consistency state where the BASE properties (basically available, soft state, and eventually consistent) can be tolerated.

We like to use a gold mining analogy to articulate the opportunity of Big Data. In the "olden days" (which, for some reason, our kids think is a time when we were their age), miners could easily spot nuggets or veins of gold, as they were visible to the naked eye. Let's consider that gold to be "high value-per-byte data"; you can see its value and therefore you invest resources to extract it. But there is more gold out there, perhaps in the hills nearby or miles away; it just isn't visible to the naked eye, and trying to find this hidden gold becomes too much of a gambling game. Sure, history has its gold rush fever stories, but nobody ever mobilized millions of people to dig everywhere and anywhere; that would be too expensive. Today's miners work differently. Gold mining leverages massive capital equipment that can process millions of tons of dirt (low value-per-byte data) to find nearly invisible strands of gold (ore grades of 30 ppm are usually needed before gold is visible to the naked eye). In other words, there's a great deal of gold (high value-per-byte data) in all of this dirt (low value-per-byte data), and with the right equipment, you can economically process lots of dirt and keep the flakes of gold that you find. The flakes of gold are taken for processing (perhaps to your data warehouse or another insight engine) and combined to make a bar of gold, which is stored and logged in a place that's safe, governed, valued, and trusted. The gold industry is working on chemical washes that aim to reveal even finer granularizations of gold to find more value out of previously extracted dirt (now think data). We think this analogy fits well into our Big Data story because we're willing to bet that if you had a corpus composed of ten years of your transaction data, new analytic approaches will let you extract more insight out of it three years from now than you can with today's technology.

In addition, if you look at the access patterns that characterize a data warehouse and a Hadoop repository, one differentiator you'll find is that a data warehouse is often characterized by response times that allow you to work with the system interactively. Indeed, terms such as "speed-of-thought response times" aren't the descriptors you're going to find associated with a batch system, which is what Hadoop is, *for now*.

A Big Data platform lets you store all of the data in its native business object format and get value out of it through mass parallelism on commodity components. For your interactive navigational needs, you'll continue to pick and choose sources, cleanse that data, and keep it in warehouses. But you can get more value out of having a large amount of lower-fidelity data by pulling in what might seem to be unrelated information to form a more robust picture. In other words, data might sit in Hadoop for a while, and when its value becomes proven and sustainable, it can be migrated to the warehouse.

The difference between observed value and discovery is not as black and white as we have described here. For example, a common use case for a

Hadoop engine is to provide database archiving services to a data warehouse, taking data that's no longer "warm" or "hot" and moving it to a lower-cost storage platform that is backed by Hadoop. For example, a customer profiling system keeps hot data for two years, but all of the data collected over the course of a 20-year relationship might still be valuable. An insurance company could benefit from understanding how your profile has evolved from being a single person, then married, then with kids, while considering current trends or events (this is especially true with wealth management portfolios).

Of course, the portability of the query API is of key importance in this scenario; for example, not having to recode your SQL-based applications when accessing cold data that was moved to Hadoop (the IBM Big Data platform lets you do this). Another example, and Big Data platform requirement, is the integration between the SQL and NoSQL worlds. You might have a consumer vulnerability job running in your relational warehouse but choose to launch a Hadoop-based sentiment job on your brand that could impact the final vulnerability assessment. At the same time, you might have a running Hadoop job that is analyzing terabytes of clickstream log data, and you now want to extract purchase information from the system of record to understand what other factors lead to a successful purchase or abandonment of past online shopping carts. (Now consider if you can take that logic and apply it to shopping carts as they are being populated in real time.)

Traditional engines and new data processing engines (Hadoop and others) will become the left and right arm of an organization. The key is ensuring that your Big Data platform provider delivers integration technologies that enable those arms to be used in tandem.

As a final analogy, consider a baseball player. A typical baseball player is very strong at throwing with one hand and catching with the other; the brain coordinates the activities of these limbs for optimized results. If a baseball player were to try to throw or catch a ball with his nondominant hand, he might be able to do it, but it won't be smooth, crisp, or look very professional. And with the exception of a few professional baseball players who have only one hand (such as Jim Abbott, www.jimabbott.net), you don't really see baseball players catch a ball, and then take their glove off to throw the ball with the same hand. This is the NoSQL and SQL analogy; each is optimized for specific tasks and data and it's important to play ball with two hands.

Wrapping It Up

In this chapter, we provided a general framework that you can use to identify Big Data. We explained why the enhanced analytic capability that can be derived from it represents an inflection point. We used the terms volume, variety, velocity, and veracity to give you an easy-to-remember way to understand and classify a Big Data opportunity. The Big Data era is all about enhancing analytics through a purpose-built Big Data platform that introduces new methods and techniques and synergizes them with just as important traditional solutions you have running today. As such, Big Data discussions should never start out with "let's migrate off our current warehouse technology." These approaches complement one another, and just like the athlete who coordinates multiple skills for superb performance, so too will the IBM Big Data platform power-up the instantiation of your successful and business-differentiating Big Data initiatives.

2

Applying Big Data to Business Problems: A Sampling of Use Cases

This chapter's title describes exactly what we're going to cover: how Big Data can be applied to help solve business problems. We'll illustrate Big Data's ability to enhance the business and solve previously insurmountable (or greatly simplify difficult) problems using selected use cases and some commentary on the mechanics of getting going with Big Data. We'll touch on how we helped clients develop new applications and what potential approaches you can use to solve previously difficult challenges. We'll also talk about how new ways of doing things can fundamentally change your approach to problem solving.

When to Consider a Big Data Solution

Are you limited by your current platform or environment because you can't process the amount of data that you want to process? Do you want to involve new sources of data in the analytics paradigm, but you can't, because it doesn't fit into schema-defined rows and columns without sacrificing fidelity or the richness of the data? Do you need to ingest data as quickly as possible and need to work with a schema-on-demand paradigm? Are you being forced into a schema-on-write approach (the schema must be created before data is loaded), but you need to ingest data quickly, or perhaps in a discovery process, and want the cost benefits of a schema-on-read approach (data is simply copied to the file store, and no special transformation is needed) until you know that you've got something that's ready for analysis? Is the data arriving too fast at your organization's doorstep for the current analytics platform to handle? If your answers to any of these questions are "yes," you need to consider a Big Data solution.

In Chapter 1, we outlined the characteristics that help you spot Big Data (velocity, volume, veracity, and variety). We also noted that most of the new Big Data solutions that you might hear about are more likely to complement, rather than replace, your current analytics platform (such as a trusted data warehouse). Together, such complementary approaches can help boost your company's Big Data IQ.

Let's begin with a good example of how we helped solve a business problem with Big Data technology. We helped a major company in the financial service sector (FSS) understand why they were experiencing increasing attrition and defection rates. We started by examining an entire month's worth of email (about 40 million messages) from their Customer Service center. In this case, the volume of stored data wasn't large by any means, but we still used IBM InfoSphere BigInsights (BigInsights)—IBM's nonforked Hadoop distribution—because the compute capacity required to perform the analytics was large. A different approach was needed to chew through the emails quickly and accurately. Moreover, we didn't know what to expect, so we wanted maximum flexibility in the scale, types of information, and methods we could use to performance the analysis. We also didn't know what we would find, and we wanted the flexibility of acquiring insight by "snapping in" other data sources; in this case, web browsing behavior, structured accounting data, and account performance history. It's this sort of flexibility that's often key in solving problems and moving projects forward. We wanted to start with this example because it highlights some of the recurring use case patterns that we often see. Specifically this use case provides examples of the following patterns:

- Need to move from a small history (months) to several years

- Inclusion of mixed information types, in this case structured account history along with email

- Cross system workflows that required specific file export formatting that was accomplished in a scripting language that was different than how the data was originally prepared

- Utilization of compute intensive NLP (natural language processing) and Machine Learning techniques.

Of course the work done on this use case led us to a set of challenges that seem to show up every time we end up recommending a Big Data solution, specifically:

- Big Data solutions are ideal for analyzing not just raw structured data, but also semistructured and unstructured data from a wide variety of sources—our insights came from the intersection of all of these sources.

- Big Data solutions are ideal when you're not content with the effectiveness of your algorithms or models; when all, or most, of the data needs to be analyzed; or when a sampling of the data isn't going to be nearly as effective. They are also helpful when you're not content to just sample the data—you want to look at every interaction because you believe it will yield a competitive advantage (it's that whole population analytics theme we talked about in Chapter 1).

- When business measures on the data are not predetermined, Big Data solutions are ideal for iterative and exploratory analysis—we deliberately took an iterative/agile approach to learning.

- Big Data solutions are ideal when you aren't completely sure where the investigation will take you, and you want elasticity of compute, storage, and the types of analytics that will be pursued—all of these became useful as we added more sources and new methods.

What's important, really important, to notice here is that we augmented the power of the existing analytics investment. It's not appropriate to rip and replace in most cases; rather, clients we work with want to increase the yields of their current investments. With this client, we used a Big Data solution to leverage data that was not suitable for their traditional warehouse environment along with what we knew from the warehouse.

Big Data technologies are also well suited for solving information challenges that don't natively fit within a traditional relational database approach. It's important to understand that conventional database technologies *are* key and relevant, and part of an overall analytic solution. In fact, they become even more vital when used in conjunction with your Big Data platform. We always say: "Big Data isn't just Hadoop." With that said, some problems can't be addressed through traditional databases, at least not at first. And there's data that we're not sure we want in the warehouse, because we don't know whether it's rich in value—it's unstructured, it's too voluminous, perhaps its shelf life is too short, or it just might simply be too early to know how to formalize its structure.

Before We Start: Big Data, Jigsaw Puzzles, and Insight

Before getting into the use cases, let's touch on how a Big Data approach to solving problems can be more effective when compared to conventional approaches. Before you read this section, we'll ask you to consider these two questions: "Is finding patterns easier or slower when dealing with Big Data?" and "Is finding outliers easier or harder as data volumes and velocity increase?" Consider your answers before reading this section, and then answer them after reading this section.

When you first open a 2,000-piece jigsaw puzzle box and empty its contents on a table, the puzzle pieces are all mixed up. By applying some basic grouping, you can easily find the straight edges and corner pieces that frame the puzzle. When the puzzle frame is complete, you still have about 1,900 pieces or so to fill in; just as with data, analytics are required to complete the picture.

You can think of this simple pattern matching as traditional reporting, which is focused on predictable, neatly shaped data that easily fits together and is ordered. If, when you opened the puzzle box, all border shapes came wrapped in a separate bag, and all the pieces that were yellow came in their own bag, and so on, the puzzle wouldn't be very hard to solve. But this isn't how puzzles are packaged, nor how data, for that matter, arrives at your organization's doorstep.

Let's assume at this point you've worked on your puzzle for a couple of hours. The outside is framed, and the middle is taking shape. You can see some of the picture. Which state of the puzzle contains more data? When it's dumped out of the box into a pile of pieces, or when you can see some (but not all) of the picture?

We suspect many people initially feel that they both contain the same amount of data—after all, the total number of puzzle pieces hasn't changed. But data isn't just about the number of rows you have, or petabytes of information; it's about context and understanding. Indeed, as the puzzle takes shape, we gain a better understanding of the problem domain. Inferences can be made, relationships spotted, and we're provided with a much richer set of information. That said, we now have more data (and metadata) to manage, even though we have the same number of puzzle pieces. Let us explain: as surely as data coming together yields more insight, new relationships and patterns must be managed (something you don't have to do with a puzzle). So, it's fair to say that when the puzzle is 35 percent complete, there's more information than when it was fresh out of the box. Although we all initially assume that dealing with more data is harder and more challenging, with patterns discovery, more data makes a problem easier to solve.

Now suppose that someone throws in some pieces from *another* puzzle without your knowledge. (This experiment comes from Jeff Jonas, IBM's Chief Scientist for Entity Analytics; his subjects were his unsuspecting family and friends. Be wary if Jeff breaks out a puzzle after dinner.) Faced with a heap of puzzle pieces in which 5 percent of the pieces don't fit, when would it be easier to determine that the puzzle was contaminated? With the initial pile, or after some of pieces had already been connected? Of course, the connected pieces help illustrate the patterns, making it easier to find the contaminated outliers and easier to solve the rest of the puzzle by eliminating those outliers. Having more data makes outliers easier to find. Think about it for a moment: the more complete the puzzle, the easier it is to identify patterns and the easier it is to spot outliers (foreign pieces). See how organizations can take advantage of more data?

Now let's suppose that we've asked you to solve the world's biggest puzzle, which has 32,256 pieces (manufactured by Ravensburger AG in 2010). How long would that take using two people? How about if we added two more people (processors) and gave them a complementary but discrete task such as looking for all the pieces that have an element of a face? How about if we added another two people whose sole task is to look at another discrete part of the puzzle, and so on? You get the idea, and that's exactly how we use machines to scale out work instead of relying on a limited number of processors. At this point, we hope you're starting to see why new Big Data technologies are so important for completing the puzzle, be it the puzzle of next best offer, next best action, curing a disease, and so on. We can't begin to fathom how many pieces would be part of a Big Data–era puzzle, and so scale-out, machine learning, and massive analytical systems are needed to frame the edge, sort and group the pieces, and discover patterns.

You might be wondering about the answers to the questions we asked you to consider at the start of this section; our answer is likely to match yours at this point—*faster* and *easier*. Solutions that utilize large data sets are often more helpful than those constrained to smaller data sets.

Big Data Use Cases: Patterns for Big Data Deployment

We debated over what use cases to cover in this chapter; we started by trying to figure out what industries don't have use case fits for Big Data. We thought we had a winner when someone blurted out "the Disc Jockey industry," but then we had one student on BigDataUniversity.com pull his entire music collection into BigInsights and subsequently build some pretty cool analytics on his music files, including a musical genomics-oriented application. So much for that approach to narrowing the field—this led us to select use cases that help tap patterns that appear to be common and cross-industry. For example, reaching for new kinds of data and applying analytics as the data streams off the collection units rigged with sensors can be used to gain better insight into traffic systems, networks, the health of a newborn baby, loan book valuations, and more.

The use patterns detailed here involve BigInsights, IBM InfoSphere Streams (Streams), and a combination of new age Big Data engines with traditional warehousing, such as the IBM PureData System for Analytics (formerly known as Netezza) or the IBM PureData System for Operational Analytics platforms. There's a common trend across all of the cases that we cover: they all involve a new way of doing things that's more practical (and now finally possible) with a Big Data platform.

You Spent the Money to Instrument It—Now Exploit It!

In Chapter 1 we gave you all kinds of metrics and examples that illustrate just how instrumented our world is: from bridges, to rail tracks, livestock, conference badges, running shoes, and more, the world can collect some kind of data from just about anything, anywhere, at any time.

Take, for example, a typical oil drilling platform that can have 20,000 to 40,000 sensors on board. All of these sensors are streaming data about the health of the oil rig, quality of operations, and so on. Not every sensor is actively broadcasting at all times, but some are reporting back many times per second. Now take a guess at what percentage of those sensors are actively utilized. If you're thinking in the 10 percent range (or even 5 percent), you're either a great guesser or you're getting the recurring theme for Big Data that spans industry and use cases: clients aren't using all of the data that's available to them in their decision-making process. Of course, when it comes to energy data (or any data for that matter) collection rates, it really begs the question: "If you've bothered to instrument the user, device, or rig, in theory, you've done it on purpose, so why are you not capturing and leveraging the information you are collecting?"

In this usage pattern, it's about applying the analytics you harvested at rest and getting them applied in motion, to better understand the domain. The University of Ontario Institute of Technology (UOIT) lead researcher (Dr. Carolyn McGregor) partnered with The Hospital for Sick Children, Toronto, to find a better way to predict the onset of a specific hospital-borne illness affecting newborn babies. You can imagine these fragile babies are connected to machines that continually collect data. Some hospitals record hourly or half hourly spot readings and discard it after 72 hours or so; thereby missing the ability to discover trends at rest and apply analytics in motion at a more granular level. UOIT's lead research, Dr. Carolyn McGregor, leveraged IBM's Streams technology to create an in-motion analytics platform that analyzes over 1,000 pieces of unique medical diagnostic information per second. Imagine the amount of sensor data for 120 babies; that's 120,000 messages per second, 178.8 million messages per day, analyzed! You can find more details on this wonderful success story on the Web (search for "IBM data baby"). Now consider expanding this approach to outpatients hooked up to a sensor who are free to go about their daily activities, or monitoring people at risk of chronic disease states. Quite simply, Big Data has the potential to be a game changer and a life saver.

Sensor data—it's amazing to see how many things the world has instrumented (electrical grids, oil rigs, traffic flows, toll routes, and more), which means their intention was to collect data: Big Data now lets you do something with it.

IT for IT:
Data Center, Machine Data, and Log Analytics

Hadoop-based log analytics has become a common use case, but that doesn't mean it's deployment is as widespread as it should be. Log analytics is actually a pattern that IBM established after working with a number of companies, initially in FSS. We've since seen this use case come up across all industries; for that reason, we'll call this pattern *IT for IT*.

Big Data–enriched IT for IT helps clients to gain better insight into how their systems are running, and when and how things break down. For example, one financial firm affectionately refers to the traditional way of figuring out how an application went sideways as "Whack-A-Mole." When things go wrong in their heavily SOA-based environment, it's hard to determine what happened, because more than 20 systems are involved in the processing of a given transaction. (We've all seen this movie, everyone running around the war room saying, "I didn't do it!" There's also a scene in that movie where everyone is pointing fingers…at you!)

One client we helped with this usage pattern ended up with the capability to analyze approximately 1TB of log data each day, with less than 5 minutes latency (this use case is just as applicable with much larger or smaller log generation rates). Today, this client is able to decipher exactly what's happening across their entire IT stack, within each and every transaction. When one of their customer's transactions, spawned from their mobile or Internet banking sites, fails, they're able to tell exactly where it happened and what component contributed to the problem. As you can imagine, this flattens time to resolution metrics.

This client could take the insights that they've harvested at-rest, and leverage Streams to investigate the health of their networks in real time. For example, if constant consumption of a memory heap in the Hibernate layer is strongly correlated with a stack overflow in the application server, being able to pick up this issue at its genesis could save the transaction or prevent the network from experiencing an outage. As an example, one of our telecommunications customers uses Streams to analyze machine data in real time to find misbehaving mobile computing applications that are harming the networks, so the offending applications can be terminated.

Sometimes, we like to refer to all those logs and the trace data that's generated by the operation of your IT solutions as *data exhaust*. Enterprises have lots of data exhaust, and like any pollutant, it gets discarded because it's viewed as waste. Log data is often too strongly associated with high storage costs. However, logs contain a great deal of potential insight, not only into what's happening to your servers now, but what *will* happen.

Take a moment to consider how your organization does infrastructure budgeting. You'd like to think that it's fact-based, but is it really? Do you have a clear view of system utilization across the end-to-end platforms, including trending? Do you understand the impact of seasonality and other events across all groups and departments? We were able to show one of our customers that they were planning new server acquisitions based on peak load volumes that could be handled by existing idle systems. We helped them to save several million dollars, resulting in a triple-digit ROI in the first year.

We helped another customer set up a central log clearinghouse rather than letting each subgroup roll their own solution. This customer was storing logs in a two-week window, then flushing them to avoid the cost of storage. Departments and application development teams that depended on these systems, knowing that the logs were going to be flushed, would grab them and place the logs on expensive SANs. There was no corporate-wide retention policy or consistency in how the logs were being used by the various departments. It's ironic when we think about it. These logs were being flushed because they incurred storage expense, yet they ended up being placed, in triplicate or more, on expensive SANs without a planned purging mechanism. This customer used BigInsights to create a centralized log clearinghouse, and realized over one million dollars in savings. Specifically, they arbitraged BigInsights storage for the SAN and implemented a nine-month rolling retention policy; after this time period, there was little value in retaining the logs. They didn't stop there, however. Now that the logs were in one place and for a reasonable amount of time, they were able to determine holistic trends and issues; in short, they were able to connect the dots.

But there's more to this use case than detecting problems. This client is now compiling a body of knowledge so that they can better anticipate failures and understand the interaction between failures. Their service bureau can generate best-practice remediation steps for specific problems, or tune the infrastructure to eliminate them. This is about discoverable preventive maintenance. Some of our large insurance and retail clients need to know the answers to such questions as "What are the precursors to failure?" or "How are these systems related?" These are the types of questions that conventional monitoring doesn't answer; a Big Data solution finally offers the opportunity to get new and better insights into the problems at hand

What, Why, and Who? Social Media Analytics

Perhaps the most talked-about Big Data use pattern involves social media and customer sentiment analysis—it's also perhaps the most overhyped and misunderstood. Although Big Data can help you to figure out what customers are saying about your brand (or your competitor's brand), we think that the current focus needs to expand.

Social media analytics is a pretty hot topic, but we're already starting to see "buyer fatigue," because the realities of current practice don't live up to the constant hype around this use case. Simply put, there's a big difference between *what* people are saying or thinking and *why* they said or thought it. Your social media Big Data analytics project should attempt to answer both the "what" and the "why" to provide you with the analytics payoff that you seek.

We were recently able to identify some negative buzz that was specifically targeted to a financial company that we were helping. We wanted to find out why the negative buzz was there in the first place—why were people in a such a state that they used technology to spread this negative sentiment? More importantly, was this impacting sales, what could be done about it, and how would we know if a particular response made things better? We call this *closed loop analytics*. If you simply listen to what people are saying, but don't have the ability to analyze the information and respond accordingly, you're still flying largely blind.

Understanding why people are saying something about your organization involves cross-correlating everything: promotions, product mixes, pricing changes, policy changes, marketing, corporate responsibility, and a whole host of other activities that contribute to consumers' opinions in the first place. There's a fundamental requirement that too few companies are talking about: you need to combine external and internal information flows in the same analytics pipeline. That's where you'll start to gain real insight and realize an uplift; as it turns out, there are few (if any) external services that provide social media offerings to do this since they can't handle the internal structured sources, or they lack the analytics to combine the two—the IBM Big Data platform can do this.

Understanding Customer Sentiment

Some industries or products have disloyal customers with very high churn rates. We worked with one telecommunications company that experiences more than 50 percent annual customer churn. They wanted to enhance retention by identifying which types of customers are most vulnerable earlier in the billing cycle. For this client, even small improvements in the conversion rate to more stable plans would double one of their offerings' revenue stream. Quite simply, they didn't have to hit a home run to be more successful; they just needed to get a base hit. Of course, that's easier said than done, however, because of how transient the opportunity is with the customer. When you're dealing with those levels of churn and massive volumes, being able to find, trap, respond, and interact is not a small challenge.

The key to making this happen is being able to detect loyalty decay and work that into your client engagements and next-best-action modeling before the next contact with the customer. It isn't quite real time, but what we call *customer time*. Customer time is simply the notion of being able to process everything needed before the next customer interaction so it looks seamless in the eyes of your client. However with Smartphones, customer time is getting close to real time because there are always opportunities such as sending an e-mail, text message, or offer.

In addition to operating in customer time, this use case provides another example of the value of capturing all of the available information to look at events that help to build context. After you've captured one aspect of the communication spectrum, you can move on to the next and start correlating that with everything from emails to social media and other things that we've talked about in this chapter; you can even correlate it with back-office service quality reports to see whether people are calling and expressing dissatisfaction with you based on your back-end systems. If you're able to identify a pattern that shows where your systems have been slow or haven't behaved properly, and that just happens to be the reason why a particular individual is calling to cancel services without explicitly mentioning it, you can establish a correlation with what the customer is saying. In fact, a goal of one of our FSS clients is to have a good idea why you're calling before they even talk to you so they can "pre-resolve" your issue and inform you of the fix rather than having to even talk to you about your problem!

We're sure that you can relate to the following scenario: You call a service provider's customer service department after getting disconnected twice. You have to reauthenticate and then repeat your whole story to yet another agent because when you got cut off, the original agent didn't finish making notes. Now imagine calling back and hearing the agent say, "We're sorry, we've been having some telephony issues and noticed that you've been disconnected twice. I apologize that I have to reauthenticate you, but I understand why you are calling and here's what we can do to help resolve it..." We're willing to bet that such a response would exceed your expectations.

Another example: How many times have you called your Internet service provider to complain about your high-speed Internet service, only to get the impression that the customer service representative's (CSR) job is to make you feel unimportant and to get you off the phone as quickly as possible? From a business perspective, you have to wonder if the service issues are really being captured. Perhaps the agent handling a call fills out a form that outlines the basic service complaint, but will it be correlated with point-in-time quantitative reports that indicate how the systems were running? If you have a Big Data platform, you can derive insight and predict issues before complaints surface. In the case of an Internet service, quality of service (QoS) is simple to measure—is the provider's technical support department analyzing Internet protocol detail records (IPDRs) to understand the health of the network, and then alerting customer service whenever there's a QoS issue in a certain part of town?

Admittedly, the previous scenario is pretty advanced for call centers today, but in the Big Data world, there's still room to grow, such as tonal change or text analysis to identify exasperation ("This is the *third* time I've called!"), or real-time correlation to identify trends in sentiment with a determination of how trends in the call center are related to the rest of the business operations. If you need to explain this is the *third* time you've had to call on the same issue, shouldn't all of the interactions with the provider reflect that, even if you chose to use a different channel?

Understanding customer sentiment is a really interesting Big Data use case, because it can be applied to what is possible today (using analytics on data that's in motion or at rest) and to emerging capabilities. You can use one of the IBM Big Data platform at-rest analytic engines, such as BigInsights, to discover and build your models and to gain business insight. Then you have the option of continuing to use at-rest analytics to harvest call interactions at much lower latency, or to build up these models and then promote them back to the frontier of the business, using Streams to examine and analyze calls as quickly as they can be converted, so that insights can be acquired in near-real time. This transforms the business from *forecasting* (we think customers will leave if…) to *nowcasting* (we know this customer is about to leave because…). The results of Streams analytics flow back into BigInsights, creating a closed-loop feedback mechanism, because BigInsights can then iterate over the results to improve the models.

Social Media Techniques Make the World Your Oyster

In the previous section we talked about social media analytics drawing a lot of chatter and fatigue—it's potentially too hyped up. We thought we'd expand your scope of where this fits in; indeed, if you have the technology to draw structure and understanding from unstructured text, you can imagine an endless number of usage patterns.

The same text analytics technology used for social media can be applied to do a number of different things. For example, one client wanted to investigate the dissemination of piracy and copyright infringement of their intellectual property (it was video-based). It's a very interesting area because in social media there are often discussions about types of piracy, and this client was able to build patterns that identify these kinds of conversations that take place in various micro-blog sites around the world. This ultimately led them to web sites that contain illegally posted copyrighted materials that belonged to our client. How did they do it? They developed dictionaries and patterns that identified the names of sports teams involved in the "stolen" materials, "pull" language that surrounds enticing links for free content, URL resolution from shortened URLS (tinyURLs) to actual sites, and so on. So while they weren't analyzing who said what, they did create structure around a problem domain from unstructured text-based data. Same technology, same toolset, same approach, just a different use case.

While we covered one vendor's move to limit the piracy of their intellectual property, you can see how a Big Data analytics platform such as the one provided by IBM could be applied in various ways. For example, one "watchdog" client sifted through countless web-posted pages of a country's parliamentary attendance and voting records to draw strong correlations and shine the spotlight on a particular representative's behavior in an elected position (which was underwhelming in this case because of the number of votes the representative missed).

Another client used the same concepts of building a dictionary of verbiage around sentiment and applied it to creating an understanding of log files (we talk about this usage pattern later in this chapter). For example, an IP address has a certain structure to it (IPv4 or IPv6), a monitoring agent has a name (such as Nagios), and so on. Is there a correlation between the name of the monitoring agent on the application server and the database server?

Finally, an investment house is scraping IT-based company's public text-based (HTML) earning reports to look for "tells" or signs within the disclosure as to the health of the business, or guidance in commentary about its future performance and so on. You can imagine comparing the services revenue stream across different companies (such as Hewlett Packard and IBM) could be very useful, but each company is likely to name these divisions differently; for example, Hewlett Packard calls it "HP Enterprise Services" and IBM calls it "IBM Global Services." It's a daunting task to manually assemble this information across a large scale of market participants, but it's a much easier one if you built text extractors that defined how to identify a company's name and services department name, then perhaps crawled the Web with Nutch (an open source web search engine based on Apache Lucene) to pull the commentary relating to that division for each company of interest.

Customer State:
Or, Don't Try to Upsell Me When I Am Mad

Studies seem to indicate that customer service is getting worse, whether it's due to outsourcing, aggressive time-to-resolution metrics, the economy, or cutbacks, among others. Many people find it hard to recall the last time they had a great customer experience. The quality of service is often up to an individual, rather than the business. (We've all had that experience: calling back with the same information or problem yields a different result, depending on the CSR's attitude and training.) Many of us have been conditioned to expect mediocre customer experiences as the rule. It doesn't have to be that way, however, and as consumers become more vocal about not wanting to be punished because the companies they do business with have been cutting service to improve their profitability in tough economic times, something is going to have to change. We've been busy helping firms with this—and the good news is that in our experience, companies *want* to provide good service, and Big Data technologies can both help improve service and lower cost at the same time.

The key is to re-image how the whole process works by making use of all the available information; to help the business do the right thing, at the right time, and in the right context. This is not a new goal, of course, but the ability to actually do it, and to do it well, is greatly facilitated by Big Data.

Most customer engagement data is ignored. Little, if any, context from call center interactions is captured. The same can be said about clickstream data that passes through your company's web site. Isn't that a form of communication? In this case, customers are saying that you've done something that's interested them enough to learn more about your company or product. This type of data is usually used at an aggregate level—we look at what customers are doing as a whole; for example, what products are your customers viewing, what's been added to a shopping cart, and what carts are being abandoned. Why not instead use this data at a more personal level to discover what the customer is actually doing? For example, are carts consistently being abandoned at the shipping calculation phase of the order process, or after searches that don't seem to yield results? This type of granular data isn't typically kept and analyzed because it requires too much storage, perhaps its considered to have too short of a shelf life to invest in, or can't be processed quickly enough to be useful at the individual customer level. As another example, consider the last time you emailed a service provider and it actually changed how they interacted with you. Shouldn't it? You bet it should! In the Big Data era, storage and processing concerns that forced a trade-off to lower service levels can start to be addressed.

Now consider a scenario in which you can combine what the warehouse knows about a customer with these communication events: you'd end up with a much richer, informed, and timely understanding of what we call the *customer state*. A great example of customer state mismatch was recently experienced by one of the authors of this book. He had an issue with a company that was incorrectly billing to his credit card, but the bank told him that he had to resolve the issue with the vendor. The bank would not stop the billing because it was a pre-authorized charge. He emailed, then chatted, then called the bank over the course of a couple days, all with increasing levels of frustration. After no luck with this resolution method, he walked into a local branch that promptly tried to upsell him on a new card feature. This clearly wasn't the right time to offer him a promotion—he wasn't in the right customer state—but the poor CSR had no idea this was the wrong time to do this. This bank experience is far from unique (and our author wants you to know they are generally pretty darn good to deal with), but it's a fact: most firms don't pick up the signals customers send them.

Fraud Detection: "Who Buys an Engagement Ring at 4 A.M.?"

When was the last time you bought an engagement ring at 4 A.M.? (We're excluding any purchases made in Las Vegas.) Not very common, is it? This is a good example of the concept of *outliers*, which are key to finding and trying to predict fraud. You search for outliers all the time. Consider your smart phone's detailed bill—you certainly don't look at hundreds of calls when trying to figure out how you blew 2,000 minutes; but we're willing to bet you spot that 70-minute phone call when the others are all measured in single-digit minutes. Fraud and risk are part of cross-industry Big Data use cases that are not restricted to the FSS. Big Data platforms, as we will see, are very well suited to finding outliers. What's more, highly dynamic environments commonly have cyclical fraud patterns that come and go in hours, days, or weeks. If the data that's used to identify new fraud detection models isn't available with low latency, by the time you discover these new patterns, it's too late and some damage has already been done.

Several challenges to fraud detection are directly attributable to the sole utilization of conventional technologies. The most common theme you'll see across all Big Data patterns are limits on what (amount and type) can be stored, and what compute resources are available to process your intentions. In other words, models to predict fraud often are either too laser focused due to compute constraints and miss things, or they are not as refined as they could (or should) be because the dimensions of the model have to be artificially constrained. After all, it's harder to find outliers when you don't store data profiling the attributes of those outliers. That said, having a larger set of data and attributes is only useful if you can handle the compute capabilities that are required to churn through them and find the signals that are buried within the noise. It's also critical to load and process data quickly enough to trap fast-moving events.

Fraud cases traditionally involve the use of samples and models to identify customers that exhibit a certain kind of profile. Although it works, the problem with this approach (and this is a trend that you're going to see in a lot of these use cases) is that you're profiling a segment and not at the individual transaction or person level. Making a forecast based on a segment is good, but making a decision that's based upon the actual particulars of an individual and correlate their transaction is obviously better. To do this, you need to work up a larger set of data than is possible with traditional approaches. We estimate that less than 50 percent (and usually much less than that) of the available information that could be useful for fraud modeling is actually being used. You might think that the solution would be to load the other 50 percent of the data into your traditional analytic warehouse. The reasons why this isn't practical seem to come up in most Big Data usage patterns, namely: the data won't fit; it'll contain data types that the warehouse can't effectively use; it'll most likely require disruptive schema changes; and it could very well slow your existing workloads to a crawl.

If stuffing the rest of the data into existing warehouses isn't going to work, then what will? We think that the core engines of the IBM Big Data platform (BigInsights, Streams, and the analytics-based IBM PureData Systems) give you the flexibility and agility to take your fraud models to the next level. BigInsights addresses the concerns we outlined in the previous paragraph, because it will scale to just about any volume and handle any data type required. Because it doesn't impose a schema on-write, you'll have maximum flexibility in how you organize your data, and your work won't impact existing workloads and other systems. Finally, BigInsights is highly scalable; you can start small and grow in a highly cost-effective manner (trust us when we say that your CIO will like this part).

Now that you have BigInsights to provide an elastic and cost-effective repository for all of the available data, how do you go about finding those outliers?

We're going to keep things simple here, because this topic itself could fill an entire book, but the first step is to load all of the useful data into BigInsights. Notice that we didn't qualify that by data type. Second, build a base customer profile with as much detail and as many dimensions of behavior as possible. Third, start building models of what "normal" looks like, and then start figuring out what an outlier looks like and how "out" it needs to lie before it's worth flagging. In the first iteration, we expect that some of your outliers will be incorrect, but iteration- and experience-based learning is what we're after. Back testing, of course, is part of this process but so is testing against current data flows, which you can do by pushing models to Streams (Predictive Model Markup Language is one way to do this) so that you can score against a live stream of data to accelerate the learning process. As models are discovered and validated, you'll promote them into your day-to-day high performance analytics platform, which brings traditional warehouse technologies into the picture. Finding outliers will provide additional insights into what your "normal" customers do, and it's rare when customer segmentation models aren't improved as a result; of course, after that happens, you'll want to unleash your teams to start working with that data too.

We said at the beginning of this chapter that there are literally hundreds of usage patterns out there, but that we can't cover them all in this chapter. In fact, fraud detection has massive applicability. Think about fraud in health care markets (health insurance fraud, drug fraud, medical fraud, and so on) and the ability to get in front of insurer and government fraud schemes (both claimants and providers). This is a huge opportunity; the US Federal Bureau of Investigation (FBI) estimates that health care fraud costs US taxpayers over $60 billion a year. Think about fraudulent online product or ticket sales, money transfers, swiped bankcards, and more.

Liquidity and Risk: Moving from Aggregate to Individual

The fact that there's room for improvement in risk modeling and management in a number of industries is probably not shocking. Risk modeling brings into focus a recurring question when it comes to the Big Data usage patterns that are discussed throughout chapter: "How much of your data do you use in your modeling?" and "How long does it take to iterate and refresh over these models?" Current modeling methodologies are held back by system constraints, which dictate the architecture and preclude pursuing the path to optimal results. It's not that companies don't recognize that there are a lot of potential insights available from undiscovered data, but their current systems don't always support them. Doubling, tripling, or quadrupling the size of an analytic warehouse isn't going to work, because they're usually already bursting at the seams or fully utilized. Capital constraints and regulatory requirements are forcing adoption of interesting new approaches in this space, and we thought we'd share some of them with you in this section.

Consider a multinational client that needed to move from line-of-business–organized stovepipes to individual-level risk management. Their current data is a month-old snapshot of their credit exposure; useful data for sure, but slow and expensive to bring through their current manual process. We proposed a new architecture that includes BigInsights, IBM Information Server, and Netezza (the name of the IBM PureData Systems for Analytics at the time). We used their existing IBM Information Server Data Stage platform to transform the raw data, and loaded the enriched data into HBase (a column-oriented data store that's included in the BigInsights product). HBase enables you to persist and present data as a key/value pair. Client credit exposure was written out as a time series that was expanded as new products were offered. Using this approach, BigInsights was able to maintain a current representation of the client's credit positions in an environment that's both elastic in sizing and performance, and significantly less expensive. The Netezza analytics environment can request data from BigInsights, whenever needed, to enrich modeling without having to be concerned with how the client evolved the process of acquiring and storing their data.

Wrapping It Up

We can't possibly do justice to this topic in such a short amount of space. The bottom line, however, is that having more data can't just give you deeper analytical insights, but actually accelerate the analytics process as a whole—you just need to have a platform that helps you to contain the side effects of more volume, variety, veracity, and velocity—more data. The IBM Big Data platform is such a platform, because it provides search, development, governance, and analytics services for Big Data in motion and Big Data at rest.

We hope that the few Big Data use cases that we included in this chapter help you to realize that adding more high-fidelity data to the analytics process and broadening the reach of data to include traditional and nontraditional sources will reward you with a highly adaptive analytics model.

3

Boost Your Big Data IQ: The IBM Big Data Platform

Today's organizations understand the value of analytics. In Chapter 1, we talked about the impact of analytics as a means of identifying the ultimate leaders in various market segments. We talked about the joint IBM/MIT Sloan study, *The New Intelligent Enterprise*, which made it quite clear that strong positive correlations exist between market leadership and an enterprise's analytics IQ (which Big Data can boost). Indeed, it's fair to say that much of the attention around Big Data is associated with companies that have a vested interest in "upping" their analytics IQ to differentiate themselves in the marketplace. So much so, that many organizations now believe that gleaning deep analytical insights from data has become a survival imperative in a global economy.

The New Era of Analytics

Now ask yourself "What happens when an increasing number of organizations embrace analytics?" Do they lose their competitive edge because they are all competing with increased insight? For example, over a decade ago, the Oakland Athletics embraced analytics and data-driven approaches to player valuation—they used this approach to gain advantage over other teams in Major League Baseball (MLB). Indeed, the A's were leaders among their peers, demonstrating exceptional *payroll to performance* and *net revenue per seat* indicators. They set themselves apart from their industry peers using analytics. In fact, their story was so compelling and generated so much

41

interest that it was told through the best-selling book and blockbuster movie hit *Moneyball*, starring Brad Pitt. Eventually, other teams caught up. Today, there isn't a single team in MLB that doesn't use sophisticated analytics. Widespread adoption of analytics within MLB has neutralized any advantage that the Oakland A's once had in this domain.

It's fair to say that we're now entering an era in which analytics will be considered to be a "table stakes" capability for most organizations. Let's look at a specific example of how an organization is taking the use of analytics to a whole new level. Using analytics to measure customer support effectiveness is a common practice among many customer-centric organizations. It enables them to monitor customer satisfaction, drive retention, and manage the cost of support. The traditional approach involves analyzing all of the data associated with a support incident, such as call duration and speed of resolution, and then identifying opportunities for improvement. It also involves conducting surveys and collecting satisfaction metrics. One such metric, the *net promoter score*, can be a very effective tool in gauging a customer's perception of the company or product based on their interactions with support personnel.

Although this traditional approach can be effective in improving customer satisfaction and reducing churn, the *analytical cycle time* (the time interval between a support call and the actual process improvements that get pushed to the front line) can be quite long. During that time, other customers might have similarly poor support experiences that could cause them to churn. The opportunity for organizations to differentiate and compete revolves around not only the use of deep analytics at the core of their business, but also the analytical cycle time. Like a giant snowball rolling down a hill, the impact of analytics on your business is slow at first, but with every rotation, the potential impact becomes greater and greater.

With this in mind, the question really becomes, "Is it possible to take the analytical models and processes that have been built on historical data sets and apply them in real time to streaming data?"

One of our clients is currently in the process of doing exactly that. They have an intelligent intercept agent that monitors all telephone conversations between customers and customer support representatives (CSRs). This agent monitors the conversation, applies sentiment analysis to that conversation, and provides recommendations to the CSR in real time. For example, if a customer uses tonal inflection to ask a question, or uses sarcasm to express displeasure, the automated agent is able to detect that immediately and provide specific guidance to the CSR. The advice could be to answer the question differently, escalate the call to the next level, provide specific incentives to the customer, or simply to be more polite.

By intercepting, monitoring, and analyzing such calls in real time, this client is able to vastly improve support effectiveness by taking immediate remedial action to improve customer satisfaction. We want to emphasize that these capabilities don't replace traditional offline analytics; rather, they augment them by incorporating new varieties of data (voice in this case) and performing analytics in real time.

Key Considerations for the Analytic Enterprise

Differentiating on analytics means using data-driven insights to enhance organizational strategies *and* using analytics in ways that were previously impossible. Limitations that used to restrict where and how organizations could run analytics are being eliminated. Moreover, some of today's most "analytic enterprises" are changing their analytic deployment models to find new competitive advantages and differentiate themselves from their peers.

In this section, we share with you the key tenet for enterprise analytics: *if you want to boost your Big Data IQ, you've got to start with the right ingredients.* We will describe these "ingredients" using real-life customer examples.

Run Analytics Against Larger Data Sets

Historically, performing analytics on large data sets has been a very cumbersome process. As a result, organizations resorted to running their analytics on a sampled subset of available data. Although the models that they built and the predictions that they generated were good enough, they felt that using more data would improve their results. They recognized that the sampling process could sometimes lead to errors or biased conclusions.

Organizations that can run analytics, at scale, against their entire data sets, definitely have an advantage over those that do not. Pacific Northwest National Lab's Smart Grid Demonstration project is a great example of this. The project hopes to spur a vibrant new smart grid industry and a more cost-effective reliable electricity supply, both of which are drivers of US economic growth and international competitiveness. They plan to collect large amounts of data—specifically event data from 60,000 metered customers across five states—and run complex analytical models on them. Using IBM's Big Data technologies, they expect to validate new smart grid technologies and business models.

Run Analytics Blazingly Fast

Running analytics is a multistep process. It involves data exploration, data cleansing and transformation, creating analytical models, deploying and scoring those models, publishing outcomes, and then refining the models. It's also an iterative process. If the underlying analytical system performs poorly while running analytical queries, this adds latency to the overall process. Hence, having the ability to run complex analytics on large data sets extremely quickly has distinct advantages.

First, it enables greater business agility and dramatically cuts down on overall decision-making times. A stock exchange client of ours, NYSE Euronext, cut the time to run deep trading analytics on 2PB of data from 26 hours to 2 minutes! They were running deep analytic queries that required significant data access and computation. This boost in performance not only helped them react to market changes faster, but it also enabled them to increase the complexity of their analytical models.

Second, it improves analyst productivity. Another client, Catalina Marketing—a large retail marketing services provider—was able to increase their analysts' productivity by a factor of six. They did this by reducing their average analytical model scoring time from 4.5 hours to 60 seconds. As a result, they were able to run more analytical models, using the same staff, and deliver deeper, transformative business insights. Pause for a moment...and consider the impact of being able to score one hundred more models while trying to predict churn, risk, fraud, weather patterns, or wildfire smoke dispersion rates—this is the opportunity of Big Data.

Run Analytics in Real Time

Having the ability to run analytics in real time, as events occur, has a profound impact on how an organization reacts to change. As we discussed in Chapter 2, UOIT employs analytics on data in motion with the goal of predicting the onset of potentially life-threatening conditions up to 24 hours earlier, which can make a huge difference in patient outcomes. They do this by analyzing streamed data from various monitors and vital sign indicators. A telecommunications client of ours is able to analyze streaming network traffic data in real time to detect bottlenecks, and is able to apply preventive maintenance to the network. By moving analytics "closer to the action," organizations create tremendous opportunities for differentiation.

Run Analytics on a Broader Variety of Data

Earlier in this chapter, we described a client who achieved enormous customer support effectiveness by analyzing voice data from support conversations in real time. The ability to incorporate newer varieties of data, such as voice, text, video, and other unstructured data types, along with structured relational sources, opens up possibilities for improving efficiencies and differentiation. One of our retail clients is now correlating social media data with their point-of-sale data in the data warehouse. Before launching a new brand, they know what type of buzz it's generating, and they use that information to forecast product sales by geography and to ensure that merchandise is stocked to that level. They are running deep analytic queries on inventory levels and models that require heavy computations.

The Big Data Platform Manifesto

To enable the key considerations of the analytic enterprise, it's important to have a checklist of the imperatives of a Big Data platform—introducing our Big Data platform manifesto. The limitations of traditional approaches have resulted in failed projects, expensive environments, and nonscalable deployments. A Big Data platform has to support all of the data and must be able to run all of the computations that are needed to drive the analytics. To achieve these objectives, we believe that any Big Data platform must include the six key imperatives that are shown in Figure 3-1.

1. Data Discovery and Exploration

The process of data analysis begins with understanding data sources, figuring out what data is available within a particular source, and getting a sense of its quality and its relationship to other data elements. This process, known as *data discovery*, enables data scientists to create the right analytic model and computational strategy. Traditional approaches required data to be physically moved to a central location before it could be discovered. With Big Data, this approach is too expensive and impractical.

To facilitate data discovery and unlock resident value within Big Data, the platform must be able to discover data "in place." It has to be able to support the indexing, searching, and navigation of different sources of Big Data. It has to be able to facilitate discovery of a diverse set of data sources, such as databases, flat files, content management systems—pretty much any persistent data store that contains structured, semistructured, or unstructured data.

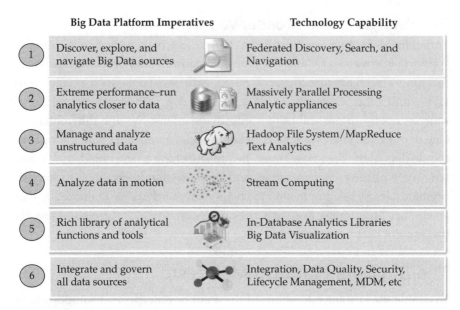

Big Data Platform Imperatives   Technology Capability

1. Discover, explore, and navigate Big Data sources — Federated Discovery, Search, and Navigation

2. Extreme performance–run analytics closer to data — Massively Parallel Processing Analytic appliances

3. Manage and analyze unstructured data — Hadoop File System/MapReduce Text Analytics

4. Analyze data in motion — Stream Computing

5. Rich library of analytical functions and tools — In-Database Analytics Libraries Big Data Visualization

6. Integrate and govern all data sources — Integration, Data Quality, Security, Lifecycle Management, MDM, etc

Figure 3-1   *The Big Data platform manifesto: imperatives and underlying technologies*

And don't forgot, the security profile of the underlying data systems needs to be strictly adhered-to and preserved. These capabilities benefit analysts and data scientists by helping them to quickly incorporate or discover new data sources in their analytic applications.

2. Extreme Performance: Run Analytics Closer to the Data

Traditional architectures decoupled analytical environments from data environments. Analytical software would run on its own infrastructure and retrieve data from back-end data warehouses or other systems to perform complex analytics. The rationale behind this was that data environments were optimized for faster access to data, but not necessarily for advanced mathematical computations. Hence, analytics were treated as a distinct workload that had to be managed in a separate infrastructure. This architecture was expensive to manage and operate, created data redundancy, and performed poorly with increasing data volumes.

The analytic architecture of the future needs to run both data processing and complex analytics on the same platform. It needs to deliver petabyte-scale performance throughput by seamlessly executing analytic models inside the platform, against the entire data set, without replicating or sampling data. It must enable data scientists to iterate through different models more quickly to facilitate discovery and experimentation with a "best fit" yield.

3. Manage and Analyze Unstructured Data

For a long time, data has been classified on the basis of its type—structured, semistructured, or structured. Existing infrastructures typically have barriers that prevented the seamless correlation and holistic analysis of this data; for example, independent systems to store and manage these different data types. We've also seen the emergence of hybrid systems that often let us down because they don't natively manage all data types.

One thing that always strikes us as odd is that nobody ever affirms the obvious: organizational processes don't distinguish between data types. When you want to analyze customer support effectiveness, structured information about a CSR conversation (such as call duration, call outcome, customer satisfaction, survey response, and so on) is as important as unstructured information gleaned from that conversation (such as sentiment, customer feedback, and verbally expressed concerns). Effective analysis needs to factor in *all* components of an interaction, and analyze them within the same context, *regardless* of whether the underlying data is structured or not. A game-changing analytics platform must be able to manage, store, and retrieve both unstructured and structured data. It also has to provide tools for unstructured data exploration and analysis.

4. Analyze Data in Real Time

Performing analytics on activity as it unfolds presents a huge untapped opportunity for the analytic enterprise. Historically, analytic models and computations ran on data that was stored in databases. This worked well for transpired events from a few minutes, hours, or even days back. These databases relied on disk drives to store and retrieve data. Even the best-performing disk drives had unacceptable latencies for reacting to certain events in real time. Enterprises that want to boost their Big Data IQ need the capability to analyze data as it's being generated, and then to take appropriate action. It's about deriving insight *before* the data gets stored on physical disks. We refer to this this type of data as *streaming* data, and the resulting analysis as *analytics of data in motion*. Depending on time of day, or other contexts, the volume of the data stream can vary dramatically. For example, consider a stream of data carrying stock trades in an exchange. Depending on trading activity, that stream can quickly swell from 10 to 100 times its normal volume. This implies that a Big Data platform not only has to be able to support analytics of data in motion, but also has to scale effectively to manage increasing volumes of data streams.

5. A Rich Library of Analytical Functions and Tool Sets

One of the key goals of a Big Data platform should be to reduce the *analytic cycle time*, the amount of time that it takes to discover and transform data, develop and score models, and analyze and publish results. We noted earlier that when your platform empowers you to run extremely fast analytics, you have a foundation on which to support multiple analytic iterations and speed up model development (the snowball gets bigger and rotates faster). Although this is the desired end goal, there needs to be a focus on improving developer productivity. By making it easy to discover data, develop and deploy models, visualize results, and integrate with front-end applications, your organization can enable practitioners, such as analysts and data scientists, to be more effective in their respective jobs. We refer to this concept as the *art of consumability*. Let's be honest, most companies aren't like LinkedIn or Facebook, with hundreds (if not thousands) of developers on hand, who are skilled in new age technologies. Consumability is key to democratizing Big Data across the enterprise. You shouldn't just *want*, you should *always demand* that your Big Data platform flatten the time-to-analysis curve with a rich set of accelerators, libraries of analytic functions, and a tool set that accelerates the development and visualization process.

Because analytics is an emerging discipline, it's not uncommon to find data scientists who have their own preferred mechanisms for creating and visualizing models. They might use packaged applications, use emerging open source libraries, or adopt the "roll your own" approach and build the models using procedural languages. Creating a restrictive development environment curtails their productivity. A Big Data platform needs to support interaction with the most commonly available analytic packages, with deep integration that facilitates pushing computationally intensive activities from those packages, such as model scoring, into the platform. It needs to have a rich set of "parallelizable" algorithms that have been developed and tested to run on Big Data. It has to have specific capabilities for unstructured data analytics, such as text analytics routines and a framework for developing additional algorithms. It must also provide the ability to visualize and publish results in an intuitive and easy-to-use manner.

6. Integrate and Govern All Data Sources

Over the last few years, the information management community has made enormous progress in developing sound data management principles. These include policies, tools, and technologies for data quality, security, governance, master data management, data integration, and information lifecycle management. They establish veracity and trust in the data, and are extremely critical to the success of any analytics program.

A Big Data platform has to embrace these principles and make them a part of the platform. It's almost scary how many times we've seen data quality and governance considered to be afterthoughts that are "bolted" onto existing processes. We need to treat these principles as foundational and intrinsic to the platform itself.

IBM's Strategy for Big Data and Analytics

In the previous section, we discussed how a new era of analytics is driving competitive differentiation within organizations and how that translates into specific considerations for an analytic enterprise. We also looked at what a Big Data platform for delivering the next generation analytic capabilities should define as its key imperatives. In this section, we cover how IBM has applied those considerations and imperatives to create the IBM Big Data platform.

1. Sustained Investments in Research and Acquisitions

IBM believes that Big Data has the potential to significantly change how organizations use data and run analytics. Business analytics and Big Data are strategic bets for IBM, who recognizes the huge potential to demonstrate leadership in this space and create shareholder value.

IBM is driving its commitment to Big Data and analytics through sustained investments and strategic acquisitions. In 2011, IBM committed a $100 million investment in the research and development of services and solutions that facilitate Big Data analytics. Look around the Big Data space. How many vendors have spent over $16 billion (as of the time this book was written—like Big Data numbers, it's out of date by the time you are reading this, and moving up), across 30 analytics-based acquisitions, in the last five years?

We often find people equating Big Data with Hadoop, and quite frankly it's a huge mistake to think that way. Hadoop is one of many technologies that is purpose-built for specific tasks. The value in Big Data (what your C-level executive branch really cares about) revolves around *how it can be monetized*. It's great to store 1PB of data, but if you can't analyze it, what do you have? A lot of data. Big Data is about analytics, and no other vendor is strategically investing in analytics like IBM. IBM's two most recent acquisitions, Netezza (whose main appliance has been rebranded as the IBM PureData System for Analytics) and Vivisimo (whose products have been rebranded as InfoSphere Data Explorer), had developed market-leading innovative technologies that have now been integrated into the IBM Big Data platform. IBM also has the largest commercial research organization on earth: hundreds of mathematicians and data scientists developing leading-edge analytics. Finally, IBM has the largest patent portfolio in the world, almost exceeding the combined total of the next four biggest patent-receiving companies!

Many of the research themes and innovations that pertain to unstructured data management, text analytics, image feature extraction, large-scale data processing have been incorporated into IBM's Big Data platform. To be frank, when you consider the strategic alignments around Big Data, there aren't many other organizations in the world that are capable of delivering a comprehensive end-to-end Big Data platform like IBM.

2. Strong Commitment to Open Source Efforts and a Fostering of Ecosystem Development

The open source community has been a major driving force for innovation in Big Data technologies. The most notable of these is Hadoop, a software framework that enables the processing of data-intensive computational tasks, in parallel and at scale. The Hadoop ecosystem consists of other related open source projects that provide supporting utilities and tools. These projects provide specialized functions that enable better access to data in Hadoop's distributed file system (HDFS), facilitate workflow and the coordination of jobs, support data movement between Hadoop and other systems, implement scalable machine learning and data mining algorithms, and so on. These technologies are all part of the Apache Software Foundation (ASF) and are distributed under a commercially friendly licensing model.

Apache Hadoop is still in early stages of its evolution. While it does provide a scalable and reliable solution for Big Data, most enterprises may find that it has missing features, lacks specific capabilities, or requires specialized skills to adopt for their needs.

Hence, technology solution providers, including IBM, are making efforts to bridge the gap and make Apache Hadoop easier for enterprise adoption. These technology solution providers can take one of two different approaches to achieving this goal. The first approach is to take the Apache Hadoop open source code base as a starting point, and then modify it appropriately to address gaps and limitations. In software development parlance, this process is known as *forking*. Vendors adopting this approach effectively create a vendor-specific proprietary Hadoop distribution that's somewhat closed and insulated from the innovations and improvements that are being applied to the open source components by the community. This makes interoperability with other complementary technologies much more difficult.

The second approach is to retain the open source Apache Hadoop components as is, without modifying the code base, while adding other layers and optional components that augment and enrich the open source distribution. IBM has taken this second approach with its InfoSphere BigInsights (BigInsights) product, which treats the open source components of Apache Hadoop as a "kernel" layer, and builds value-added components around it. This enables IBM to quickly adopt any innovations or changes to the core open source projects in its distribution. It also makes it easy for IBM to certify third-party technologies that integrate with open source Apache Hadoop.

This modular strategy of incorporating other open source–based Hadoop distributions into its own offering enables IBM to both maintain the integrity of the open source components and to address their limitations. BigInsights is an IBM-certified version of Apache Hadoop. Moreover, many of the value components that BigInsights offers (such as BigSheets and the Advanced

Text Analytics Toolkit) are supported for use on Cloudera's distribution of Hadoop components. (Other distributions are currently under consideration.)

Sometimes we field questions about IBM's commitment to open source. This kind of catches us off-guard, not because the question is hard—on the contrary, we're caught off-guard because we realize that perhaps IBM hasn't done a good enough job of evangelizing what it does in this space, so we decided to do it here (albeit briefly). For the record, IBM is 100 percent committed to open source, and IBM is 100 percent committed to Hadoop.

A number of our engineers contribute pieces of code to the Apache Hadoop open source project and its associated ecosystem (they are called *committers* in the open source world). IBM has a long history of inventing technologies and donating them to the open source community as well; examples include Apache Derby, Apache Geronimo, Apache Jakarta, DRDA, XERCES; the list goes on and on. The *de facto* tool set for open source, Eclipse, came from IBM. Text analytics is a major use case around Big Data, and IBM contributed the Unstructured Information Management Architecture (UIMA). Search is a Big Data prerequisite enabler, and IBM is a major contributor to Lucene (search technology that was showcased in the winning Watson technology on the television program *Jeopardy!*). We don't have the space to detail IBM's commitment to open source in this book, but we think we made our point.

IBM has also built a strong ecosystem of solution providers in the Big Data space. Currently, its partners—including technology vendors and system integrators that are trained and certified on the IBM Big Data platform—number in the triple digits.

3. Support Multiple Entry Points to Big Data

Big Data technologies can solve multiple business problems for an organization. As a result, organizations often grapple with the best approach to adoption. As practitioners, we sometimes see IT organizations embark on a Big Data initiative as though it were a science experiment in search of a problem; and we'll tell you, in our experience, lack of focus and unclear expectations typically lead to unfavorable outcomes (it's not good for job security). In our opinion, the most successful Big Data projects start with a clear identification of a business problem, or a pain point, followed by the application of appropriate technology to address that problem. After all, we've yet to see a client get excited about software because they love the look of it. (Although we think that Netezza was definitely the first product to make hardware look cool.) Getting started in the right place is crucial. In fact, the success of your first Big Data project can determine how widely and how quickly this technology is adopted across the rest of your organization.

We've identified some of the most common pain points (that effectively act like Big Data project "triggers") that we come across in our client engagements. For this reason, we refer to the IBM Big Data platform as having five Big Data entry points, as shown in Figure 3-2.

The IBM Big Data platform provides quantifiable benefits as you move from an entry point to a second and third project, because it's built on a set of shared components with integration at its core. We find it typical that assets being used in one Big Data project not only increase your chances of success with downstream projects, but accelerate their delivery as well. For

Figure 3-2 *IBM's Big Data platform supports multiple entry points.*

example, you might develop a sentiment analysis package for an application that crunches millions of emails for a service desk application. A subsequent project could take this asset (data harvested at rest) and transparently deploy it to a data-in-motion application that assesses a live Twitter stream for trending sentiment.

Finally, it's worth noting that the IBM Big Data platform is not an all-or-nothing proposition. Quite the contrary: you can get started with a single product, a subset of products, or the entire platform, giving you the flexibility and agility that you need to successfully deliver that initial project, and then incrementally "up" your Big Data IQ from there. In the remainder of this section, we discuss each of the IBM Big Data platform entry points.

Unlock Big Data

How many times have you not been able to find content on your laptop that you knew you had? How many times have you stumbled across one file while you were looking for another file that you had completely forgotten about? If you can't really get a handle on the data assets that are on your own laptop, imagine this pain point for a large enterprise! To be honest, we find that enterprises are often guilty of not knowing what they could already know because they don't know what they have. In other words, they have the data, but they can't get to it. This is the pain point that's associated with "unlock Big Data."

This problem is compounded for organizations that have access to multiple sources of data, but don't have the infrastructure to get all of that data to a central location, or the resources to develop analytical models to gain insights from it. In these cases, the most critical need might be to quickly unlock the value resident in this data without moving it anywhere, and to use the Big Data sources in new information-centric applications. This type of implementation can yield significant business value, from reducing the manual effort to search and retrieve Big Data, to gaining a better understanding of existing Big Data sources before further analysis. The payback period is often short. This entry point enables you to discover, navigate, view, and search Big Data in a federated manner.

Reduce Costs with Hadoop

Organizations might have a particular pain point around reducing the overall cost of their data warehouse. They might be retaining certain groups of data that are seldom used but take up valuable storage capacity. These data groups could be possible candidates for extension (sometimes called *queryable archive*) to a lower-cost platform that provides storage and retrieval, albeit with poorer performance. Moreover, certain operations, such as transformations, could be offloaded to a more cost-efficient platform to improve the efficiency of either the ETL (extract, transform, and load) process or the data warehouse environment. An entry point for this type of problem might be to start with Hadoop, a data-at-rest engine. The primary area of value creation here is cost savings. By selectively pushing workloads and data sets onto a Hadoop platform, organizations are able to preserve their queries and take advantage of Hadoop's cost-effective processing capabilities for the *right* kinds of data and workloads.

Analyze Raw Data

There might be situations in which an enterprise wants to extend the value of its data warehouse by bringing in new types of data and driving new types of analysis. Their primary need might be to analyze unstructured data from one or multiple sources. They might want to overcome the prohibitively high cost of converting unstructured data sources to a structured format by analyzing data in its raw format. A Hadoop-based analytics system could be the right entry point for this type of problem. Enterprises often gain significant value with this approach, because they can unlock insights that were previously unknown. Those insights can be the key to retaining a valuable customer, identifying previously undetected fraud, or discovering a game-changing efficiency in operational processes.

Simplify Your Warehouse

We often come across situations in which business users are hampered by the poor performance of analytics in a general-purpose enterprise warehouse because their queries take hours to run. The cost associated with improving the performance of the data warehouse can be prohibitively high. The enterprise might want to simplify its warehouse and get it up and running quickly. In such cases, moving to a purpose-built, massively parallel, data warehousing and analytics appliance could be the perfect entry point to Big Data. Many organizations realize a 10- to-100-fold performance boost on deep analytics, with reduced cost of ownership and improved employee efficiency, by using our technology.

Analyze Streaming Data

An organization might have multiple sources of streaming data and want to quickly process and analyze perishable data, and take action, in real time. Often they will be unable to take full advantage of this data simply because there might be too much of it to collect and store before analysis. Or the latency associated with storing it on disk and then analyzing it might be unacceptable for the type of real-time decisions that they want to drive. The ability to harness streaming data and turn it into actionable insight could be another Big Data entry point. The benefits would be the ability to make real-time decisions and to drive cost savings by analyzing data in motion and only storing what's necessary.

A Flexible, Platform-Based Approach to Big Data

We finish this chapter by mapping the services that are available from the IBM Big Data platform (shown in Figure 3-3) to the products that deliver them, with pointers to more detailed information elsewhere in the book.

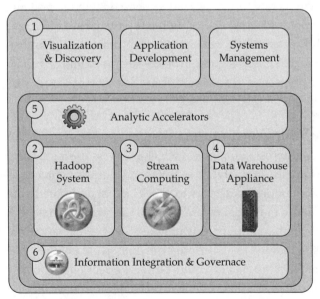

Figure 3-3   *The IBM Big Data platform*

1. Visualization and Discovery:
IBM InfoSphere Data Explorer Powered by Velocity

For organizations that need to understand the scope and content of their data sources, IBM InfoSphere Data Explorer (Data Explorer) is a good starting point. It enables them to unlock the data that they have available, both inside and outside of the enterprise, through federated search, discovery, and navigation. It enables everyone—from management to knowledge workers to front-line employees—to access all of the information that they need in a single view, regardless of format or location. Rather than wasting time accessing each silo separately, Data Explorer enables them to discover and navigate seamlessly across all available sources, and provides the added advantage of cross-repository visibility. It secures the information, so that users see only the content that they are permitted to see as if they were logged directly into the target application. In addition, Data Explorer gives users the ability to comment, tag, and rate content, as well as to create folders for content that they would like to share with other users. All of this user feedback and social content is then fed back into Data Explorer's relevance analytics to ensure that the most valuable content is presented to users. Enterprises like Procter and Gamble have been able to streamline their support and operations by providing employees visibility into over 30 data repositories using this technology.

Data Explorer is a great place to start the Big Data journey, because you can quickly discover and examine the data assets that you have on hand to determine what other parts of the platform you will need next. We talk about this technology in Chapter 7.

2. Hadoop System: IBM InfoSphere BigInsights

Hadoop is an ideal technology for organizations that want to combine a variety of data types, both structured and unstructured, in one place for deep analysis. It also enables organizations to reduce the cost of their data management infrastructure by offloading data and workloads. IBM's Info-Sphere BigInsights builds on top of open source Hadoop and augments it with mandatory capabilities that are needed by enterprises. It has optimizations that automatically tune Hadoop workloads and resources for faster performance. It has an intuitive spreadsheet-style user interface for data scientists to quickly examine, explore, and discover data relationships. It provides security and governance capabilities to ensure that sensitive data is protected and secured. BigInsights is prepackaged with development tooling that makes it easier for technical teams to create applications without first having to go through exhaustive training to become Hadoop experts. We will describe IBM's Hadoop distribution in Chapter 5.

3. Stream Computing: IBM InfoSphere Streams

Stream computing enables organizations to immediately respond to changing events, especially when analyzing stored data isn't fast enough. It also enables them to be more efficient in prefiltering and selectively storing high-velocity data. IBM InfoSphere Streams (Streams) delivers this capability by enabling organizations to analyze streaming data in real time. Streams has a modular design that has unlimited scalability and can process millions of events per second. It has the ability to analyze many data types simultaneously and to perform complex calculations in real time. We will describe Streams and analytics in motion in Chapter 6.

4. Data Warehouse Appliance: IBM PureData System for Analytics Powered by Netezza Technology

We often find enterprises struggling with the complexity of their data warehousing environments. Their data warehouses tend to be glutted with data and not suited for one particular task. Gaining deep analytical insights might be too complex or expensive. IBM addresses this pain point through an anaytics-based IBM PureData System. The IBM PureData System for Analytics (the new name for the latest generation Netezza appliance) is a purpose-built appliance for complex analytical workloads on large volumes of structured data. It's designed with simplicity in mind and needs minimal administration and no performance tuning. It uses a unique hardware-assisted query processing mechanism that enables users to run complex analytics at blistering speeds. We talk about this technology in Chapter 4.

5. Analytic Accelerators

One of the objectives of IBM's platform-based approach is to reduce time to value for Big Data projects. The IBM Big Data platform achieves this by packaging prebuilt analytics, visualization, and industry-specific applications as part of the platform. The analytic accelerators contain a library of pre-built functions that analyze data in its native format, where it lives, and with the appropriate engine: InfoSphere BigInsights, InfoSphere Streams, or an analytics-based IBM PureData System. The library of prebuilt functions includes algorithms for processing text, image, video, acoustic, time series, geospatial, and social data. The functions span mathematical, statistical, predictive, and machine learning algorithms. The accelerators also include the appropriate development tools to enable the market to develop analytic applications for the Big Data platform. We cover text analytics in Chapter 8, and in Chapter 9, we talk about the three Big Data analytic accelerators that are designed to get you moving on a Big Data project…fast. Discovery tools, such as BigSheets, are covered in Chapter 5, along with the BigInsights product.

6. Information Integration and Governance

The IBM Big Data platform includes purpose-built connectors for multiple data sources. It has adapters for common file types, databases, and sources of unstructured and streaming data. It also has deep integration between its data processing engines, which enables data to be moved seamlessly between an analytics-based IBM PureData System, InfoSphere BigInsights, and InfoSphere Streams.

Security and governance are key aspects of Big Data management. The Big Data platform might contain sensitive data that needs to be protected, retention policies that need to be enforced, and data quality that needs to be governed. IBM has a strong portfolio of information lifecycle management, master data management, and data quality and governance services. These services are integrated and available for use within the Big Data platform. We cover this topic in Chapters 10 and 11.

Wrapping It Up

We started this chapter by describing the foundational components of any enterprise. We believe that these core capabilities are the DNA of any Big Data platform—whether you are looking at IBM's offering in this space, or another vendor's, our vast experiences suggest that this is what you're going to need to boost your Big Data IQ. Our Big Data manifesto sits on top of these foundational components.

We concluded this chapter by introducing you to the IBM Big Data platform, a solution that provides you with a flexible adoption plan for Big Data that's aligned with specific business challenges. The real benefit of the platform is the ability to leverage reusable components (analytics, accelerators, and policies) as you adopt new capabilities from one implementation to the next. The platform gives you the ability to manage all of your enterprise data with a single integrated platform, provides multiple data engines (each optimized for a specific workload), and uses a consistent set of tools and utilities to operate on Big Data. The preintegrated components within the platform also reduce implementation time and costs. IBM is the only vendor with this broad and balanced view of Big Data and the needs of a Big Data platform.

IBM has delivered its Big Data platform through a "Lego block" approach. For example, if a customer has challenges with an existing data warehouse and is unable to process structured data at scale, their initial starting point would be a purpose-built data warehousing appliance. This can then be expanded to either include Hadoop to analyze raw data at rest, or stream computing to analyze data in motion. Finally, IBM delivers distinct capabilities that are aligned with each of the trigger pain points. We believe that there is no comparably complete, consumable, and capable Big Data platform in the marketplace.

Part II

Analytics for Big Data at Rest

4

A Big Data Platform for High-Performance Deep Analytics: IBM PureData Systems

Data warehousing systems and technologies are intended to give organizations access to information on demand, help them react to it faster, and facilitate quicker decisions. Indeed, the language used to describe the size of data warehouses has changed from gigabytes to terabytes and petabytes, workloads have evolved from being primarily operational to increasingly analytic, and numbers describing concurrency have gone from hundreds to thousands. These changes create a realization for many that the traditional approaches to data warehousing can't scale to meet today's challenges.

Organizations expect that when they need critical information urgently, the platform that delivers it should be the last thing on their minds. After all, when you turn on the lights at your house, do you consider the wiring and circuitry that makes it happen? Obviously not. You expect to be able to consume what you need to get the job done without effort (well, you have to flip the light switch, but you get the point). To support the escalating complexity, concurrency, and volumes of today's data warehouses, IT organizations are demanding a platform that's simple, reliable, and able to handle almost any workload without complexity getting in the way.

The first generation of data warehouse technologies was modeled after OLTP-based databases running on large symmetric multiprocessing (SMP) machines. These machines had inherent architectural limitations that prevented them from becoming a viable platform for analytics. Subsequent iterations tried to incorporate parallel processing techniques and distributed storage subsystems into the architecture. The resulting complexity of operation (various kinds of indexes, indexes on indexes, optimization hints, and the like) made these systems even more complex to operate and expensive to maintain.

Achieving consistent performance against increasing data volumes and diverse workloads without a significant increase in total cost of ownership (TCO) has always been the biggest challenge in data warehousing technologies. Invariably, the biggest bottleneck across all data warehouse operations was the speed at which the database engine could read from and write data to disk, known as *disk I/O bottleneck*.

When warehouses were piece-parts, various providers delivered a number of I/O innovations in an attempt to address this bottleneck; however, these innovations were brought to market independently and exhibited little synergy across warehouse tiers: the relational database management system (RDBMS), storage subsystem, and server technologies. For example, using caching in the storage subsystem, faster network fabric on the servers, and software optimizations, such as partitioning and indexing, are all optimizations that were brought to market to minimize disk I/O. And although they addressed the issues *locally* and that helped a bit, they weren't collectively optimized to significantly improve disk I/O. In addition, these optimization techniques relied on the data warehouse designers to second-guess query patterns and retrieval needs up-front so that they could tune the system for performance. This not only impacted business agility in meeting new reporting and analytics requirements, but it also required significant manual effort to maintain, tune, and configure the data warehouse tiers. As a result, collectively these systems became expensive to manage and brutal to maintain.

The IBM PureData System for Analytics appliance—formerly known as the IBM Netezza Data Warehouse Appliance, often just referred to as Netezza—was developed to overcome these specific challenges. (Since this chapter talks about the history of the Netezza technology that is the genesis for this IBM PureData System appliance, we'll refer to both the appliance and technology simply as Netezza for the remainder of this chapter.) In fact, it's fair to say that Netezza started what has now become the appliance revolution in data warehousing by integrating the database, processing, and storage components in a flexible, compact, purpose-built, and optimized system for analytical workloads. This innovative platform was built to deliver an industry-leading price-performance ratio with appliance simplicity. As a purpose-built appliance for high-speed Big Data analytics, its power comes not from the most powerful and expensive components (which would increase the slope of its cost-benefit curve) but from how the right components are assembled and work together to maximize performance. In short, the goal wasn't to build a supercomputer, but rather an elegantly designed system to address commonplace bottlenecks with the unequalled ability to perform analytics. Netezza did this by combining massively parallel processing (MPP) stream and multicore CPUs with Netezza's unique hardware acceleration (we refer to this as Netezza's secret sauce) to minimize disk I/O bottlenecks and deliver performance and expert tuning that much more expensive systems could never match, or even approach. We want to clarify the word *streams* in the previous sentence. In this context, we are talking about streaming data from database components on disk into memory for processing. You will learn about streams that reference continuous processing of data in motion using InfoSphere Streams in Chapter 6.

It's important to note that Netezza didn't take an old system with known shortcomings and balance it with a storage tier. It was built from the ground up, specifically for running complex analytics on large volumes of structured data. As an easy-to-use appliance, the system delivers its phenomenal results out of the box, with no indexing or tuning required. Appliance simplicity extends to application development, enabling rapid innovation and the ability to bring high-performance analytics to the widest range of users and processes. For users and their organizations, it means the best intelligence to all who seek it, even as demands escalate from all directions.

Looking back at the history of Netezza and today's Big Data era, we think it's safe to assert that Netezza took the CFO/CIO discussion from "spending money to save money," to "spending money to make money": it handed businesses, both large and small, the ability to democratize deep analytics, while flattening the cost curve that was once associated with this domain.

In this chapter we're going to get a little more technical than the previous chapters you've read. This will allow us to better explain concepts and illustrate the "secret sauce" that's made the industry-leading Netezza technology so special.

Netezza's Design Principles

Netezza's approach to data analysis is patented and proven. Its goal has always been to minimize data movement, while processing it at "physics speed," in parallel, and on a massive scale—all delivered within an easy-to-use appliance at a low cost. The Netezza appliance has undergone multiple iterations since its inception (it's latest refresh includes a name change to the IBM PureData System for Analytics), but its architecture has always been based on a core set of design principles. These design principles have been a hallmark of Netezza's price-performance leadership in the industry, and we'll cover them in this section.

Appliance Simplicity: Minimize the Human Effort

Enterprises are spending more and more money to pay people to manage their systems. Now consider this observation in an environment where cheaper labor is presumably available through a globally distributed delivery model, and you can see that the required amount of human effort is a problem.

Appliances are dedicated devices that are optimized for a very specific purpose. They are self-contained and ready to go. They are very fast to install and easy to operate. They have standard interfaces that enable other systems to interoperate with them. All of these characteristics make appliances a very elegant vehicle for delivering IT solutions. In certain areas, such as network and storage solutions, appliances are the preferred means for delivering specific capabilities.

Netezza pioneered the concept of appliances in the data warehousing and analytics realm. All of its technologies are delivered in an appliance form, shielding end users from the underlying complexity of the platform. Simplicity rules whenever there is a design tradeoff with any other aspect of the appliance. Unlike other solutions, the appliance just runs, handling demanding queries and mixed workloads at blistering speeds. Even normally time-consuming tasks, such as installation, upgrade, and ensuring high-availability and business continuity, are vastly simplified, saving precious time and resources, and mitigates operational risk.

Hardware Acceleration: Process Analytics Close to the Data Store

Netezza's architecture is based on a fundamental principle of computer science: when operating on large data sets, don't move data unless you absolutely have to. Moving large data sets from physical storage units to compute nodes increases latency and affects performance. Netezza minimizes data movement by using innovative hardware acceleration; for example, it uses field-programmable gate arrays (FPGA) to filter out extraneous data as early in the data stream as possible, and basically as fast as data can be streamed off the disk. This process of data elimination close to the data source removes I/O bottlenecks and keeps downstream components, such as the CPU, memory, and network, from having to process superfluous data; this produces a significant multiplier effect on system performance.

Balanced, Massively Parallel Architecture: Deliver Linear Scalability

Every component of Netezza's architecture, including the processor, FPGA, memory, and network, is carefully selected and optimized to service data as fast as the physics of the disk allows, while minimizing cost and power consumption. The Netezza software orchestrates these components to operate concurrently on the data stream in a pipeline fashion, thus maximizing utilization and extracting the utmost throughput from each MPP node. Although the use of open, blade-based components enables Netezza to incorporate technology enhancements very quickly, the turbo-charger effect of the FPGA, a balanced hardware configuration, and tightly coupled intelligent software combine to deliver overall performance gains far greater than those of the individual elements. In fact, Netezza has delivered more than four-fold performance improvements every two years since its introduction, far outpacing other well-established vendors.

Modular Design: Support Flexible Configurations and Extreme Scalability

One of the key concerns with traditional appliance-based architectures has been their ability to scale after data volumes outgrow the physical capacity of the appliance. Netezza addresses this concern with a modular appliance design that simply scales from a few hundred gigabytes to tens of petabytes of user data *that can be queried*. In fact, the system has been designed to be highly adaptable, and to serve the needs of different segments of the data warehouse and analytics market. The use of open blade-based components enables the disk-processor-memory ratio to be easily modified in configurations that cater to performance or storage-centric requirements. This same architecture also supports memory-based systems that provide extremely fast, real-time analytics for mission-critical applications. In the remainder of this chapter, we'll delve into just how these design principles translate into practice.

What's in the Box? The Netezza Appliance Architecture Overview

Netezza architecture is based on an asymmetric massively parallel processing (AMPP) methodology that combines the best elements of symmetric multiprocessing (SMP) and MPP to create a purpose-built appliance for running blazingly fast analytics on petabytes of data.

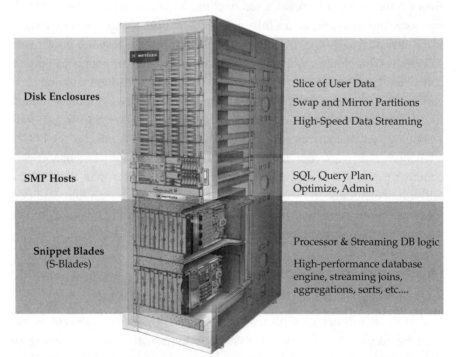

Figure 4-1   *The IBM Netezza appliance (now known as the IBM PureData System for Analytics)*

A single rack Netezza system is shown in Figure 4-1. As you can see, it has two high-end rack-mounted servers called *hosts*, which function both as the external interface to the Netezza appliance and the controller for the massively parallel infrastructure. The hosts are connected through an internal network fabric to a set of *snippet blades* (we'll often refer to them simply as *S-blades*), where the bulk of the data processing is performed. The S-blades are connected through a high-speed interconnect to a set of disk enclosures where the data is stored.

If any component fails, be it the host, disk, or S-blade, recovery is automatic. The range of automatic failure detection and recovery options demonstrates the advantages of an appliance approach. Netezza has built-in component and operational redundancy, and the system responds automatically and seamlessly to the failure of critical components.

A Look Inside the Netezza Appliance

Every component of Netezza's AMPP architecture, including the processor, FPGA, memory, and network is carefully selected and integrated to yield a balanced overall system. In addition to raw performance, this balanced architecture can deliver linear scalability to more than a thousand processing streams executing in parallel, while offering a very economical TCO. These parallel streams work together to "divide and conquer" the workload. Let's examine the key components of a Netezza system, as shown in Figure 4-2.

Netezza Hosts

Hosts are the primary interfaces to the system. The hosts are high-performance Linux servers that are set up in an active-passive configuration for high availability (note that Figure 4-2 has two of them stacked on top of each other). The host compiles SQL queries into executable code segments called *snippets*, creates optimized query plans, and distributes the snippets to the MPP nodes for execution. The active host presents a standardized interface to external tools and applications, such as business intelligence reporting tools, data integration and ETL tools, advanced analytics packages, backup and recovery tools, and so on. These external applications use ubiquitous protocols, such as JDBC, ODBC, and OLE DB, to interface with the Netezza host.

Hosts run both high-availability (HA) clustering software and mirroring technology. All write operations to the active host are mirrored to the standby host, preparing it to take over system processing at any moment if a failure should occur. The standby host monitors the active host through Ethernet links and assumes the primary role should the active host fail.

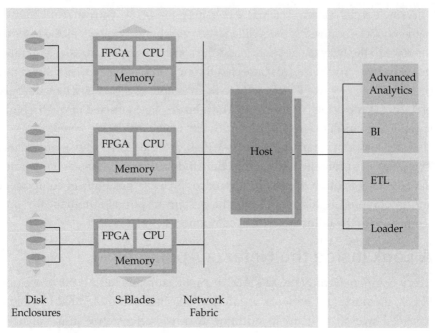

IBM Netezza data warehouse appliance   External Applications
(IBM PureData System for Analytics)

Figure 4-2   *The Netezza AMPP architecture*

S-blades

S-blades are intelligent processing nodes that make up the MPP engine of the Netezza appliance. Each S-blade is an independent server that contains powerful multicore CPUs, multiengine FPGAs, and gigabytes of RAM, all balanced and working concurrently to deliver peak performance.

Netezza protects against S-blade failures as well. The system management software continuously monitors each S-blade and, if a failure is detected, the S-blade is taken out of service and its processing load is automatically transferred to the spare S-blade. Monitoring of the S-blade includes error correction code (ECC) checking on the blade memory. If the system management software detects that ECC errors have exceeded a failure threshold, it takes the S-blade out of service.

Disk Enclosures

The system's disk enclosures (which each contain slices of a table's data) contain high-density, high-performance disks that are RAID protected. Disk enclosures are connected to the S-blades through high-speed interconnects that enable all of the disks in Netezza to simultaneously stream data to the S-blades at the maximum rate possible.

There are two independent data paths from each S-blade in the chassis to each disk. Each drive is mirrored in a RAID 1 configuration. In the event of a disk failure, processing is completed on the mirror without any interruption of service. I/O is simply redirected to the mirror drive by the storage subsystem. Spare drives are included in each appliance so that it can transparently self-heal by selecting a spare to take the place of the failed drive and regenerating its contents to restore redundancy.

Network Fabric

Internode communication across Netezza's MPP grid occurs on a network fabric running a customized IP-based protocol that fully utilizes the total cross-sectional bandwidth of the fabric and eliminates congestion even under sustained, bursty network traffic. The network is optimized to scale to more than a thousand nodes, while allowing each node to initiate a large data transfer to every other node simultaneously.

Netezza's custom network protocol is designed specifically for the data volumes and traffic patterns that are associated with high-volume data warehousing. It ensures maximum utilization of the network bandwidth without overloading it, thereby allowing predictable performance close to the data transmission speed of the network.

Traffic in a Netezza system flows smoothly in three distinct areas:

- From the host to the snippet processors (1 to 1000+) in broadcast mode

- From snippet processors to the host (1000+ to 1), with aggregation in the S-blades and at the system rack level

- Between snippet processors (1000+ to 1000+), with data flowing freely on a massive scale for intermediate processing

The Netezza network fabric infrastructure has the same level of redundancy as the other major components. In fact, each Netezza appliance has two completely independent networks, and because each of the redundant hosts is connected to one of these redundant networks, the loss of any piece of the network fabric can be overcome by switching to the standby host. The data network is not only redundant, but also physically distinct from the separate management network, enabling the system to assess the health of its components even if the data network experiences problems.

The Secret Sauce: FPGA-Assisted Analytics

The FPGA is a critical enabler of the price-performance advantages of the Netezza appliance. An FPGA is a semiconductor chip equipped with a large number of internal gates that can be programmed to implement almost all logical functions. After an FPGA is programmed, it operates more like special-built hardware than a general-purpose processor giving it optimum performance for narrowly defined tasks. FPGAs are particularly effective at managing special purpose stream processing tasks, and are extensively used in such applications as digital signal processing, medical imaging, and speech recognition. In fact, it's likely the case that you've got an FPGA in your house and didn't even know it! Do you watch DVDs or Blu-ray discs? An FPGA is likely behind the scenes, facilitating reads of high-quality compressed digital data off the spinning disc without the jitters. An FPGA is tiny in size (about 1" × 1" of square silicon) but performs programmed tasks with enormous efficiency, drawing little power and generating little heat.

Figure 4-3 illustrates FPGA-enabled processing within each S-blade. A dedicated high-speed interconnect from the storage array enables data to be delivered to memory as quickly as it can stream off the disk. Compressed data is cached in memory using a smart algorithm, which ensures that the most commonly accessed data is served right out of memory instead of requiring disk access.

Each FPGA contains embedded engines that perform filtering and transformation functions on the data stream. These engines are dynamically reconfigurable (enabling them to be modified or extended through software), are customized for *every snippet* through instructions provided during query execution, and act on the data stream at extremely high speeds. All of the engines that you see in the FPGA box in Figure 4-3 run in parallel and deliver the net effect of decompressing and filtering out 95 to 98 percent of table data at physics speed, thereby only keeping the data that's relevant

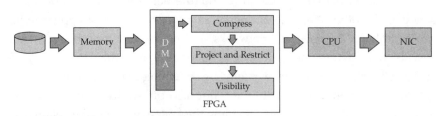

Figure 4-3 *FPGA-assisted snippet processing in Netezza*

to the query. The CPU cores shown in the figure also run in parallel and process the remaining data in the stream concurrently. We kept this figure simple to make it easy to read, but the process described here is repeated on about one hundred of these parallel snippet processors running in the appliance. On a ten-rack system, this would represent up to one thousand parallel snippet processors, with performance that exceeds that of much more expensive systems by orders of magnitude.

The FPGA includes the following embedded engines:

- **The compression engine**   All data in Netezza is stored compressed on disk. The compression engine resides inside the FPGA and decompresses data at the transmission speed of the network, instantly transforming each block on disk into 4 to 8 blocks in memory. The use of semiconductor-based technology, and not software, to achieve compression and decompression of data boosts system performance by a factor of 4 to 8, which results in significant acceleration of the slowest component in any data warehouse, the disk.

- **The project and restrict engine**   This engine further enhances performance by filtering out columns and rows, based on parameters in the SELECT and WHERE clauses of an SQL query.

- **The visibility engine**   Netezza maintains ACID (atomicity, consistency, isolation, and durability) compliance at streaming speeds, and uses its visibility engine to filter out rows that should not be "seen" by a query (for example, rows belonging to a transaction that's not yet committed).

Query Orchestration in Netezza

All queries and analyses enter Netezza through the host machine where the optimizer, the compiler, and the scheduler decompose them into many different snippets whose instructions are subsequently distributed into the multiple S-blades (all of which then process their workload simultaneously against their locally managed slice of data). In this section, we discuss these individual steps in greater detail using Figure 4-4.

Query Optimization

The intelligence of the Netezza optimizer is one of its greatest strengths. It was engineered to create query execution plans specifically optimized for

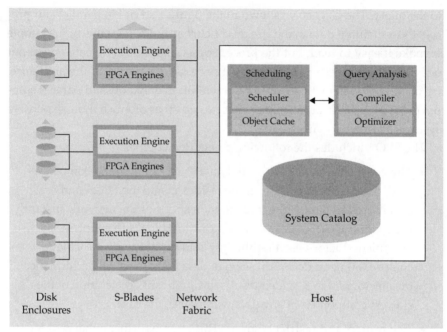

Figure 4-4 *Query orchestration in Netezza*

Netezza's AMPP architecture. The optimizer makes use of all MPP nodes in the system to gather detailed up-to-date statistics on every database table that is referenced in a query. A majority of these metrics are captured during query execution with very low overhead, yielding just-in-time statistics that are specific to each query. The optimizer uses these statistics to transform queries before processing begins, which helps to minimize disk I/O and data movement. Typical transformation operations performed by the optimizer include: determining the correct join order, rewriting expressions, and removing redundancy from SQL operations.

The appliance nature of Netezza, with integrated components that are able to communicate with each other, enables its cost-based optimizer to more accurately measure disk, processing, and network costs associated with an operation. By relying on accurate data, instead of heuristics alone, the optimizer is able to generate query plans that utilize all components with extreme efficiency. One example of optimizer intelligence is the ability to determine the best join order in a complex join. For example, when joining multiple small tables to a large fact table, the optimizer can choose to broadcast the small tables in their entirety to each S-blade, while keeping the large table distributed across all snippet processors. This approach minimizes data movement while taking advantage of the AMPP architecture to parallelize the join.

Snippet Compilation

A compiler converts a query plan into executable code segments, called *snippets*. Query segments are executed by snippet processors in parallel across all of the data streams in the appliance. Each snippet has two elements: compiled code that's executed by individual CPU cores, and a set of FPGA parameters that customize the embedded engines' filtering for that particular snippet. This snippet-by-snippet customization enables Netezza to provide, in effect, a hardware configuration that is optimized on the fly for individual queries.

The host uses a feature called the *object cache* to further accelerate query performance. This is a large cache of previously compiled snippet code that supports parameter variations. For example, a snippet with the clause WHERE NAME='Bob' might use the same compiled code as a snippet with the clause WHERE NAME='Jim' but with settings that reflect the different name. This approach eliminates the compilation step for over 99 percent of snippets.

Just-In-Time Scheduling

The Netezza scheduler balances execution across complex workloads to meet the objectives of different users, while maintaining maximum utilization and throughput. It considers a number of factors, including query priority, size, and resource availability in determining when to execute snippets on the S-blades. The appliance architecture enables the scheduler to gather more up-to-date and accurate metrics about resource availability from each component of the system. Sophisticated algorithms are at the heart of this scheduler and empower Netezza to maximize system throughput by utilizing close to 100 percent of the disk bandwidth while ensuring that memory and network resources don't get overloaded and cause the system to lose efficiency. This important characteristic of the Netezza appliance ensures that the system keeps performing at peak throughput even under very heavy loads. When the scheduler gives the "green light," the snippet is broadcast to all snippet processors throughout the intelligent network fabric.

Massively Parallel Snippet Processing

Every S-blade's snippet processor receives the specific instructions that it needs to execute its portion of the snippet. In addition to the host scheduler, the snippet processors have their own smart pre-emptive scheduler that allows snippets from multiple queries to execute simultaneously. This scheduler takes into account the priority of the query and the resources set aside for the user or group that issued the query to decide when and for how long to schedule a particular snippet for execution. The following steps outline the sequence of events associated with snippet processing:

1. The processor core on each snippet processor configures the FPGA engines with parameters contained in the query snippet and sets up a data stream.

2. The snippet processor reads table data from the disk array into memory. It also interrogates the cache before accessing the disk for a data block, avoiding a scan if the data is already in memory. The snippet processor uses a Netezza innovation called *ZoneMap acceleration* to reduce disk scans.

   ZoneMap acceleration exploits the natural ordering of rows in a data warehouse to accelerate performance by orders of magnitude. The technique avoids scanning rows with column values outside the start and end range of a query. For example, if a table contains two years of weekly records (~100 weeks), and a query is looking for data for only one week, ZoneMap acceleration can improve performance up to 100 times. Unlike typical indexes associated with optimizations in traditional data warehousing technology, ZoneMaps are automatically created and updated for each database table, without incurring any administrative overhead.

3. The FPGA acts on the data stream. First, it accelerates it four- to eight-fold by decompressing data stream at the transmission speed of the network. Next, its embedded engines filter out any data that's not relevant to the query. The remaining data is streamed back to memory for concurrent processing by the CPU core (as we show in Figure 4-3). The resultant data at this stage is typically a tiny fraction (2 to 5 percent) of the original stream, greatly reducing the execution time that's required by the processor core.

4. The processor core picks up the data stream and performs core database operations such as sorts, joins, aggregations, and so on. It also applies complex algorithms that are embedded in the snippet processor for advanced analytics. Results of each snippet processor's work are assembled in memory to produce a subresult for the entire snippet. With more than a thousand snippet processors working simultaneously, hundreds or thousands of query snippets can execute in parallel. Snippet processors use the intelligent network fabric to communicate with the host (and with each other) and perform intermediate calculations and aggregations. Some highly complex algorithms, such as matrix computations, require communication among nodes. For this reason, Netezza engineered a message-passing interface to communicate interim results and to produce the final result.

5. Finally, the host assembles the intermediate results received from the snippet processors, compiles the final result set, and returns it to the application. Of course, during this time, other queries are streaming through the system at various stages of completion. This gives Netezza another point of optimization: because the original compressed data blocks are still in memory, they can be automatically reused in later queries requiring similar data through the table cache—an automated mechanism requiring no administrator involvement.

Platform for Advanced Analytics

Traditionally, analytics had to be built and deployed on separate analytics servers. These servers would run computationally intensive analytical algorithms and interface with a data repository, such as a data warehouse, on the back end. This architecture lengthens the time from model inception to deployment, and requires data movement from the data repository to the analytics server. Not only does this process take too much time, but it's inefficient, limits the data that can be used to derive insight, constrains the scope of the analytic modeling, and impedes the ability to experiment iteratively.

Netezza offers a distinctive and simple-to-use approach for serious analytics on structured data with IBM Netezza Analytics, an advanced analytics platform that's shipped free inside every Netezza appliance. With IBM Netezza Analytics, analytic activities such as data exploration, discovery, transformation, model building, and scoring can all be performed right where the data resides—in the data warehouse. This reduces the time that it takes to build and deploy analytic models throughout an enterprise. By shrinking the time from model inception to deployment, companies can move to enterprise-wide, fact-based decisions by infusing more of their decisions with insightful on-demand analytics. This also enables practitioners to experimentally iterate through different analytical models more quickly to find the best fit. After a model is developed, it can seamlessly be executed against all of the relevant data in the enterprise. The prediction and scoring can be done right where the data resides, inside the data warehouse. Users can get the results of prediction scores in near-real time, helping to *operationalize* advanced analytics and making it available throughout the enterprise.

IBM Netezza Analytics supports multiple tools, languages, and frameworks. It enables analytic applications, visualization tools, and business intelligence tools to harness parallelized advanced analytics through a variety of programming methods such as SQL, Java, MapReduce, Python, R, C, C++, and Fortran; all can be used to deliver powerful, insightful analytics. The comprehensive advanced analytics environment makes it easy to derive benefit from this platform, giving you the flexibility to use your preferred tools for ad-hoc analysis, prototyping, and production deployment of advanced analytics.

The Netezza analytics platform enables the integration of its robust set of built-in analytics with leading analytics tools from such vendors as Revolution Analytics (who ship a commercial version of R), SAS, IBM SPSS, Fuzzy Logix, and Zementis. Additionally, you can develop new capabilities using the platform's user-defined extensions. The entire Netezza analytics platform is shown in Figure 4-5.

IBM Netezza Analytics includes a built-in library of parallelized analytic functions, purpose-built for large data volumes, that flattens the time-to-development curve for any analytics project. Table 4-1 summarizes some of these key built-in analytic functions and their benefits.

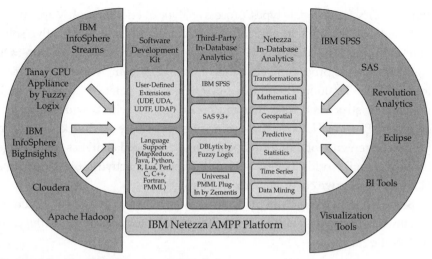

Figure 4-5 *The IBM Netezza analytics platform*

Transformations	Execute in-database data transformations to realize significant performance gains.
Mathematical	Perform deep in-database mathematical calculations to leverage MPP processing.
Statistics	Calculate rich statistics without moving the data.
Time series	Create forecasts and identify trends using rich histories to improve model accuracy.
Data mining	Use more data, or all of the data, to discover new and emerging insights.
Predictive	Move from batch processing to near-real-time speed-of-thought analytics to predict with great accuracy and speed.
Geospatial	Implement location-based analytics on Big Data with immediate feedback.

Table 4-1 *In-Database Analytics Built into IBM Netezza Analytics*

Extending the Netezza Analytics Platform with Hadoop

As previously mentioned, the principle of massive parallelism and close-to-source data processing (embodied by all parts of the IBM Big Data platform, including Netezza, InfoSphere BigInsights [Hadoop], InfoSphere Streams, and InfoSphere Data Explorer) provides enormous benefits for advanced analytics running on large data sets. Because Hadoop and Netezza both work on stored data, we want to explain when to use each, and how the two technologies work together. Hadoop's ability to run on commodity servers, store a wide variety of data types, process analytic queries through MapReduce, and predictably scale with increased data volumes is a very attractive solution set for Big Data analytics. Netezza's ability to embed complex non-SQL algorithms in the processing elements of its MPP stream, without the typical intricacies of Hadoop programming, enables low-latency access to high volumes of structured data that can be integrated with a wide variety of enterprise BI and ETL tools. These principles make Netezza the ideal platform for the convergence of data warehousing and advanced analytics. To leverage the best of both worlds, Netezza offers different connectivity solutions with a Hadoop cluster (we cover Hadoop in Chapter 5).

Because the IBM Big Data platform is so flexible, we thought it would be worthwhile to discuss some typical scenarios that use Hadoop *in conjunction* with Netezza.

Exploratory Analysis

Sometimes an organization encounters a new source of data that needs to be analyzed. They might have little to no knowledge about the format of this new data source, the data types that it contains, or the relationships it encapsulates. For example, suppose that the marketing department has launched a new multichannel campaign and wants to integrate responses from Facebook and Twitter with other sources of data that they might have. If you've never used Facebook or Twitter APIs, or are not familiar with their data feed structures, it might take some experimentation (data discovery) to figure out what to extract from this feed and how to integrate it with other sources. Hadoop's ability to process data feeds for which a schema has not yet been defined is ideal in this scenario. So if you want to explore relationships within data, especially in an environment where the schema is constantly evolving, Hadoop provides a mechanism by which you can explore the data until a formal, repeatable ETL process is defined. After that process is defined and structure is established, the data can be loaded into Netezza for standardized reporting or ad-hoc analysis.

Hadoop Is the New Tape: The Queryable Archive

Big Data analytics tend to bring large volumes of data under investigation. Quite often we find that a significant percentage of this data might not be of interest on a regular basis. Such data might be of an historical nature or very granular data that has subsequently been summarized within the data warehouse. Putting all of this data within an infrastructure that is primarily optimized for performance might not be economically viable. For this reason, enterprises might want to optimize their analytics footprint and store the less frequently accessed data on infrastructure that's optimized for price per terabyte of storage, and leverage the higher performing infrastructure as needed.

Since Hadoop's fault-tolerant distributed storage system runs on commodity hardware, it could serve as a repository for this type of data. Unlike tape-based storage systems that have no computational capability, Hadoop provides a mechanism to access and analyze data. Because moving computation is cheaper than moving data, Hadoop's architecture is better suited as a *queryable* archive for Big Data. In fact, the number one use case that countless enterprise customers have described to us involves the architecture of "hot-cold" data storage schemes between Netezza and Hadoop, where the most actively used data is warehoused in Netezza, and everything else is archived in Hadoop. Of course, in addition to the native connectors that are built into Hadoop, IBM provides a whole information integration and governance platform (which we cover in Chapters 10 and 11) that can help to facilitate and govern this process.

Unstructured Data Analysis

Relational data warehouses provide limited capabilities for storing complex data types and unstructured data. What's more, performing computations on unstructured data through SQL can be quite cumbersome and limited. Hadoop's ability to store data in any format and analyze that data using a procedural programming paradigm, such as MapReduce, makes it well suited for storing, managing, and processing unstructured data. You could use Hadoop to preprocess unstructured data, extract key features and metadata, and then load that data into your Netezza data warehouse for further analysis.

Customers' Success Stories: The Netezza Experience

It's a fact: hundreds of organizations have escaped the frustrations of their first-generation data warehouses by replacing older database technologies with IBM Netezza's data warehousing and analytic appliances. The systems that were replaced forced users to deal with too much complexity; the warehouses demanded constant attention and administration from highly trained specialists. This complexity is doubly corrosive: the costs of administration spiral upward and out of control as data volumes grow, while the business, distanced from its data, must seek technical expertise to manage its interactions with its information.

As we noted earlier, Netezza revolutionized the data warehousing market and caused traditional data warehouse providers to change their strategies. Why did the market change its course, or accelerate plans, when Netezza took the marketplace by storm? Simple: customers were able to refocus their time away from the technical aspects of managing data and toward the business and the greater role that data can play in its success. Individuals who previously spent as much as 90 percent of their time consumed in low-level technical work now rarely interact with the technology, but constantly interact with the business and its data to investigate new ways to create value from their data. We thought it'd be worthwhile to share with you just a few customer stories that highlight why and how Netezza blazed the trail for data warehouse appliances.

T-Mobile: Delivering Extreme Performance with Simplicity at the Petabyte Scale

Every day, T-Mobile processes more than 17 billion events, including phone calls, text messages, and data traffic over its networks. This translates to upward of 2PB of data that needs to be crunched. T-Mobile needed a Big Data solution that could store and analyze multiple years worth of call detail records (CDRs) containing switch, billing, and network event data for its millions of subscribers. T-Mobile wanted to identify and address network bottlenecks and to ensure that quality and capacity would be provisioned when and where they are needed.

Netezza proved to be the right solution for T-Mobile to manage its massive growth in data. More than 1,200 users access its Netezza system. They analyze over 17 billion events per day and perform network quality of experience (QoE) analytics, traffic engineering, churn analysis, dropped session analytics, as well as voice and data session analytics. Since deploying Netezza, T-Mobile has realized a significant reduction in data warehouse administrative activities compared to its previous solution, and has also been able to reduce tax and call-routing fees by using the greater volume of granular data to defend against false claims. To top it off, T-Mobile has been able to increase network availability by identifying and fixing network bottlenecks and congestion issues whenever they arise.

State University of New York: Using Analytics to Help Find a Cure for Multiple Sclerosis

The State University of New York (SUNY) at Buffalo is home to one of the leading multiple sclerosis (MS) research centers in the world. MS is a devastating, chronic neurological disease that affects nearly one million people worldwide. The SUNY team has been looking at data obtained from scanned genomes of MS patients to identify genes whose variations could contribute to the risk of developing MS. Their researchers postulated that environmental factors, along with genetic factors, determine a person's MS risk profile.

SUNY's goal was to explore clinical and patient data to find hidden trends among MS patients by looking at factors such as gender, geography, ethnicity, diet, exercise, sun exposure, and living and working conditions. Their data sources for this analysis included medical records, lab results, MRI scans, and patient surveys; in short, a wide variety of data in enormous volumes. The data sets used in this type of multivariable research are very large, and the analysis is computationally very demanding because the researchers are looking for significant interactions among thousands of genetic and environmental factors. The computational challenge in gene-environmental interaction analysis is due to a phenomenon called *combinatorial explosion*. Just to give you a sense of the number of computations necessary for data mining in this scenario, think about a 1 followed by 18 zeroes (we're talking *quintillions* here)!

SUNY researchers wanted to not only see which variable is significant to the development of MS, but also which combinations of variables are significant. They decided to use Netezza as their data platform. By using Revolution R Enterprise for Netezza, in conjunction with the IBM Netezza Analytics system, they were able to quickly build models using a range of variable types and to run them against huge data sets spanning more than 2,000 genetic and environment factors that might contribute to MS. This solution helped the SUNY researchers to consolidate all reporting and analysis into a single location to improve the efficiency, sophistication, and impact of their research, and to reduce the time required to conduct this analysis from 27 hours to 11 minutes!

NYSE Euronext: Reducing Data Latency and Enabling Rapid Ad-Hoc Searches

NYSE Euronex is a Euro-American corporation that operates multiple securities exchanges, most notably the New York Stock Exchange (NYSE) and Euronext. NYSE ingests about 8 billion transactions per day. On certain days, for example when we had the financial market "flash crash," they process over 15 billion transactions. This is 2TB to 4TB of data that needs to be ingested into their data warehouse each day. Their analysts track the value of a listed company, perform trend analysis, and search for evidence of fraudulent activity. NYSE and Euronext perform market surveillance and analyze each and every transaction from a trading day, which translates into full table scans on massive volumes of data. As is the case with many enterprises, NYSE and Euronext's traditional data warehouse was moving data back and forth between the storage systems and their analytic engine, and took over 26 hours to complete certain types of processing. They also have global customers and need 24/7 access without any downtime. How did they address these challenges? They chose Netezza. Netezza's core tenet of running compute close to data minimized network traffic and reduced the time needed to access business critical data from 26 hours to 2 minutes. It facilitated rapid ad-hoc searches over a petabyte of data and opened up new analytical capabilities.

5

IBM's Enterprise Hadoop: InfoSphere BigInsights

Few technologies have gotten more buzz over the past few years than Hadoop and NoSQL. Couple that with Big Data, and you have enough hype to write a whole library of trendy technical books. There's a reason for all the excitement around these technologies. Traditional data storage and analytics tools have not been cutting it when dealing with Big Data. From a *volume* perspective, many tools start being impractical when thresholds in the dozens of terabytes are exceeded. Sometimes "impractical" means that the technology simply won't scale any further, or that a tipping point is reached in terms of how much time it takes to transfer a data set over the network for processing. And other times, impractical means that although the technology can scale, the licensing, administrative, and hardware costs to deal with increased volume become unpalatable. From a *variety* perspective, traditional analytic tools only work well with structured data, which represents, at most, 20 percent of the data in the world today. Finally, there is the issue of how fast the data is arriving at your organization's doorstep—Big Data velocity—which we detail in the next chapter.

Considering the pressing need for technologies that can overcome the volume and variety challenges for data at rest, it's no wonder that business magazines and online tech forums alike are buzzing about Hadoop and NoSQL. And it's not all talk either. The IT departments in most Fortune 500 companies have done some level of experimentation with Hadoop and the like.

The problem is that many of these initiatives have stagnated in the "science project" phase. The challenges are common: it's easy and exciting to start dumping data into these repositories; the hard part comes with what to do next. Meaningful analysis of data that is stored in Hadoop requires highly specialized programming skills—and for many algorithms, it can be very challenging to put them into a parallelizable form so that they can run in Hadoop. And what about information governance concerns, such as security and data lifecycle management, where new technologies like Hadoop don't have a complete story?

IBM sees the tremendous potential for technologies such as Hadoop to have a transformative impact on businesses. This is why IBM has scores of researchers, developers, and support staff continually building out a platform for Hadoop, called IBM InfoSphere BigInsights (BigInsights). BigInsights was released in October, 2010, with a relatively straightforward goal: make Hadoop enterprise-ready. We describe three main aspects of enterprise readiness in this chapter:

- **Analytics support**   Enable different classes of analysts to get value out of data that is stored in BigInsights without asking them to pass requirements over the fence to Hadoop programmers, or buying expensive consulting hours to procure custom Hadoop applications that no one in your organization understands. Think consumability!

- **Data integration**   If your business is analyzing data that is stored in Hadoop, you'll need to ensure that your Hadoop system integrates with the rest of your IT infrastructure. For example, you'll need to be able to query Hadoop data from your warehouse environment, and, inversely, query warehouse data from your Hadoop environment.

- **Operational excellence**   After you start depending on analytics that is generated by Hadoop, you will need to govern and administer the data that is stored in Hadoop. BigInsights includes a number of key features for security, governance, administration, and performance.

Before we describe the BigInsights extensions to Hadoop, you'll need to understand what Hadoop is in the first place.

What the Hadoop!

At a very high level, Hadoop is a distributed file system and data processing engine that is designed to handle extremely high volumes of data in any structure. In simpler terms, just imagine that you've got dozens, or even hundreds (or thousands!) of individual computers racked and networked together. Each computer (often referred to as a *node* in Hadoop-speak) has its own processors and a dozen or so 2TB or 3TB hard disk drives. All of these nodes are running software that unifies them into a single cluster, where, instead of seeing the individual computers, you see an extremely large volume where you can store your data. The beauty of this Hadoop system is that you can store anything in this space: millions of digital image scans of mortgage contracts, days and weeks of security camera footage, trillions of sensor-generated log records, or all of the operator transcription notes from a call center. This ingestion of data, without worrying about the data model, is actually a key tenet of the NoSQL movement (this is referred to as "schema later"). In contrast, the traditional SQL and relational database world depends on the opposite approach ("schema now"), where the data model is of utmost concern upon data ingest. This is where the flexibility of Hadoop is even more apparent. It's not just a place where you can dump many files. There are Hadoop-based databases where you can store records in a variety of models: relational, columnar, and key/value. In other words, with data in Hadoop, you can go from completely unstructured to fully relational, and any point in between. The data storage system that we describe here is known as the *Hadoop distributed file system (HDFS)*.

Let's go back to this imaginary Hadoop cluster with many individual nodes. Suppose that your business uses this cluster to store all of the clickstream log records for its e-commerce site. Your Hadoop cluster is using the BigInsights distribution, and you and your fellow analysts decide to run some of the sessionization analytics against this data to isolate common patterns for customers who leave abandoned shopping carts—we call this use case *last mile optimization*. When you run this application, Hadoop sends copies of your application logic to each individual computer in the cluster, to be run against data that's local to each computer. So instead of moving data to a central computer for processing (bringing data to the function), it's the application that gets moved to all of the locations in which the data is stored (bringing function to the data). This programming model is known as Hadoop MapReduce.

Where Elephants Come From: The History of Hadoop

Now that you've got a high-level sense of what Hadoop is, we can get into why it's revolutionizing IT. First, let's look at Hadoop's origins.

Hadoop was inspired by Google's work on its Google (distributed) file system (GFS) and the MapReduce programming paradigm. IBM has long been involved with MapReduce, as it teamed up with Google in October 2007 to do some joint university research on MapReduce and GFS for large-scale Internet problems. Shortly after Google published papers describing GFS and MapReduce (in 2003 and 2004 respectively), people in the open source community (led by Doug Cutting) applied these tools to the open source Nutch search engine. It became quickly apparent that the distributed file system and MapReduce modules together had applications beyond just the search world. It was in early 2006 that these software components became their own research project, called Hadoop. Hadoop is quite the odd name (and you'll find a lot of odd names in the Hadoop world). Read any book on Hadoop today and it pretty much starts with the name that serves as this project's mascot, so let's start there too. Hadoop is actually the name that creator Doug Cutting's son gave to his stuffed toy elephant. In thinking up a name for his project, Cutting was apparently looking for something that was easy to say and stands for nothing in particular, so the name of his son's toy seemed to make perfect sense.

Much of the work in building Hadoop was done by Yahoo!, and it's no coincidence that the bulk of the inspiration for Hadoop has come out of the search engine industry. Hadoop was a necessary innovation for both Yahoo! and Google, as Internet-scale data processing became increasingly impractical on large centralized servers. The only alternative was to scale out and distribute storage and processing on a cluster of thousands of nodes. Yahoo! reportedly has over 40,000 nodes spanning its Hadoop clusters, which store over 40PB of data.

The Hadoop open source team took these concepts from Google and made them applicable to a much wider set of use cases. Unlike transactional systems, Hadoop is designed to scan through large data sets and to produce its results through a highly scalable, distributed *batch* processing system. Hadoop is not about speed-of-thought response times, real-time warehousing, or blazing transactional speeds; however, it *is* about discovery and making the once-nearly-impossible possible from a scalability and analytics perspective.

Components of Hadoop and Related Projects

As mentioned earlier, Hadoop is generally seen as having two parts: a file system (HDFS) and a programming paradigm (MapReduce). One of the key components of Hadoop is the redundancy that is built into the environment. Not only is data redundantly stored in multiple places across the cluster, but the programming model is such that failures *are expected* and are resolved automatically by running portions of the program on various servers in the cluster. Because of this redundancy, it's possible to distribute the data and programming across a very large cluster of commodity components, like the cluster that we discussed earlier. It's well known that commodity hardware components will fail (especially when you have very large numbers of them), but this redundancy provides fault tolerance and the capability for the Hadoop cluster to heal itself. This enables Hadoop to scale out workloads across large clusters of inexpensive machines to work on Big Data problems.

There are many Hadoop-related projects, and some of the more notable ones include: Apache Avro (for data serialization), Cassandra and HBase (databases), Hive (provides ad-hoc SQL-like queries for data aggregation and summarization), Mahout (a machine learning library), Pig (a high-level Hadoop programming language that provides a data-flow language and execution framework for parallel computation), and ZooKeeper (provides coordination services for distributed applications). We don't cover these related projects due to the size of the book, but there's lots of information available on the Web, and of course, BigDataUniversity.com.

Hadoop 2.0

For as long as Hadoop has been a popular conversation topic around IT water coolers, the NameNode single point of failure (SPOF) has inevitably been brought up. Interestingly enough, for all the talk about particular design limitations, there were actually very few documented NameNode failures, which is a testament to the resiliency of HDFS. But for mission-critical applications, even one failure is one too many, so having a hot standby for the Name-Node is extremely important for wider enterprise adoption of Hadoop.

The MapReduce processing layer (the JobTracker server) also has a single point of failure.

In Hadoop 1.0 deployments, you can address the NameNode availability problem through active/passive failover solutions. One option is to automatically replicate data between two separate Hadoop clusters. Another option is to have a dedicated backup for the master node (which includes the NameNode, and can also include the JobTracker service), so that all of the Hadoop cluster's NameNode metadata is backed up. In the event of a NameNode failure, the Hadoop cluster can restart, using the backup NameNode.

In Hadoop 2.0 (which was in alpha state at the time of writing), there are two significant availability improvements: the ability to designate a hot standby for the HDFS NameNode, and YARN (also known as MapReduce2), which distributes JobTracker functionality so that this server is no longer a SPOF. IBM committers are working with the open source community to make Hadoop 2.0 production-ready, and, of course, IBM intends to keep BigInsights current with the latest enterprise-ready open source innovations.

In the open source community, there is some controversy as some vendors have released Hadoop 2.0 code in the Generally Available (GA) editions of their products. The point of contention is that the Hadoop 2.0 code being included here is not classified as production-ready. Other vendors, including IBM and Hortonworks, have shied away from this approach, reaffirming their policies to release only production-ready open source code in their distributions.

We'd love to get into more depth and describe how HDFS and MapReduce work, not to mention the additional projects in the Apache Hadoop ecosystem, but space is limited. To learn about Hadoop in greater detail, visit BigDataUniversity.com, where you can find a number of quality online courses for free!

What's in the Box: The Components of InfoSphere BigInsights

Before describing the enterprise-readiness capabilities of BigInsights, we'd like to establish a context, and go over the product's main components from both a licensing and packaging perspective, and a software component perspective. We'll describe the Hadoop components included in BigInsights, the main user interface for BigInsights (the BigInsights Web Console), the developer tooling, and the various editions that are available.

Hadoop Components Included in InfoSphere BigInsights 2.0

BigInsights features Apache Hadoop and its related open source projects as a core component. This is informally known as the IBM Distribution for Hadoop. IBM remains committed to the integrity of these open source projects, and will ensure 100 percent compatibility with them. This fidelity to open source provides a number of benefits. For people who have developed code against other 100 percent open source–compatible distributions, their applications will also run on BigInsights, and vice versa. This open source compatibility has enabled IBM to amass over 100 partners, including dozens of software vendors, for BigInsights. Simply put, if the software vendor uses the libraries and interfaces for open source Hadoop, they'll work with BigInsights as well.

IBM also releases regular product updates for BigInsights so that it remains current with the latest releases of the open source components.

The following table lists the open source projects (and their versions) that are included in BigInsights 2.0, which was the most current version available at the time of writing.

Component	Version
Hadoop (common utilities, HDFS, and the MapReduce framework)	1.0.3
Avro (data serialization)	1.6.3
Chukwa (monitoring large clustered systems)	0.5.0
Flume (data collection and aggregation)	0.9.4
HBase (real-time read and write database)	0.94.0
HCatalog (table and storage management)	0.4.0
Hive (data summarization and querying)	0.9.0
Lucene (text search)	3.3.0
Oozie (work flow and job orchestration)	3.2.0
Pig (programming and query language)	0.10.1
Sqoop (data transfer between Hadoop and databases)	1.4.1
ZooKeeper (process coordination)	3.4.3

With each release of BigInsights, updates to both the open source components and IBM components go through a series of testing cycles to ensure that they work together. That's another special point that we want to clarify: You can't just drop new code into production. In our experience, backward-compatibility issues are always present in open source projects. BigInsights pretty much takes away all of the risk and guesswork that's associated with typical open source projects for your Hadoop components. It goes through the same rigorous regression and quality assurance testing processes used for other IBM software. So ask yourself this: Would you rather be your own systems integrator, repeatedly testing all of the Hadoop components to ensure compatibility? Or would you rather let IBM find a stable stack that you can deploy without worry?

IBM's tradition of open source support continues with Hadoop. The Big Insights development team includes a set of committers to the Hadoop project and its related projects. These committers contribute to the leadership of the open source projects, and have the task of donating IBM code to the open source code base. By having committers on the BigInsights development team, IBM is more involved in the continuing evolution of open source Hadoop. IBM is also able to find and eliminate bugs in the open source code faster than would otherwise be possible. The hope that we share with the open source Hadoop community is that collectively, we've learned lessons from the UNIX wars, in which decades of development effort were wasted when technology firms built their own UNIX flavors to solve the same problems. With open source Hadoop, even though the companies involved are competitors, there is a shared interest in making Hadoop better.

The BigInsights Web Console

One of the nice features BigInsights brings to Hadoop is a rich interface called the BigInsights Web Console (see Figure 5-1). Whether you're running on a public cloud instance in a cluster half-way across the world, or on a 1,000-node cluster in your firm's server farm, this console is the focal point of the entire cluster, because all administration, application deployment, and application execution activities are performed there. The BigInsights Web Console has a number of capabilities that we cover in later sections, but for now take note of the task assistance on the left side of Figure 5-1, designed for consumability.

What you're able to see in the console depends on your level of access as a BigInsights user. For example, if you have an administrator account, you can see the administrative dashboards, such as Application Status and Cluster Status. And if you have a user account, you'll only be able to see the dashboards that are applicable to browsing files, running applications, and doing analysis work, namely the File Explorer, the Application Dashboard, and the BigSheets interface.

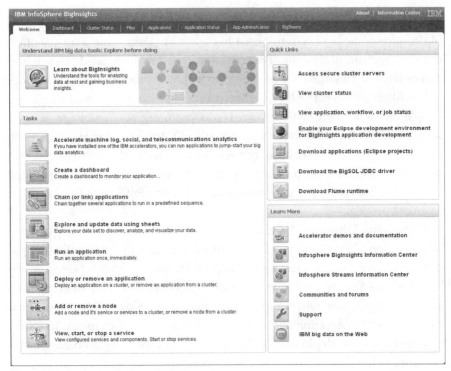

Figure 5-1 *The BigInsights Web Console*

The BigInsights Development Tools

In addition to the Web Console, BigInsights includes a set of Eclipse plug-ins for the development of applications that work with Big Data. This package of plug-ins can be downloaded from the Web Console, complete with installation instructions. This development tooling includes two Eclipse perspectives: BigInsights (which is oriented toward developing data processing applications using SQL, Jaql Hive, HBase, Pig, or MapReduce); and BigInsights Text Analytics (which directs you through a workflow for building text analytics applications). The Big Data platform comes with other perspectives as well, such as one for building applications for IBM InfoSphere Streams.

The BigInsights development tools can connect to the Web Console to gain cluster awareness. This enables developers to easily test and deploy applications, and to work directly with the cluster. In the upcoming section on analytics, we show you how the BigInsights Web Console and the development tools work together to provide a full lifecycle for building, testing, and deploying applications.

BigInsights Editions: Basic and Advanced

BigInsights comes in two editions: a free offering (Basic), and a for-fee offering (Enterprise). BigInsights Basic Edition is IBM's integrated, tested, and preconfigured download for anyone who wants to experiment with Hadoop. This edition includes the BigInsights installer, which gives you a quick and simple clickable path to your own Hadoop cluster. As a package of open source components, this represents the IBM Distribution for Hadoop. With the exception of a few database connectors and some of the tooling functions, none of the analytics, integration, or operational excellence features are included in this distribution. If you ever want to move to the Enterprise Edition, it's a seamless process.

BigInsights Enterprise Edition includes all of the features in BigInsights Basic Edition plus the analytics, integration, and operational excellence capabilities that we describe later in this chapter. Included with this license is also a limited use license for Streams, which entitles you to run streaming data jobs in conjunction with your data-at-rest processing using BigInsights (there's lots of integration here—more on that in the next chapter). To reflect different kinds of deployments, BigInsights Enterprise Edition also has a non-production license, and a starter kit license.

Deploying BigInsights

Hadoop—and by extension, BigInsights—is designed to be deployed on a cluster of many individual computers with dedicated storage and processing resources. Failover and redundancy capabilities are built into Hadoop with the expectation that it is to be deployed on inexpensive and eventually unreliable hardware. We refer to this kind of computing resource as *commodity hardware*, specifically, Intel chipsets with standard spinning disk storage. This is in contrast to the robust, high-quality, and, of course, expensive hardware that we see deployed in data warehouse servers, for example.

Ease of Use: A Simple Installation Process

The BigInsights installer was designed with simplicity in mind. IBM's development teams asked themselves, "How can IBM cut the time-to-Hadoop curve without the effort and technical skills normally required to get open source software up and running?" They answered this question with the BigInsights installer.

The main objective of the BigInsights installer is to insulate you from complexity. As such, you don't need to worry about software prerequisites or determining which Apache Hadoop components to download. You don't need to worry about the configuration between these components or the overall setup of the Hadoop cluster. The BigInsights installer does all of this for you, and all you need to do is click a button. Hadoop startup complexity is all but eliminated with BigInsights. Quite simply, your experience is going to be much like installing any commercial software.

What's more, you can use IBM's installation program to graphically build a response file, which you can subsequently use to deploy BigInsights on all of the nodes in your cluster in an automated fashion.

A Low-Cost Way to Get Started: Running BigInsights on the Cloud

With the rise of virtualization technologies, the Cloud has become a popular platform for businesses to leverage IT resources. Given the significant work involved in procuring and building a moderately sized Hadoop cluster, it would seem that Cloud technologies were designed with Hadoop in mind.

Let's say that you're interested in seeing what BigInsights can do for your business. You have a large data set, and you have analysts and developers ready to experiment with it. If you're considering an on-site experimental Hadoop installation, it could take weeks, if not months, for the procurement process to run its course, and for the hardware to finally be installed. On the other hand, you could have a made-to-order Cloud-based BigInsights cluster up and running within hours. Let's take this scenario a little further, and imagine that your data is loaded on this Cloud-based cluster, and that your analysts are working away. If some aspect of performance is poor, no problem! Additional resources (memory, data nodes, CPU) can be added dynamically to your cluster. This is another reason why the Cloud is such a great option for trial deployments: there's no need to spend a lot of time ironing out reference architecture details. With the Cloud, if it doesn't work, make adjustments in real time.

Like other components in the IBM Big Data platform, BigInsights works well in Cloud deployments. From a technology perspective, BigInsights supports virtualization, which is a must in Cloud environments. BigInsights also has an excellent security story, whereby the entire cluster can be isolated behind a single point of access through the Web Console. From a licensing perspective, it couldn't be easier, because the pricing model for BigInsights is based on the volume of data that is stored in the cluster (before replication and after compression). Finally, the BigInsights licenses have no restrictions around virtualization. Again, you only pay for how much you use, which is the same pricing model as Cloud services!

BigInsights has been successfully deployed on some of the most notable Cloud providers; for example, Amazon EC2, RackSpace, and IBM Smart-Cloud. IBM has also partnered with RightScale, the leading Cloud management platform. This partnership enables IBM to deliver trials for BigInsights and several other IBM products on both public Clouds and private Clouds that are built on open source Cloud stacks from Eucalyptus and Cloud.com.

Higher-Class Hardware: IBM PowerLinux Solution for Big Data

Although commodity hardware deployments have been the norm for Hadoop clusters up to this point, we're seeing some alternatives. One compelling option is the IBM PowerLinux Solution for Big Data. This is a Linux on Power hardware solution that's been optimized for Hadoop.

One of the most significant benefits of Power hardware is reliability, which makes it well suited to be deployed as master nodes in your cluster. If you need higher energy efficiency, or need to concentrate DataNodes to fewer tiles, or simply need more processing power, Power can most definitely be a great way to go.

In 2011, the IBM Watson system beat the two greatest champions of the American quiz show *Jeopardy!* Linux on Power was the underlying platform for Watson, which also leveraged Hadoop for some of its subsystems. During the development of the IBM PowerLinux Solution for Big Data, customizations and lessons learned from the Watson project were applied to this offering.

Cloudera Support

With the release of BigInsights 1.4, IBM expanded its Big Data platform to run on other distributions of Hadoop, beginning with Cloudera. The Cloudera brand has become synonymous with Hadoop, largely through the reach of their Cloudera Distribution for Hadoop (CDH). Although BigInsights includes the IBM Distribution for Hadoop, extending support to CDH does not reflect a contradictory approach. Rather, it's another way in which IBM supports a strong and unified Hadoop community. Because it's all based on open source code, the IBM Distribution for Hadoop and CDH are really not too different.

The main purpose behind IBM's support for Cloudera (and eventually, other open source Hadoop distributions) is to emphasize the value of the IBM Big Data platform. In short, even if you're not using the IBM Distribution for Hadoop, you can take advantage of the advanced analytics, integration, and tooling capabilities in BigInsights. Clients obtain CDH from Cloudera, install their CDH cluster, and then BigInsights enterprise features can be layered on top of CDH. For CDH users, this is a great story: they no longer have to make a difficult choice to leave the comfort of their installation to use BigInsights. The point here is that the choice of which distribution you use is less important than your approach to analytics higher in the stack.

Analytics: Exploration, Development, and Deployment

The biggest challenge facing organizations that have adopted Hadoop is how to quickly and easily derive value from the data that's stored in their clusters. There are many factors to consider here, some of which we've touched on earlier. For example: the difficulty of parallelizing many analytics algorithms; making data stored in Hadoop accessible for business analysts and data scientists; and dealing with really messy data. BigInsights addresses all of these issues by applying an integrated platform-based approach across its various components.

As an analytics platform for Hadoop, BigInsights supports three classes of analytic users: line-of-business analysts, data scientists, and application developers. In addition, the analytics and development components of BigInsights feature lifecycle management tooling, which enables developers to easily deploy analytic applications to line-of-business users and data scientists. Figure 5-2 shows all of the analytic components in BigInsights. We describe each of these components in this section. We also cover the application lifecycle

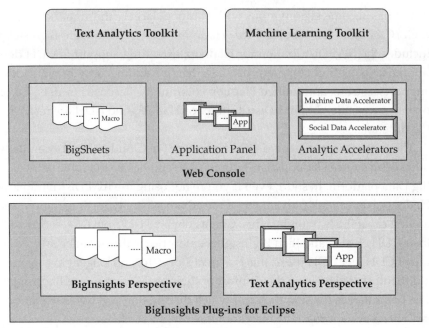

Figure 5-2   *Data analysis components in BigInsights*

methodology and the corresponding features that are baked into the BigInsights components.

Advanced Text Analytics Toolkit

One of our favorite examples of the deep integration that characterizes the IBM Big Data platform is the Advanced Text Analytics Toolkit. Although the BigInsights analytics components all connect to this toolkit, it's also integrated into the Streams product. This means that the text extractors that you write for your organization's data can be deployed on data at rest (through BigInsights), or data in motion (through Streams). The Text Analytics Toolkit is also integrated throughout the BigInsights components. As we describe in the section "The BigInsights Application Lifecycle" later in this chapter, you have the ability to deploy text extractors for easy execution in the Web Console. Because the Advanced Text Analytics Toolkit is not just a BigInsights feature, we gave it a dedicated chapter—see Chapter 8 for a detailed description.

Machine Learning for the Masses: Deep Statistical Analysis on BigInsights

BigInsights includes a Machine Learning Toolkit, which provides a platform for statisticians and mathematicians to conduct high-performance statistical and predictive analysis on data in a BigInsights cluster. It includes a high-level machine learning language, which is semantically similar to R (the open source language for statistical computing), and can be used by analysts to apply statistical models to their data processing. A wealth of built-in data-mining algorithms and statistical models are included as well. The Machine Data Accelerator and the Social Data Accelerator (introduced in the next section) both make use of these statistical algorithms for their reports and visualizations. A number of machine learning algorithms and utilities are available as apps in the Applications panel of the BigInsights Web Console. This includes data processing utilities such as pivoting delimited numeric data into a matrix format, and algorithms such as linear regression and multi-class support vector machines (SVM).

The Machine Learning Toolkit includes an engine that converts the statistical workloads that are expressed in machine learning language into parallelized MapReduce code, which means it not only hides this complexity from analysts—it lets the analysts be analysts. In short, analysts don't need to be Java programmers, and they don't need to factor MapReduce into their analytics applications, and more.

The Machine Learning Toolkit was developed in IBM Research by a team of performance experts, statisticians, and mathematicians. Their primary goals were high performance and ease of use for analysts needing to perform complex statistical analyses in a Hadoop context. As such, this toolkit features optimization techniques for the generation of low-level MapReduce execution plans. This enables statistical jobs to achieve up to orders-of-magnitude performance improvements, when compared to algorithms that are directly implemented in MapReduce or other Hadoop languages, like Pig. Not only can analysts avoid MapReduce coding techniques in their analytics applications, but the machine learning code that they write is highly optimized for excellent Hadoop performance. Quite simply, it's hard to write parallel programs—IBM has delivered a declarative language to open up the building of parallel-driven statistical applications in the same manner that it did for relational databases when it invented SQL.

BigInsights also features integration with R in the form of an app available in the Applications panel of the BigInsights Web Console. With this app, users can run ad-hoc R scripts against their data.

Analytic Accelerators: Finding Needles in Haystacks of Needles?

In recognizing the importance of tools that reflect specific use cases, IBM has built a set of Big Data Analytic Accelerators—tools designed to enable analysts and data scientists to productively explore data. The initial set of accelerators are: the Social Data Accelerator, Telecommunications Data Accelerator, and the Machine Data Accelerator. These accelerators are configured to provide out-of-the-box value and can be further customized. For example, you can tailor the text analytics extractors for the Machine Data Accelerator to your company's log data. See Chapter 9 for a detailed description of these analytic accelerators.

Apps for the Masses: Easy Deployment and Execution of Custom Applications

The BigInsights Web Console has a tab called "Applications," where you can see a number of apps that are ready for you to run. IBM has modeled this panel after the "app store" concept that is common today for mobile devices. Running these apps takes a simple common approach: click on the app, enter the path from which the data to be analyzed will be read, enter another path where you want the result sets to be stored (and any of the app's additional fields) and you're ready to run the application. You don't have to spend precious budgets on app deployment with installers and such—just click and run.

BigInsights ships with a number of apps, which you can use to test the cluster, and to get an idea of the kinds of apps you can build. In fact, the code to write every app that's shipped with BigInsights can be downloaded from the console as an Eclipse BigInsights project, so you have a ready-made starting point for your own app project! Another nice thing about this feature is that you can use it as a front-end scheduler for end users to run Big Data apps distributed in your enterprise.

Your business analysts and data scientists can leverage existing apps as building blocks to create new apps. Users can do this by using a graphical drag-and-drop tool to chain existing apps together in a workflow. You can easily direct the outputs from one app into the inputs of the next app in the chain.

The emphasis on security in BigInsights shows through here, because someone with an Application Administrator role can determine which users are to be authorized to run specific apps. Given that there are data sources or services where security credentials are required, the apps interface lets you leverage the BigInsights credentials store, enabling you to securely pass authentication information to the data source or service to which you're connecting.

Data Discovery and Visualization: BigSheets

Although Hadoop makes analyzing Big Data possible, you pretty much need to be a programmer with a good understanding of the MapReduce paradigm to explore the data. We've seen what happens when you try to explain parallel programming concepts to nontechnical people, so clearly there's a big barrier that keeps most business analysts from being able to make sense of data that's stored in Hadoop. BigInsights has the answer: a browser-based visualization tool called BigSheets. This tool enables line-of-business users to harness the power of Hadoop using a familiar spreadsheet interface. BigSheets requires no programming (it automatically generates Hadoop code underneath the covers) or special administration. If you can use a spreadsheet (pivot, slice, dice, and so on), you can use BigSheets to perform analysis on vast amounts of data, in any structure.

Three easy steps are involved in using BigSheets to perform Big Data analysis:

1. *Collect data.* You can collect data from multiple sources, using apps that are deployed in BigInsights to crawl the Web, local files, or files on your network. Multiple protocols and formats are supported, including HTTP, HDFS, Amazon S3 Native File System (s3n), and Amazon S3 Block File System (s3), and more. There's also a facility to extend BigSheets with custom plug-ins for importing data. For example, you could build a plug-in to harvest Twitter data and include it in your BigSheets collections.

2. *Extract and analyze data.* After you have collected the data, you can see a sample of it in the spreadsheet interface, such as that shown in Figure 5-3. At this point, you can manipulate your data by using the spreadsheet-type tools that are available in BigSheets. For example, you can combine columns from different collections, run formulas, or filter data. You can also deploy custom macros for BigSheets. For example, you can deploy a text extractor that you

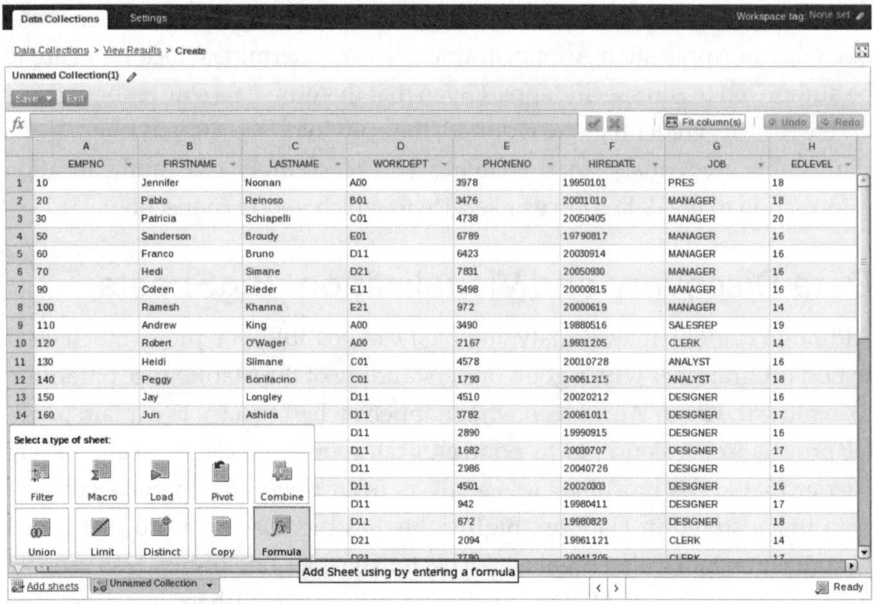

Figure 5-3   *The BigSheets spreadsheet-like interface*

built with the BigInsights development tools as a BigSheets macro.
As you build your sheets and refine your analysis, you can see the
interim results in the sample data. It's only when you click the Run
button that your analysis is applied to the complete data collection.
Because your data could range from gigabytes to terabytes to
petabytes in size, working iteratively with a small data set is the
best approach.

3. *Explore and visualize data.* After running the analysis from your
   sheets against the data, you can apply visualizations to help you
   make sense of your data. BigSheets provides a number of traditional
   and new age Big Data visualizations, including:

   • **Tag Cloud**   Shows word frequencies; the larger the letters, the
     more occurrences of data referencing that term were found. See
     Figure 5-4 for an example.

   • **Pie Chart**   Shows proportional relationships, where the relative
     size of the slice represents its proportion of the data

   • **Map**   Shows data values overlaid onto either a map of the world
     or a map of the United States

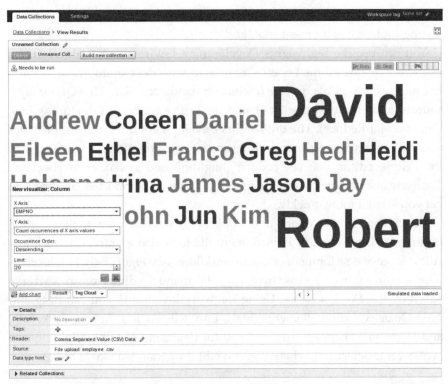

Figure 5-4   *Data visualization in BigSheets*

- **Heat Map**   Similar to the Map, but with the additional dimension of showing the relative intensity of the data values overlaid onto a Map

- **Bar Chart**   Shows the frequency of values for a specified column

BigSheets is fully extensible with respect to its visualization tools. As such, you can include custom plug-ins for specialized renderings of your data.

The BigInsights Development Environment

As we briefly mentioned earlier in this chapter, one of the main components of BigInsights is a set of Eclipse plug-ins that provide a rich development environment for creating BigInsights applications. This includes all of the usability features that you'd typically associate with an integrated development environment (IDE), namely: content completion, context-sensitive assistance, design-time assistance and error detection, a breakpoint and debugging console, code editors, workflow assistants, testing tools, a deployment tool, and more.

You can use the BigInsights Development Environment to develop text extractors (we detail the benefits associated with developing these artifacts in Chapter 8), Big Data queries (including standalone SQL, HiveQL for Hive sources, and HBase expressions), and Big Data applications (including Jaql, Pig, and MapReduce). The BigInsights Development Environment provides you with an enriched experience when you use any of these languages. In the Eclipse editor, you see code highlighting and syntax error checking. There are also templates and integrated help for the supported languages to get you started more quickly.

In addition to the query and application development tooling in the BigInsights Development Environment, there is also a graphical workflow editor for easy development of Oozie workflows (see Figure 5-5). This is otherwise a painstaking process, involving the manual editing of an XML file based on the Oozie schema. Using the workflow editor, you can drag and drop Oozie workflow elements (Start, End, Kill, Action, Action, Fork, Join, and Decision). There is also a code editor (featuring code highlighting and syntax error detection), where you can edit the generated Oozie XML.

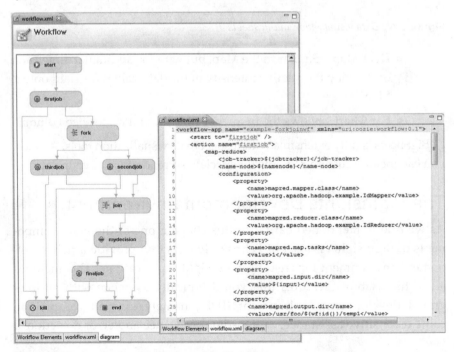

Figure 5-5   *Application chaining graphical interface*

To speed up application deployment, you can configure the BigInsights Development Environment to be aware of your BigInsights cluster, so that pushing application code to the cluster is as easy as clicking a button.

The fact is that the population of specialized programmers for Hadoop is quite small, but the number of developers who know Eclipse, or SQL, is very large. Think about that as you start from a proof of concept and move to enterprise production; you will move from a handful of developers to a full development, architecture, and QA team—potentially hundreds of developers. The BigInsights Development Environment has been designed to cater to the skill set of an average developer. So if your business is making the jump to BigInsights, you have integrated tooling that will help your development team get up to speed more quickly.

The BigInsights Application Lifecycle

Now that we've covered the full range of analysis and application development tools in BigInsights, let's step back and see how the big picture of application lifecycle management has been baked into BigInsights. The following details lifecycle steps and their impacted components (see also Figure 5-6).

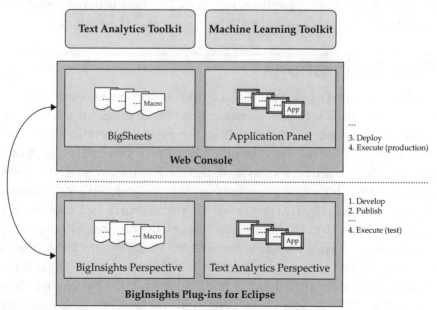

Figure 5-6   *The BigInsights application lifecycle*

1. **Develop**   Using the BigInsights development tools for Eclipse, you can, for example, create text extractors to isolate connection failures in your web server logs.

2. **Publish**   From Eclipse, you can push your text extractor to be available in the Web Console as either an app (through the Applications panel) or a macro for BigSheets.

3. **Deploy**   From the Web Console, someone with the Application Administrator role can deploy and configure an application for execution on the BigInsights cluster.

4. **Execute**   An end user can run the text extractor in the console (either as an app or as a macro, depending on how it was published). Alternatively, a developer can run the app from the Web Console, and download the results for testing in the Text Analytics debugging tool.

These are all steps that an IT organization needs to take to develop and deploy applications in a Hadoop context. In BigInsights, IBM has provided extensive automation and orchestration to make this process much faster, simpler, and more reliable. Without this tooling, not only would you have to manually move files around and set configurations, you would also have to develop wrappers and interfaces for your applications so that your users can execute them.

Data Integration

A key value of IBM's vision for Big Data is the importance of integrating data from a variety sources. Hadoop is not a one-size-fits-all solution to meet all your storage and processing needs, so you'll also continue to have other repositories in the enterprise. But once you make the commitment to add a Hadoop cluster to your IT infrastructure, it's inevitable that some of these other systems will need access to it. It's with this in mind that IBM has developed a SQL interface for data in BigInsights. This eliminates the learning curve for DBAs needing to query Hadoop data. In addition, BigInsights supports data exchange with a number of sources, including the IBM PureData System for Analytics (formerly known as Netezza), the IBM PureData System for Operational Analytics (formerly known as the IBM Smart Analytics System, which is powered by DB2); DB2 for Linux, UNIX, and Windows; other relational data stores via a Java Database Connectivity (JDBC) interface; InfoSphere Streams; InfoSphere Information Server (specifically, DataStage); and more. In this section, we'll delve into the details of some of the integration points, and merely highlight others; where we simply highlight an integration point, we cover details in the corresponding chapters later in this book.

The Analytics-Based IBM PureData Systems and DB2

You can exchange data between BigInsights and any of the analytics-based IBM PureData Systems (both the Analytics and Operational Analytics versions, or earlier versions of Netezza, or DB2 for Linux, UNIX, and Windows) in two ways: from your database server, or from your BigInsights cluster. These IBM database technologies can both connect and interact with BigInsights through a set of user-defined functions (UDFs) that can be installed on the database server. BigInsights can connect to the IBM PureData System for Analytics and Netezza through a special high-speed adapter. BigInsights can connect to the IBM PureData System for Operational Analytics or DB2 through the JDBC module (described in a later section).

BigInsights UDFs

The integration with BigInsights, the analytics-based IBM PureData Systems, Netezza, and DB2 has two main components: a set of UDFs installed on the database server, and a Jaql server (to listen for requests from these UDFs) on the BigInsights cluster. The Jaql server is a middleware component that can accept Jaql query processing requests from any system that's powered by Netezza (running Netezza Analytics version 2.0 or later) or DB2 server (version 9.5 or later) technology. Specifically, the Jaql server can accept the following kinds of Jaql queries from a supported database DB2 server:

- Read data from the BigInsights cluster.
- Upload (or remove) modules of Jaql code in the BigInsights cluster.
- Submit Jaql jobs (which can refer to modules you previously uploaded from supported database servers) to be run on the BigInsights cluster.
- (IBM PureData System for Analytics only) Write data from the data warehouse to the BigInsights cluster.

Running these BigInsights functions gives you an easy way to integrate with Hadoop from your traditional application framework. With these functions, database applications (which are otherwise Hadoop-unaware) can access data in a BigInsights cluster using the same SQL interface they use to get relational data out of them. Such applications can now leverage the parallelism and scale of a BigInsights cluster without requiring extra configuration or other overhead. Although this approach incurs additional performance overhead as compared to a conventional Hadoop application, it is a very useful way to integrate Big Data processing into your existing IT application infrastructure.

The IBM PureData System for Analytics Adapter

BigInsights includes a connector that enables data exchange between a BigInsights cluster and IBM PureData System for Anlaytics (or its earlier incarnation, the Netezza appliance). This adapter supports splitting tables (a concept similar to splitting files). This entails partitioning the table and assigning each divided portion to a specific mapper. This way, your SQL statements can be processed in parallel.

The adapter leverages the Netezza technology's external table feature, which you can think of as a materialized external UNIX pipe. External tables use JDBC. In this scenario, each mapper acts as a database client. Basically, a mapper (as a client) will connect to the database and start a read from a UNIX file that's created by the IBM PureData System's infrastructure.

JDBC Module

The Jaql JDBC module enables you to read and write data from any relational database that has a standard JDBC driver. This means you can easily exchange data and issue SQL statements with every major database warehouse product in the market today.

With Jaql's MapReduce integration, each map task can access a specific part of a table, enabling SQL statements to be processed in parallel for partitioned databases.

InfoSphere Streams for Data in Motion

As you'll discover in Chapter 7, Streams is the IBM solution for real-time analytics on streaming data. Streams includes a sink adapter for BigInsights, which lets you store streaming data directly into your BigInsights cluster. Streams also includes a source adapter for BigInsights, which lets Streams applications read data from the cluster. The integration between BigInsights and Streams raises a number of interesting possibilities. At a high level, you can create an infrastructure to respond to changes detected in data in real time (as the data is being processed in-motion by Streams), while using a wealth of existing data (stored and analyzed at rest by BigInsights) to inform the response. You could also use Streams as a large-scale data ingest engine to filter, decorate, or otherwise manipulate a stream of data to be stored in the BigInsights cluster.

Using the BigInsights sink adapter, a Streams application can write a control file to the BigInsights cluster. BigInsights can be configured to respond to the appearance of such a file so that it would trigger a deeper analytics operation to be run in the cluster. For more advanced scenarios, the trigger file from Streams could also contain query parameters to customize the analysis in BigInsights.

InfoSphere DataStage

DataStage is an extract, transform, and load (ETL) platform that is capable of integrating high volumes of data across a broad, heterogeneous range of source and target systems. It offers an easy-to-use interface and design tools; supports massive scalability; transforms data from multiple, disparate information sources; and delivers data in batch or in real time. Expanding its role as a data integration agent, DataStage has been extended to work with BigInsights and can push and pull data to and from BigInsights clusters. The DataStage connector to BigInsights integrates with HDFS, taking advantage of the clustered architecture so that any bulk writes to the same file are done in parallel. The result of DataStage integration is that BigInsights can quickly exchange data with any other software product able to connect with DataStage.

Increasingly we're seeing Hadoop being leveraged as a dynamic ETL engine, especially for unstructured data. ETL is not just about the transformation, though. Orchestration, debugging, lifecycle management, and data lineage are but a few important considerations. DataStage, and the rest of the InfoSphere Information Server platform provide means to deal with all these items and more. Plans are in place for even tighter connections between Information Server and BigInsights, such as the ability to choreograph BigInsights jobs from DataStage, making powerful and flexible data transformation scenarios possible. We talk about Hadoop optimizations, including DataStage's Big Data File Stage (BDFS), in Chapter 10 and Chapter 11.

Operational Excellence

As more organizations come to depend on Hadoop for their business analytics, the demand for additional governance and administrative capabilities increases. People have grown accustomed to the rich data management features in enterprise relational databases and want to see them in their Hadoop clusters as well. At the same time, Hadoop is entering an era in which the understanding of data governance is highly evolved. Relational databases had the advantage of "growing up" with a lot of the thinking about data. As a result, many experienced IT people look at Hadoop with high expectations. The trouble is that open source software focuses more on core capability than on rounding out a lot of administrative features. In IBM, there are hundreds of researchers and developers who are industry-leading experts on governance, workload management, and performance optimization. Since the Apache Hadoop project took off, many of these experts have been developing Hadoop solutions that have been incorporated into BigInsights.

Securing the Cluster

Security is an important concern for enterprise software, and in the case of open source Hadoop, there are limitations to consider before moving to production. The good news is that BigInsights addresses these issues by reducing the security surface area through securing access to the administrative interfaces, key Hadoop services, lockdown of open ports, role-based security, integration into InfoSphere Guardium Database Security (Guardium), and more.

The BigInsights Web Console has been structured to act as a gateway to the cluster. It features enhanced security by supporting Lightweight Directory Access Protocol (LDAP) authentication. LDAP and reverse-proxy support help administrators restrict access to authorized users. In addition, clients outside of the cluster must use secured REST interfaces to gain access to the cluster through the gateway. In contrast, Apache Hadoop has open ports on every node in the cluster. The more ports you need to have open (and there are a lot of them in open source Hadoop), the less secure the environment and the more likely you won't pass internal audit scans.

BigInsights can be configured to communicate with an LDAP credentials server for authentication. All communication between the console and the LDAP server occurs using LDAP (by default) or both LDAP and LDAPS (LDAP over HTTPS). The BigInsights installer helps you to define mappings between your LDAP users and groups and the four BigInsights roles (System Administrator, Data Administrator, Application Administrator, and User). After BigInsights has been installed, you can add or remove users from the LDAP groups to grant or revoke access to various console functions.

Kerberos security is integrated into open source Hadoop, and offers services and some operational tooling, but does not support alternative authentication. BigInsights uses LDAP as the default authentication protocol. BigInsights emphasizes the use of LDAP because when compared to Kerberos and other alternatives, it's a much simpler protocol to install and configure. Finally, BigInsights supports alternate authentication options such as Linux Pluggable Authentication Modules (PAM). You can use this to deploy Kerberos token authentication, or even biometric authentication.

Putting the cluster behind the Web Console's software firewall and establishing user roles helps to lock down BigInsights and its data, but a complete security story has to include regulatory compliance. For example, any business that accepts credit cards must be in compliance with the Payment Card Industry Data Security Standard (PCI DSS), which requires customer data to be secured and any accesses logged. Guardium is the market leader in the compliance market, and processes the audit logs generated by relational databases. IBM has built extensions to BigInsights, to store audit logs for data accesses in the cluster. Audit logs are generated for any data access activity involving the following components: Hadoop RPC, HDFS, MapReduce, Oozie, and HBase.

Recent changes to Apache Hadoop have improved security for HDFS; however, there are still some limitations. As such, the experience that IBM has with locking down the enterprise, which is baked into BigInsights, enables you to build a more secure, robust, and easily maintainable multitenant solution.

Monitoring All Aspects of Your Cluster

To aid in the administration of your cluster, the BigInsights Web Console provides a real-time, interactive view of your cluster's components. The BigInsights console includes graphical tools for examining the health of your BigInsights environment, including the nodes in your cluster, the Hadoop and BigInsights services, HDFS metadata, MapReduce metrics, and the status of your jobs (applications).

Monitoring the Cluster

BigInsights features a rich monitoring dashboard that enables you to tailor your view of administrative metrics. There are predefined dashboards for the following areas: System (covering CPU utilization and load average), Cluster, HDFS (covering total files and corrupted blocks), and MapReduce (covering map and reduce tasks running, and tasks failed). Each of the dashboards contains monitoring widgets that you can configure to a high degree of granularity, ranging from a range of time to the refresh rate (see Figure 5-7).

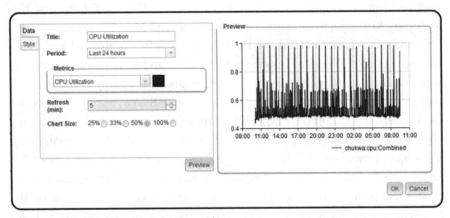

Figure 5-7   *Customizing monitoring widgets*

Monitoring Applications

The BigInsights Web Console provides context-sensitive views of the cluster, so that people only see what they need to based on their associated role. If someone with the security role of "user" runs an application, they only see their own statistics in the Application History view. This particular view is optimized to show a high level of application status information, hiding the lower-level workflow and job information.

People with administrator roles can see the state of all applications in the Application History view and the Application Status monitoring dashboard, and are able to drill into individual workflows and jobs for debugging or performance testing reasons. The Application Status pane has views for Workflows and Jobs. Each of those views lists every active and completed workflow and job. You can drill into each workflow or job to get further details, and from there also see related elements.

Compression

When dealing with the large volumes of data that are expected in a Hadoop setting, the idea of compression is appealing. On the one hand, you can save a great deal of space (especially when you consider that every storage block is replicated three times by default in Hadoop); on the other hand, data transfer speeds are improved because of lower data volumes on the wire. You should consider two important items before choosing a compression scheme: *splittable compression* and the *compression and decompression speeds* of the compression algorithm that you're using.

Splittable Compression

In Hadoop, files are split (divided) if they are larger than the cluster's block size setting (normally one split for each block). For uncompressed files, this means that individual file splits can be processed in parallel by different mappers. Figure 5-8 shows an uncompressed file with the vertical lines

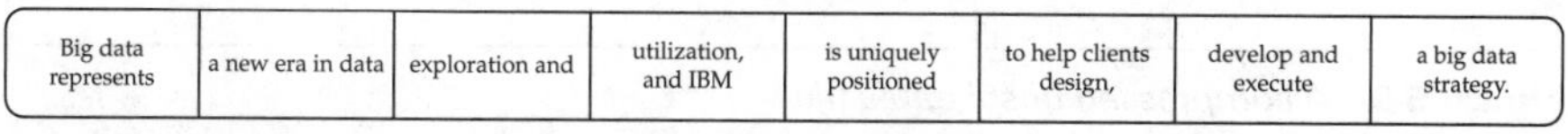

Big data represents	a new era in data	exploration and	utilization, and IBM	is uniquely positioned	to help clients design,	develop and execute	a big data strategy.

Figure 5-8 *An uncompressed splittable file in Hadoop*

representing the split and block boundaries (in this case, the split and block size are the same).

When files (especially text files) are compressed, complications arise. For most compression algorithms, individual file splits cannot be decompressed independently of other splits from the same file. More specifically, these compression algorithms are not *splittable* (remember this key term when discussing compression and Hadoop). In the current production release of Hadoop (1.0.3 at the time of writing), no support is provided for splitting compressed text files. For files in which the Sequence or Avro formats are applied, this is not an issue, because these formats have built-in synchronization points, and are therefore splittable. For unsplittable compressed text files, MapReduce processing is limited to a single mapper.

For example, suppose that the file in Figure 5-8 is a 1GB text file in your Hadoop cluster, and that your block size is set to the BigInsights default of 128MB, which means that your file spans eight blocks. When this file is compressed using the conventional algorithms available in Hadoop, it's no longer possible to parallelize the processing for each of the compressed file splits, because the file can be decompressed only as a whole, and not as individual parts based on the splits. Figure 5-9 depicts this file in a compressed (and binary) state, with the splits being impossible to decompress individually. Notice the mismatch? (The split boundaries are dotted lines, and the block boundaries are solid lines.)

Because Hadoop 1.0.3 doesn't support splittable text compression natively, all the splits for a compressed text file are processed by only a single mapper. For many workloads, this would cause such a significant performance hit that compression wouldn't be a viable option. However, Jaql is configured to understand splittable compression for text files and will process them automatically with parallel mappers. You can do this manually for other environments (such as Pig

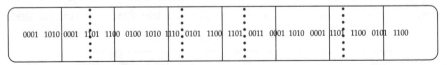

Figure 5-9 *A compressed unsplittable file*

and MapReduce programs) by using the TextInputFormat input format instead of the Hadoop standard.

Compression and Decompression Speeds

The old saying "nothing in this world is free" is surely true when it comes to compression. There's no magic going on; in essence, you are simply consuming CPU cycles to save disk space. So let's start with this assumption: There could be a performance penalty for compressing data in your Hadoop cluster, because when data is written to the cluster, the compression algorithms (which are CPU-intensive) need CPU cycles and time to compress the data. Likewise, when reading data, any MapReduce workloads against compressed data can incur a performance penalty because of the CPU cycles and the time required to decompress the compressed data. This creates a conundrum: You need to balance priorities between storage savings and additional performance overhead.

We should note that if you've got an application that's I/O bound (typical for many warehouse-style applications), you're likely to see a performance gain in your application, because I/O-bound systems typically have spare CPU cycles (found as idle I/O waits in the CPU) that can be used to run the compression and decompression algorithms. For example, if you use idle I/O wait CPU cycles to do the compression, and you get good compression rates, you could end up with more data flowing through the I/O pipe, and that means faster performance for those applications that need to fetch a lot of data from disk.

A BigInsights Bonus: IBM CMX Compression

BigInsights includes the IBM CMX compression (an IBM version of the LZO compression codec), which supports splitting compressed files and enabling individual compressed splits to be processed in parallel by your MapReduce jobs.

Some Hadoop online forums describe how to use the GNU version of LZO to enable splittable compression, so why did IBM create a version of it, and why not use the GNU LZO alternative? First, the IBM CMX compression codec *does not* create an index while compressing a file, because it uses fixed-length compression blocks. In contrast, the GNU LZO algorithm uses variable-length compression blocks, which leads to the added complexity of needing an index file that tells the mapper where it can safely split a compressed file. (For GNU LZO compression, this means that mappers would need to perform index look-ups during decompression and read operations. There is administrative overhead with this index, because if you move the compressed file, you will need to move the corresponding index file as well.) Second, many companies, including IBM, have legal policies that prevent them from purchasing or releasing software that includes GNU Public License (GPL) components. This means that the approach that is described in online Hadoop forums requires additional administrative overhead and configuration work. In addition, there are businesses with policies restricting the deployment of GPL code. The IBM CMX compression is fully integrated with BigInsights and under the *same* enterprise-friendly license agreement as the rest of BigInsights, which means that you can use it with less hassle and none of the complications associated with the GPL alternative.

In a future release of Hadoop, the bzip2 algorithm will support splitting. However, decompression speed for bzip2 is much slower than for IBM CMX, so bzip2 is not a desirable compression algorithm for workloads where performance is important.

Figure 5-10 shows the compressed text file from the earlier examples, but in a splittable state, where individual splits can be decompressed by their own mappers. Note that the split sizes are equal, indicating fixed-length compression blocks.

In the following table, you can see the four compression algorithms that are available on the BigInsights platform (IBM CMX, bzip2, gzip, and DEFLATE) and some of their characteristics.

Compression Codec	File Extension	Splittable	Degree of Compression	Decompression Speed
IBM CMX	.cmx	Yes	Medium	Fastest
bzip2	.bz2	Yes, but not yet available	Highest	Slow
Gzip	.gz	No	High	Fast
DEFLATE	.deflate	No	High	Fast

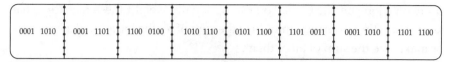

| 0001 1010 | 0001 1101 | 1100 0100 | 1010 1110 | 0101 1100 | 1101 0011 | 0001 1010 | 1101 1100 |

Figure 5-10   *A splittable compressed text file*

Improved Workload Scheduling: Intelligent Scheduler

Open source Hadoop ships with a rudimentary first in, first out (FIFO) scheduler and a pluggable architecture supporting alternate scheduling options.
There are two pluggable scheduling tools available through the Apache Hadoop
project: the Fair Scheduler and the Capacity Scheduler. These schedulers are
similar in that they enable a minimum level of resources to be available for
smaller jobs to avoid starvation. These schedulers don't provide adequate
controls to ensure optimal cluster performance or offer administrators the
flexibility that they need to implement customizable workload management.
For example, Fair is pretty good at ensuring that resources are applied to
workloads, but it doesn't give you SLA-like granular controls.

As you might imagine, IBM has decades of experience and research expertise in workload management. From the mainframe to distributed systems,
there are continually repeating proof points of this expertise. For example,
IBM is the only database vendor that we know of to integrate database-level
workload management (in DB2) with the underlying host operating system's
workload management capabilities such that they work in unison. Workload
management for data in a database or data in a file system is still workload
management.

Performance experts in IBM Research have studied the workload scheduling problems in Hadoop and have crafted a solution called the Intelligent
Scheduler (previously known as the FLEX Scheduler). This scheduler extends
the Fair Scheduler and manipulates it by constantly altering the minimum
number of slots that are assigned to jobs. The Intelligent Scheduler includes a
variety of metrics that you can use to optimize your workloads. These metrics
can be chosen by an administrator on a cluster-wide basis, or by individual

users on a job-specific basis. You can optionally weight these metrics to balance competing priorities, minimize the sum of all the individual job metrics, or maximize the sum of all of them.

The following are examples of the Intelligent Scheduler settings that you can use to tune your workloads:

- **average response time**   The scheduler allocates maximum resources to small jobs, ensuring that these jobs are completed quickly.

- **maximum stretch**   The scheduler allocates resources to jobs in proportion to the amount of resources that they need. Big jobs have higher priority.

- **user priority**   The scheduler allocates maximum resources to jobs for a particular user.

Adaptive MapReduce

In their efforts to further optimize Hadoop performance, IBM Research has developed a concept called Adaptive MapReduce, which extends Hadoop by making individual mappers self-aware and aware of other mappers. This approach enables individual map tasks to adapt to their environment and make efficient decisions. (If you consider what connection pooling and connection concentration did for database scalability and apply that to Adaptive MapReduce for Hadoop, you'll have a good analogy to work from if you are new to this space.)

In normal MapReduce, when a job is about to begin, Hadoop divides the data into many pieces, called *splits*. Each split is assigned a single mapper. To ensure a balanced workload, these mappers are deployed in waves, and new mappers start after old mappers finish processing their splits. In this model, a small split size means more mappers, which helps ensure balanced workloads and minimizes failure costs. However, smaller splits also result in increased cluster overhead due to the higher volumes of startup costs for each map task. For workloads with high startup costs for map tasks, larger split sizes tend to be more efficient. An adaptive approach to running map tasks gives BigInsights the best of both worlds.

One component of Adaptive MapReduce is the concept of an *adaptive mapper*. Adaptive mappers extend the capabilities of conventional Hadoop mappers by tracking the state of file splits in a central repository. Each time an adaptive mapper finishes processing a split, it consults this central repository and locks another split for processing until the job is completed. This means that for adaptive mappers, only a single wave of mappers is deployed, because the individual mappers remain open to consume additional splits. The performance cost of locking a new split is far less than the startup cost for a new mapper, which accounts for a significant increase in performance. The left side of Figure 5-11 shows the benchmark results for a set-similarity join workload, which had high map task startup costs that were mitigated by the use of adaptive mappers. The adaptive mappers result (see the AM bar) was based on a low split size of 32MB. Only a single wave of mappers was used, so there were significant performance savings based on avoiding the startup costs for additional mappers.

For some workloads, any lack of balance could get magnified with larger split sizes, which would cause additional performance problems. When using adaptive mappers, you can (without penalty) avoid unbalanced workloads by tuning jobs to use a smaller split size. Because there will only be a single wave of mappers, your workload will not be crippled by the mapper startup costs of many additional mappers. The right side of Figure 5-11 shows the benchmark results for a join query on TERASORT records, in which an imbalance occurred between individual map tasks that led to an unbalanced workload for the larger split sizes. The adaptive mappers result (again, see the AM bar) was based on a low split size of 32MB. Only a single wave of mappers was

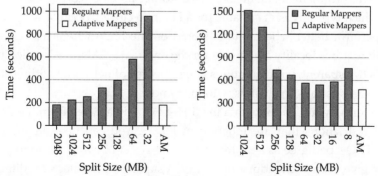

Figure 5-11 *Benchmarking a set-similarity join workload with high map task startup costs reduced through the use of adaptive mappers*

used, so there were significant performance savings based on the startup costs for additional mappers.

A Flexible File System for Hadoop: GPFS-FPO

The General Parallel File System (GPFS) was developed by IBM Research in the 1990s for high-performance computing (HPC) applications. Since its first release in 1998, GPFS has been used in many of the world's fastest supercomputers, including Blue Gene, Watson (the *Jeopardy!* supercomputer), and the reigning fastest supercomputer in the world, IBM Sequoia. In addition to HPC, GPFS is commonly found in thousands of other mission-critical installations worldwide. Needless to say, GPFS has earned an enterprise-grade reputation and pedigree for extreme scalability, high performance, and reliability.

The design principles behind HDFS were defined by use cases that assumed Hadoop workloads would involve sequential reads of very large file sets (and no random writes to files already in the cluster—just append writes). In contrast, GPFS has been designed for a wide variety of workloads and for a multitude of uses.

Extending GPFS for Hadoop: GPFS File Placement Optimization

In 2009, IBM extended GPFS to work with Hadoop. GPFS-Shared Nothing Cluster was eventually renamed to GPFS-FPO (File Placement Optimization). GPFS was originally available only as a storage area network (SAN) file system, which typically isn't suitable for a Hadoop cluster, because MapReduce jobs perform better when data is stored on the node where it's processed (which requires locality awareness for the data). In a SAN, the location of the data is transparent, which requires a high degree of network bandwidth and disk I/O, especially in clusters with many nodes.

By storing your Hadoop data in GPFS-FPO, you are free from the design-based restrictions that are inherent in HDFS. You can take advantage of GPFS-FPO's pedigree as a multipurpose file system in your Hadoop cluster, which gives you tremendous flexibility. A significant architectural difference between GPFS-FPO and HDFS is that *GPFS-FPO is a kernel-level file system, whereas HDFS runs on top of the operating system.* Many limitations in HDFS stem from the fact that it's not fully POSIX-compliant. On the other hand, GPFS-FPO is 100 percent POSIX-compliant, which can give you significant flexibility.

Because GPFS is POSIX-compliant, files that are stored in GPFS-FPO are visible to all applications, just like any other files stored on a computer. For example, when copying files, any authorized user can use traditional operating system commands to list, copy, and move files in GPFS-FPO. This isn't the case in HDFS, where users need to log into Hadoop to see the files in the cluster. As for replication or backups, the only mechanism available for HDFS is to copy files manually through the Hadoop command shell.

The full POSIX compliance of GPFS-FPO enables you to manage your Hadoop storage just as you would any other computer in your IT environment. That's going to give you economies of scale when it comes to building Hadoop skills, and just make life easier. For example, your traditional file administration utilities will work, as will your backup and restore tooling and procedures. GPFS-FPO will actually extend your backup capabilities because it includes point-in-time (PiT) snapshot backup, off-site replication, and other utilities.

With GPFS-FPO, you can safely manage multitenant Hadoop clusters with a robust separation of concern infrastructure for your Hadoop cluster, allowing other applications to share the cluster resources. This isn't possible in HDFS. This also helps from a capacity planning perspective, because without GPFS-FPO, you would need to design the disk space that is dedicated to the Hadoop cluster up front. If fact, not only do you have to estimate how much data you need to store in HDFS, but you're also going to have to guess how much storage you'll need for the output of MapReduce jobs, which can vary widely by workload. Finally, don't forget that you need to account for space that will be taken up by log files created by the Hadoop system too! With GPFS-FPO, you only need to worry about the disks themselves filling up; there's no need to dedicate storage for Hadoop.

All of the characteristics that make GPFS the file system of choice for large-scale mission-critical IT installations are applicable to GPFS-FPO. After all, this is still GPFS, but with Hadoop-friendly extensions. You get the same stability, flexibility, and performance in GPFS-FPO, as well as all of the utilities that you're used to. GPFS-FPO also provides hierarchical storage management (HSM) capabilities, whereby it can manage and use disk drives with different retrieval speeds efficiently. This enables you to manage multitemperature data, keeping "hot" data on your best-performing hardware. HDFS doesn't have this ability.

GPFS-FPO is such a game changer that it won the prestigious Supercomputing Storage Challenge award in 2010 for being the "most innovative storage solution" submitted to this competition.

NOTE   GPFS-FPO is currently available only for beta testing.

Wrapping It Up

We said it earlier in this book, but it's really important to understand that Big Data does not solely equal Hadoop. Hadoop is but one of multiple data processing engines you will need to address today's challenges (and the ones you don't yet know about yet). For this reason, IBM has been long committed to Hadoop, with contributions to the Apache project and continual engineering around the ecosystem. With its long history of enterprise-grade infrastructure and optimization, IBM has taken this experience and applied it to Hadoop through BigInsights. BigInsights includes open source Hadoop and adds some operational excellence features such as Big Data optimized compression, workload management, scheduling capabilities, and even an app development and deployment ecosystem.

While operational excellence delivers economics of scale and infrastructure trust, the true potential of Hadoop lies in the analytic capabilities—more accurately, the consumability of the analytic capabilities. For this reason, BigInsights includes toolkits, accelerators, and tools such as BigSheets, which seek to democratize the use of Big Data so it isn't bottled up in deeply skilled tech departments that require an army of Java programmers to monetize the data. In addition, BigInsights provides an end-to-end text extraction framework. Quite simply, Hadoop doesn't provide anything here, so IBM builds a high-value stack that treats Hadoop as a first-class citizen and integrates it across the IBM Big Data platform.

We don't think anything illustrates the kind of analytic value that's required for today's Hadoop clusters more than IBM supporting the analytic capabilities found in BigInsights in Cloudera's Hadoop distribution. We think that sums it up—it illustrates the kind of partner you want to start your Big Data journey with: one who can help you get value from your data. After all, we've yet to see anyone think highly of a 100-node cluster that provided no value.

Part III

Analytics for Big Data
in Motion

6

Real-Time Analytical Processing with InfoSphere Streams

Why are we willing to wait for actionable insight? How did we learn to tolerate days, weeks, or months before we identify new opportunities, understand the health of our businesses, or identify customer concerns with our products and services? With the world speeding up, it is simply not acceptable to wait any more. Just as IBM has delivered technology to uniquely handle the largest analytical problems for *data at rest* with InfoSphere BigInsights (BigInsights) and the IBM PureData System for Analytics (the new IBM branding for Netezza announced in 4Q2012), IBM also delivers the ability to derive value from data instantly with the analysis of *data in motion*. Using BigInsights and any of the analytic-based IBM PureData Systems gives you enormous capabilities when it comes to navigating the oceans of information that are available to enterprises today, while IBM InfoSphere Streams (Streams) gives you enormous insights from the rivers of data flowing through your enterprise. You can choose to tap into those rivers to gain time-sensitive competitive advantages for your business, or you can stand by and watch the opportunities be washed away. This is where Streams comes in. Its design lets you leverage massively parallel processing (MPP) techniques to analyze data *while it is streaming by*, so you can understand what is happening in real time, and optionally take action, make better decisions, and improve outcomes.

By this point in the book, we're sure that you understand the importance of the Big Data velocity characteristic, and how the integration of at-rest analytics, moved to the frontier of your business through an in-motion platform, can really boost your Big Data IQ. For this reason, this chapter is a little more detailed, from a technology perspective, than the other chapters in this book. But let's start by clarifying what we mean by *Streams* and *stream*; the capitalized form refers to the IBM InfoSphere Streams product, and the lowercase version refers to a stream of data. With that in mind, let's look at the basics of Streams, some of the technical underpinnings that define how it works, and its use cases.

The Basics: InfoSphere Streams

Streams is a powerful analytic computing software platform that continuously analyzes and transforms data in memory before it is stored on disk. Instead of gathering large quantities of data, manipulating and storing it on disk, and then analyzing it, as is the case with other analytic approaches, Streams enables you to apply the analytics directly on data in motion. When you analyze data in motion with Streams, you get the fastest possible results, huge potential hardware savings, and the highest throughput.

With all of those advantages, you might ask "What's the catch?" To achieve these benefits, Streams operates primarily on "windows" of data that are maintained in memory across a cluster. Nevertheless, large memory sizes enable windows of data to represent analytics over a few seconds to a few days of data, depending on the data flow rates. This data can be enriched with context that has been accumulated during processing and with data from an at-rest engine, such as Hadoop, or a database.

We generally recommend Streams for the following use cases:

- Identifying events in real time, such as determining when customer sentiment in social media is becoming more negative

- Correlating and combining events that are closely related in time, such as a warning in a log file followed by a system outage

- Continuously calculating grouped aggregates, such as price trends per symbol per industry in the stock market

We don't generally recommend Streams for analytics that require multiple passes over a large data set, so scoring a regression model is possible, but building one should be done using BigInsights or one of the purpose-built IBM analytic data warehousing engines with data at rest. However, Streams can take advantage of rich historical context by using models built by BigInsights, the IBM PureData System for Operational Analytics (formerly know as the IBM Smart Analytics System), the IBM PureData System for Analytics, or other analytic tools, such as SPSS.

If you're already familiar with Complex Event Processing (CEP) systems, you might see some similarities in Streams. However, Streams is designed to be much more scalable and dynamic, to enable more complex analytics, and to support a much higher data flow rate than other systems. Many CEP or stream processing systems, including new open source projects like Storm, advertise a few *hundred thousand* events per second within a whole *cluster*. In contrast, the IBM Streams technology has been demonstrated to handle a *few million* events per second on a single *server*—it is *fast*. (Don't forget, you can deploy Streams in a cluster with near-linear scalability).

In addition, Streams has much better enterprise-level characteristics, such as high availability, a rich and easy-to-use application development tool set, numerous out-of-the box analytics, and integration with many common enterprise systems. In fact, Streams provides nearly 30 built-in operators in its standard toolkit, dozens of operators in extension toolkits such as data mining and text analytics, and literally hundreds of functions to facilitate application development. There is even a CEP toolkit that provides Streams functions normally found in CEP systems. Even though other systems can't match the power of Streams, the emergence of CEP systems and open source projects, such as Storm, highlights the growing importance of data-in-motion analysis.

You can think of a Streams application as a set of interconnected operators. Multiple operators are combined into a single, configurable deployment unit called a *job*, and an application is made up of one or more jobs. An application is normally deployed until it is cancelled, continuously processing the data that flows through it. The operators that bring data into Streams applications are typically referred to as *source adapters*. These operators read the input stream and then produce a stream that can be consumed by downstream operators. The analytical steps include various *operators* that perform specific actions based on input from one or more streams. Finally, for every way *into* the continuous analytics platform, there are multiple ways *out*, and in Streams, these outputs are called *sink adapters*. (Think of water flowing out of the tap and into your kitchen sink.) Any operator can simultaneously be a source adapter, standard operator, and sink adapter, but it is helpful to think of them as being distinct. We cover all of these operators later in this chapter.

Streams applications generally fall into one of two types. The first keeps up with the most current data no matter what happens, even if it means dropping older data. For these applications, *now* is more important than processing every bit of data. Examples of applications that need to keep up with the most current data include detecting and responding to cyber attacks, making buy-and-sell decisions on the stock market, or monitoring a person's vital signs. For these applications, you need to make decisions based on the most current data. Streams supports this type of application by delivering scalability and high throughput, load-shedding operators to intelligently shed data when necessary, and maintaining system-level high availability to keep applications running.

The second type of application requires every bit of data to be processed, no matter what. These applications typically have used database technology in the past, but for reasons of efficiency, timeliness, or the inability to keep up, a portion of the application is moved to Streams. One example of this type of application is processing call detail records (CDRs) for the telecommunications industry. For compliance and business reasons, these CDRs need to be de-duplicated, transformed, and stitched together without losing a single record. By moving processing to Streams while the CDRs are still in motion, significant efficiency gains are realized and new business opportunities arise. For these kinds of applications, the inherently high throughput coupled with system-level high availability and application patterns make Streams an excellent choice.

As with a web application server or a database, you can customize Streams to deliver applications that solve business problems. Streams provides many enterprise-class features, such as the ability to deploy applications across a cluster of dozens or hundreds of servers to improve availability, scalability, and performance (similar to Hadoop but for real-time applications). Streams also provides an easy-to-use, drag-and-drop tooling environment to help you design and build your streaming applications (covered in the "Programming Streams Made Easy" section in this chapter). Another nice feature is that Streams shares the same Text Analytics Toolkit with BigInsights, enabling you to reuse skills and code snippets across your entire Big Data platform (we talk about that in Chapter 8).

You can build your applications for a single server or a cluster, and Streams automatically fuses sets of operators into highly optimized processing elements (PEs) that transmit streaming data point-to-point in the cluster for optimal throughput. When you're ready to deploy your streaming application, Streams autonomically decides, at run time, where to run the PEs based on cluster-based load balancing and availability metrics, enabling it to reconfigure operators to run on other servers to ensure the continuity of the stream in the event of server or software failures. If you want more placement control, you can also have fine-grained control over the placement of one or more operators by programmatically specifying which operators run on which servers and which operators should run together or separately.

This autonomic streaming and customizable platform enables you to increase the number of servers performing analysis on the stream simply by adding additional servers and assigning operators to run on those servers. The Streams infrastructure ensures that the data flows successfully from one operator to another, whether the operators are running on distinct servers or on the same server. Not only can you add or remove servers, but you can also dynamically add applications that will automatically connect to running applications and that can be reconfigured programmatically. Of course, you can also remove applications on the fly, which enables you to change priorities and improve analysis over time. These features provide a high degree of agility and flexibility to let you start small and grow the platform as needed.

Much like BigInsights, Streams is ideally suited for both structured data and for the nontraditional semistructured or unstructured data coming from sensors, voice, text, video, and financial sources, and many other high-volume sources. Because Streams and BigInsights are part of the IBM Big Data platform, you'll find enormous efficiencies with being able to apply the same Big Data analytics you build to both in-motion or at-rest data. For example, the extractors that are built from the Text Analytics Toolkit can be deployed in both Streams and BigInsights.

How InfoSphere Streams Works

As previously mentioned, Streams is all about analytics on data in motion. In Streams, data flows continuously through a sequence of operators in a pipeline fashion, much like ingredients flowing through an assembly line in a chocolate factory. Some operators discard data that isn't useful or relevant in the same way that a sorter of cocoa beans might discard beans that are too small. Other operators might transform data into a derived data stream in the same way that cocoa beans are crushed and liquefied. Some operators combine different types of data in the same way that nuts are combined with a chocolate mixture in just the right proportions.

When operators are too slow to keep up, a data stream can be split up and sent to parallel instances of those operators, in much the same way that a factory might arrange its assembly line to have parallel molding machines. Some operators might send different kinds of data to different downstream operators, like sending a candy bar with nuts to one wrapping station, and the candy bar without nuts to another wrapping station. Operators might even send signals to earlier stages of analysis to change behavior, in much the same way that quality control in the factory might increase the nuts-to-chocolate mixture if samples are not meeting specifications.

Unlike an assembly line that can be changed only during a temporary plant shutdown, however, Streams operators can be improved, added, or removed dynamically without stopping the analysis. Streams is an excellent approach for high-throughput, timely analysis; it enables businesses to leverage just-in-time intelligence to perform actions in real time, ultimately yielding better results for the business. Streams provides operators to store data and results in an at-rest engine, to send action signals, or to just toss out the data if it's deemed to be of no value during in-flight analysis.

What's a Lowercase "stream"?

A *stream* is a continuous sequence of data elements. A Streams application can be viewed as a *graph of nodes connected by directed edges*. Each node in the graph is an *operator* or *adapter* that processes the data from a stream. Operators can have zero or more inputs and zero or more outputs. The output (or outputs) from one operator connects to the input (or inputs) of another operator (or operators). The edges of the graph that join the nodes together represent the stream of data moving between the operators. Each output of an operator defines a new stream, and other operators can connect to the stream. Operators occurring early in a pipeline can even connect to a stream that is produced by "downstream" operators, enabling control flows to change the computation of upstream operators as new insights are uncovered. Figure 6-1 represents a simple stream graph that reads data from a file, sends the data to an operator known as a *functor* (this operator transforms incoming data in some programmatic manner), and then feeds that data to another operator. In this figure, the streamed data is fed to a *split operator*, which then feeds data to either a file sink or a database (depending on what goes on inside the split operator).

The data elements in a stream are known as *tuples*. In a relational database sense, you can think of a tuple as similar to a row of data. However, when Streams works on semistructured and unstructured data, a tuple is an abstraction that represents a package of data, and that's why we think of a tuple as a set of attributes for a given object. Each element in the tuple contains the value for that attribute, which can be a character string, a number, a date, or even some sort of binary object, such as a video frame. For applications with semistructured data, it is common for Streams applications to start with tuples that consist of a small amount of metadata coupled with an unstructured payload in each tuple, with subsequent operators progressively extracting more information from the unstructured payload.

The simplest operators work on one tuple at a time. These operators can filter a tuple based on characteristics of its attributes, extract additional information from the tuple, and transform the tuple before sending data to an output stream. Because a stream consists of a never-ending sequence of tuples, how can you correlate across different streams, sort tuples, or compute aggregates?

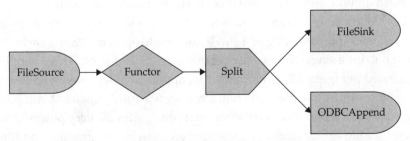

Figure 6-1 *A simple data stream that applies a transformation to data and splits it into two possible outputs based on predefined logic*

The answer is *windows of data*. A window of data is a finite sequence of tuples and looks a lot like a database view. Windows are continuously updated as new data arrives, by eliminating the oldest tuples and adding the newest tuples. Windows can be easily configured in many ways. For example, the window size can be defined as N tuples long or M seconds long. Windows can be advanced in many ways, including one tuple at a time, or by replacing an entire window at once. Each time the window is updated, you can think of it as a temporarily frozen view. It's easy to correlate a frozen view with another window of data from a different stream, or compute aggregates using similar techniques for aggregates and joins in relational databases. The windowing libraries in Streams provide incredible productivity for building applications. We discuss *windowing* later in this chapter where we talk about the various operators, but it's an important concept to understand, because Streams *is not* just about manipulating one tuple at a time, but rather analyzing large sets of data in real time and gaining insight from analytics across multiple tuples, streams, and context data.

Streams also has the concept of *composite operators*. A composite operator consists of a reusable and configurable Streams subgraph. Technically, all Streams applications contain at least one composite (the main composite for the application), but they can include more than one composite (composites can also be nested). A composite defines zero or more input streams and zero or more output streams. Streams can be passed to the inputs of the composite and are connected to inputs in the internal subgraph. Outputs from the internal subgraph are similarly connected to the composite outputs. A composite can expose parameters that are used to customize its behavior. An extreme example of nested composites is the Matryoshka sample application in Streams, which is inspired by the Matryoshka (or Russian) dolls, the famous wooden dolls of decreasing size that are stored inside one another.

Consider a simple example in which a composite operator, PetaOp, contains a subgraph consisting of a single composite operator TeraOp, which in turn contains a single composite operator GigaOp, and so on. This example is illustrated in Figure 6-2, which shows an application deployed with just the PetaOp operator (on the top) contrasted with a fully expanded composite operator (on the bottom). You can see that composites are very powerful and useful for big applications, because subtasks can be encapsulated and hidden, enabling developers to focus on the broader goals.

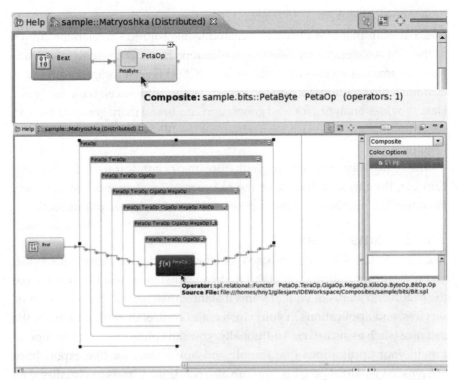

Figure 6-2   *The Matryoshka sample application with the PetaOp composite operator on the top and the PetaOp composite operator fully expanded (showing all internal composite operators) on the bottom*

Programming Streams Made Easy

For the last several years, enterprises have been delighted by the speed, reliability, and cost savings provided by Streams. Additionally, developers have found that the analytic toolkits and programming tools provide a high level of agility when building applications. However, it has been difficult for non-programmers to use Streams—that is, until now.

Streams 3.0 is focused completely *on ease of use*. Streams 3.0 (herein simply referred to as Streams) includes an integrated development environment (IDE) that provides a drag-and-drop work-as-you-think programming experience, new operational and data visualizations, new analytic toolkits, new management console features, and installation enhancements that all serve to deliver a *dramatically* improved user experience. Not every company can hire waves of new programmers, and this is why the consumability of the Big Data platform is just as important as its capabilities.

Streams has also surfaced the most popular use cases as solution accelerators. For example, IBM provides a customizable solution accelerator known as the IBM Accelerator for Telecommunications Event Data Analytics, which uses Streams to process call detail records (CDR) for telecommunications. A customizable solution accelerator known as the IBM Accelerator for Social Data provides analytics for lead generation and brand management based on social media. You can learn more about all the IBM Big Data accelerators in Chapter 9.

Most end-user interactions with Streams occur through the Streams Console, the Streams Studio, or the `streamtool` command-line interface. We cover the highlights of these powerful tools in the rest of this section.

The Streams Console

The Streams Console is a web-based tool that provides management services and a wealth of information about a Streams instance. You can quickly see the health and status of your Streams instance; manage and monitor servers, services, and applications in your cluster; and control overall settings for the instance (such as security). Additionally, you can configure Views for operators in your applications that sample and buffer data for live export from Streams to visualization tools. You can also configure Charts to visualize data directly in the Streams Console.

The bottom of Figure 6-3 illustrates host (server) management through the Streams Console. A sortable and filterable table shows each available host in the cluster. At a glance, you can see host health in the `Status` field. You can also see the status of services on each host, whether the host is available for running applications, and metrics for the host, including load average and number of CPU cores when metrics collection is enabled. Tags, such as `IngestServer`, can be added to hosts to facilitate optimal application placement in the cluster. When something goes wrong with a host, you can view or download logs with the click of a button for problem determination. It's also possible to quiesce workloads on a server so that it can be taken out of service for maintenance. Similar features for jobs, operators, and processing elements are available as well; for example, the top of Figure 6-3 shows the console's jobs view.

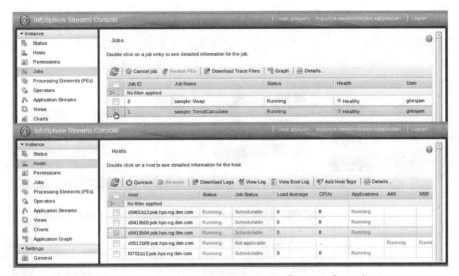

Figure 6-3   *The management of jobs and hosts in the Streams Console*

Operations Visualized

A great new feature in the Streams Console is the ability to monitor results of
Streams applications in a very natural way, using graphs. The Application
Graph feature displays all running applications and run-time metrics from a
Streams instance in an interactive and customizable window.

For example, Figure 6-4 illustrates two running financial services applications, one calculating trend metrics and one calculating the volume-weighted
average price (VWAP) for every stock symbol on a tick-by-tick basis. At the
top of Figure 6-4, you can see that the graph is configured to continuously
update the color of the operator based on the tuple rate. The thickness of the
lines is also updated to be proportional to the data flow rate to give you a
quick idea of how much data is flowing. The bottom of Figure 6-4 illustrates
a different view, in which the operators are grouped by job. By clicking on an
operator in the TrendCalculator application, additional information, such as
tuples processed by the operator, is displayed. Clicking on other objects, such
as ports or a stream, also provides significant detail. These graphs are similar
to Streams Live Graph in previous versions of Streams, but they are now also
exposed through the Streams Console, making them easier for administrators
to access.

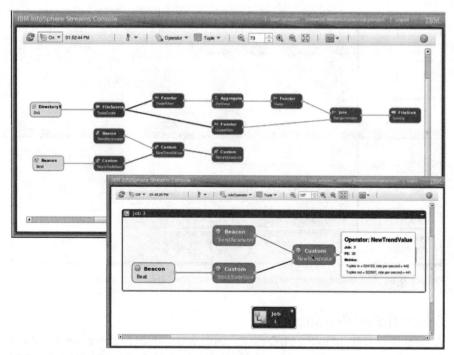

Figure 6-4 *The Streams Console showing an Application Graph with two running jobs at the top, and a grouping by jobs showing details about the NewTrendValue custom operator at the bottom*

Data Visualized

One of the most important new features in the Streams Console is *data visualization*. In addition to making live data available for external visualization tools, live streaming data can be visualized directly in the Streams Console. Tables and graphs can be extensively configured by selecting and rearranging attributes from the tuples, as well as filtering. Figure 6-5 shows a chart for the IBM ticker with VWAP, Min Price, Max Price, and Average Price. (Our lawyers want us to mention that this is old data from a sample application, so don't use these charts if you're a day trader.)

The data visualization widgets found in Streams are very rich; see some other examples in Figure 6-6.

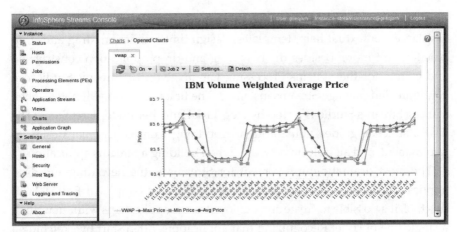

Figure 6-5   *Chart displaying VWAP calculations for symbol IBM*

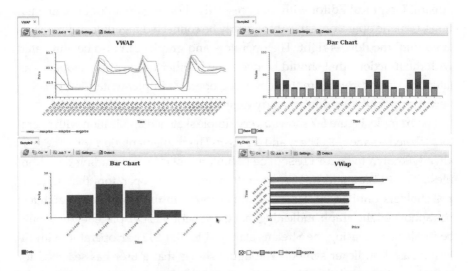

Figure 6-6   *Examples of charts that are available in the Streams Console*

An Integrated Development Environment for Streams: Streams Studio

Streams Studio is an interactive tool set that's used for creating and deploying Streams applications. It's a typical IDE, so if you have experience in application development, you will love what you're getting here: content assist, design-time assistance, contextual help, templates, design-time validation, drag-and-drop palettes, and more. Besides the new drag-and-drop application construction and editors for the Streams Processing Language (SPL), Streams Studio can configure and manage Streams instances. The first thing you will notice when starting Streams Studio is a step-by-step Task Launcher under First Steps. The Task Launcher guides you through everything from conceptual design to deployment, and all tasks in between, when building a Streams application.

The most dramatic improvement for Streams is the new drag-and-drop application development tooling called the Streams Graphical Editor. With this tool, it's possible to create and deploy Streams applications without writing a single line of code! Recognizing that applications often start by sketching a graph on paper, Streams Studio lets users sketch an application flow in the Streams Graphical Editor without necessarily choosing operator implementations. Generic operators can subsequently be connected together and manipulated until the flow is right. The operators and graphs can also be annotated with the functions that should be performed. Other users, or developers, can later choose and configure the remaining operator implementations, creating new operators if they don't already exist in one of the extensive toolkits.

For example, Figure 6-7 shows a very simple sketched application with operators labeled Reader, Filter, and Writer. The implementation for Reader is already known to be a FileSource (a built-in operator for reading data from files). The Filter and Writer operators are generic operators that serve as placeholders until an implementation is chosen. In this example, an architect has annotated the graph, indicating that the generic Filter placeholder should be implemented using the Streams standard toolkit Filter operator, with filtering based on ticker symbol. The figure shows that a user has searched for operators starting with "fil" and is dragging the standard toolkit Filter operator onto the graph to provide an implementation for the Filter placeholder. If the implementation needs to be changed to another operator later, it can be overwritten in the same way. After choosing an operator for the Writer placeholder and configuring the properties, a complete application is ready to run.

Extending existing applications is also a snap. Figure 6-8 shows the volume-weighted average price (VWAP) sample application that comes with Streams. In this example, a user extended the sample application so that the QuoteFilter stream is written to a file. This is one of the greatest benefits

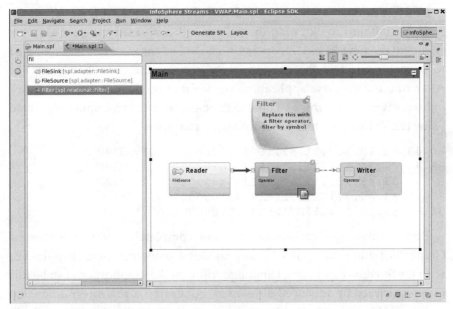

Figure 6-7 *Application building is as simple as dragging and dropping with the Streams Graphical Editor.*

associated with all of the samples that are shipped with Streams: You can extend and customize them to build your application.

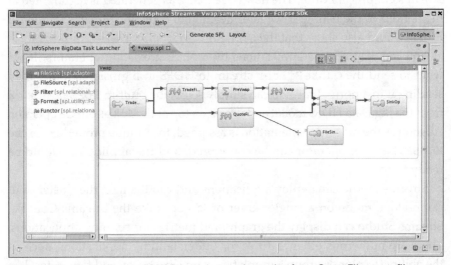

Figure 6-8 *Extending the VWAP sample to write tuples from QuoteFilter to a file*

In this example, a user simply dragged a `FileSink` operator from the Streams standard toolkit onto the palette and connected the `QuoteFilter` stream to the new `FileSink` operator. The `FileSink` operator was renamed to `QuoteWriter` and the `file` property is set to the `QuoteFile.txt` file. After running the new application, we see that by default, the tuple attributes are written one row at a time to `QuoteFile.txt` in a comma-separated value (CSV) form, such as in the following example:

```
80.43,83.49,10,(1135711808,117000000,0),"IBM"
83.43,83.46,10,(1135711813,283000000,0),"IBM"
83.42,83.46,10,(1135711813,718000000,0),"IBM"
83.42,83.45,1,(1135711814,731000000,0),"IBM"
81.42,83.45,3,(1135711815,751000000,0),"IBM"
```

Even though applications can be built completely within the Streams Graphical Editor, this tool set also provides a powerful round-trip linkage with the Streams Processing Language editor so that applications can be further customized by advanced developers. For example, this integration gives you the ability to implement custom operators, which didn't initially exist in the Streams toolkits. Developers often find it convenient to start with the Streams Graphical Editor and switch back and forth between it and the SPL editor after the initial application has been sketched. Figure 6-9 shows the SPL editor with the new `QuoteWriter` operator that we added using the Streams Graphical Editor. The new code that was generated is highlighted at the bottom of the listing. If we later delete that code, the Streams Graphical Editor would also show that the `QuoteWriter` operator was removed.

You can also change applications by replacing existing operators. If we want to send the `QuoteFilter` stream to HDFS in BigInsights rather than sending it to a normal file, we can simply select the built-in `HDFSFileSink` from the Big Data HDFS toolkit and drag it on top of the `FileSource` operator. As soon as the new implementation is assigned, the unique properties for the `HDFSFileSink` operator can be configured, and the application would be ready to go.

Streams Studio can deploy applications and run them on the cluster or in stand-alone mode on a single server or laptop. Like the Streams Console, Streams Studio can display the graphs and metrics for running applications. There are numerous other features for understanding applications, such as the ability to color or group a graph based on jobs, hosts, and flow rates. It is

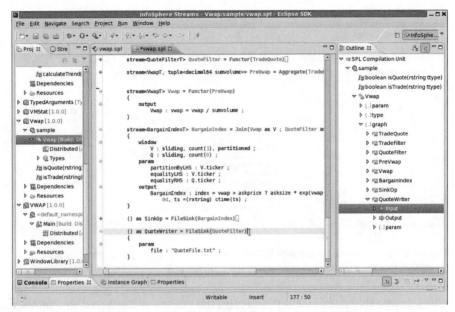

Figure 6-9 *The Streams Graphical Editor and SPL editor are linked for round-trip updates.*

also possible to quickly gather and display logs from the cluster if an application is not behaving as expected. For example, Streams Studio applies colorization to a job and its operators, and even colors the PE containing the operator, so that different PEs have different colors.

Additionally, by clicking on any operator, it is possible to highlight upstream or downstream operators to understand provenance (the origin of the data and any changes applied to it in the stream). The ability to quickly see the upstream operators is extremely useful for debugging large applications when an operator is not receiving the data that is expected. For example, if an operator is not receiving data, by highlighting upstream operators you can quickly trace back to the problem in the application. Figure 6-10 shows an Instance Graph with both the VWAP and TrendCalculator job running. Operators that are upstream from the QuoteWriter operator are highlighted to determine what generates its data.

One of the most useful new features in Streams Studio for debugging applications is the ability to click on a stream in an Instance Graph to display the data that is flowing on that stream. As in the Table view in the Streams

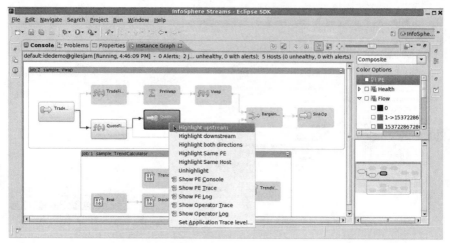

Figure 6-10 *Instance Graph with VWAP and TrendCalculator applications; operators upstream from the QuoteWriter operator are highlighted.*

Console, the live data that is flowing on the stream is displayed in a tabular form that can be filtered and manipulated. Figure 6-11 shows a user selecting Show Data for the NewTrendValue stream. It also shows the live data from the stream after the user runs through a wizard to configure the attributes and filters that should be applied. Data in the table can be paused for closer examination without impacting the running applications; after updates are resumed, the latest data in the view buffer is displayed. Because you can quickly see the data elements as they pass by in the stream, it is much easier to extend and debug applications.

The Up-and-Running Experience: Getting the Environment Installed and Configured

Clusters can be very challenging to install and configure. Although we can't go into detail about the Streams installer and streamtool command-line tools, we've invested a lot to ensure that the up-and-running experience is as seamless as possible. If you've ever installed and configured a Hadoop cluster from Apache, and compared that with the Cloudera or BigInsights experience, then you'll appreciate what we've done here. After a quick and easy installation program, the user accesses the Streams First Steps configuration tool. This tool vastly simplifies complex tasks, such as setting up ssh keys, setting environment variables, configuring public and private keys, and verifying

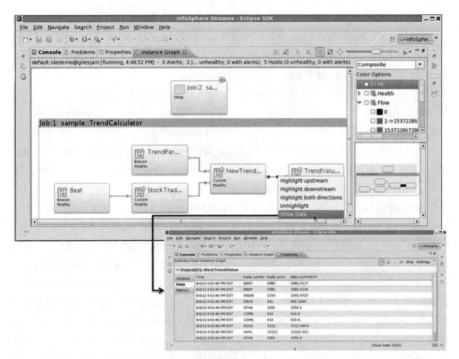

Figure 6-11   *Display live data being fed from the NewTrendValue stream by clicking directly on the Instance Graph*

the installation. In many cases, the user simply needs to click on the task and it is completed automatically with minimal configuration. (You can also launch First Steps any time using the `streamtool launch -firststeps` command.)

As you can see, there are many powerful tools that help users and developers to assemble, deploy, run, and debug Streams applications. There are also tools to effectively install and manage a cluster, which provide detailed health and metrics information. Built-in operators make it easy to assemble applications without writing a program. It is easier than ever to visualize live streaming data using Streams Console and Streams Studio.

The Streams Processing Language

With the new Streams Graphical Editor, many applications can be created without looking at any source code. However, under every Streams application is the Streams Processing Language (SPL). SPL is a structured application development language that can be used to build Streams applications. It's supported by both the Streams Graphical and the Streams Processing Language editors, which are integrated with "round-trip ability" so that it's possible to go back and forth between both editors.

SPL is a very powerful declarative language that provides a higher level of abstraction for building Streams applications than using lower-level languages or APIs, in the same way that Jaql or Pig makes development easier for Hadoop compared to writing MapReduce applications directly. Streams 3.0 introduces a new XML data type and operators to process XML natively. Source and sink adapters support XML data, XML can be queried and manipulated with new operators and functions, and Streams tuples can be converted to and from XML. Additionally, SPL has been extensively enhanced with new built-in functions and operators; in fact, one of our partners, Dr. Alex Philp, Founder and CTO of TerraEchos, Inc., noted that their developers can "deliver applications 45 percent faster due to the agility of [the] Streams Processing Language." We think that Bó Thide, a professor at Sweden's top-ranked Uppsala University, said it best when referring to SPL: "Streams allows me to again be a Space Physicist instead of a Computer Scientist." After all, technology is great, but if you can't quickly apply it to the business need at hand, what's the point?

Streams-based applications built with the Streams Graphical Editor or written in SPL are compiled using the Streams compiler, which turns them into binary (`bin`) executable code—this executable code runs in the Streams environment to accomplish tasks on the various servers in the cluster. An SPL program is a text-based representation of the graph that we discussed in the preceding section: It defines the sources, sinks, and operators, as well as the way in which they are interconnected with a stream. For example, the following SPL code reads data from a file line by line into tuples, converts each line to uppercase, and then writes each line to standard output.

```
composite toUpper {
    graph
      stream<rstring line> LineStream = FileSource() {
        param   file              : "input_file";
                format            : line;
      }
      stream<LineStream> upperedTxt = Functor(LineStream) {
```

```
      output upperedTxt        : line = upper(line);
   }
   () as Sink = FileSink(upperedTxt) {
   param  file        : "/dev/stdout";
   format             : line;
   }
}
```

In this SPL snippet, the built-in `FileSource` operator reads data from the specified file one line at a time and puts it into a stream called `LineStream` that has a single tuple attribute called `line`. The built-in `Functor` operator consumes the `LineStream` stream, converts the `line` attribute from each streamed tuple to uppercase text, and creates a new output stream called `upperedTxt` using the same tuple format as `LineStream`. The `Sink` operator then reads the `upperedTxt` stream of data and sends the tuples to standard output (`STDOUT`). Notice that the application is wrapped in a composite operator that encapsulates the function, as described in the previous sections; again, all applications consist of one or more composite operators.

This snippet represents the simplest stream with a single source, a single operation, and a single sink. Of course, the power of Streams is that it can run massively parallel jobs across large clusters of servers, where each operator, or a group of operators, can be running on a separate server. But before we get into the enterprise class capabilities of Streams, let's look at some of the most popular adapters and operators that are available in this product. As described earlier in this chapter, Streams provides nearly 30 built-in operators in the standard toolkit, dozens of operators from special toolkits, such as data mining and text analytics, and literally hundreds of functions out-of-the-box for developers.

Source and Sink Adapters

It goes without saying that in order to perform analysis on a stream of data, the data has to enter a stream. Of course, a stream of data has to go somewhere when the analysis is done (even if that "somewhere" is defined as a *void* where bits get dumped into "nowhere"). Let's look at the most basic source adapters available to ingest data along with the most basic sink adapters to which data can be sent. Perhaps the most powerful adapters we describe are `import` and `export`—these operators provide dynamic connections for jobs that can be configured at deployment time and at run time.

FileSource and FileSink

As the names imply, `FileSource` and `FileSink` are standard built-in adapters that are used to read from or write to a file. You use parameters to specify the name and location of the file that is to be used for the read or write operation. Another parameter identifies the format of the file's contents, which could be any of the following formats:

- **txt**   Simple text files, where each tuple is a row in the file

- **csv**   Files that contain comma-separated values

- **bin**   Files that contain binary data tuples

- **line**   Files that contain lines of text data

- **block**   An input stream made up of binary data blocks (much like a BLOB)

There are a number of other optional parameters that can be used to specify column separators, end-of-line markers, delimiters, compression, and more.

TCPSource/UDPSource and TCPSink/UDPSink

The `TCPSource` and `TCPSink` adapters are the basic TCP adapters used in Streams to read from and write to a socket. When you use these adapters, you specify the IP address (using either IPv4 or IPv6) along with the port, and the adapter will read from the socket and generate tuples into the stream. Parameters for these adapters are the same as those for the `FileSource` and `FileSink` adapters, in terms of the format of the data flow (txt, csv, and so on). The `UDPSource` and `UDPSink` adapters read from and write to a UDP socket in the same manner as the TCP-based adapters.

Export and Import

The `export` and `import` adapters work together to connect jobs within a Streams instance. An `export` adapter can be used to make data from a job available to other jobs that are already deployed or that might be deployed in the future. You can export data using the `export` adapter and assign a `streamID` to the exported stream, as well as optional name/value pairs to further characterize the stream.

After the stream is assigned these export properties, any other Streams applications that are deployed to the same Streams instance can import this data using an `import` operator and a subscription expression that matches the export properties—assuming the application is authorized to access the exported data stream. Using built-in APIs, both export properties and import subscriptions can be changed dynamically at run time. This means that applications can be built to evolve in powerful ways over time, depending on the jobs that are submitted and the processing that is being done. For example, a sentiment analysis job might subscribe to all streams with the parameter `textForSentimentAnalysis=true`. There might be jobs processing email and blog text that export that parameter. At some time in the future, if you decide to process instant messaging text for sentiment, you just need to deploy the job to process the instant messages and export the `textForSe ntimentAnalysis=true` parameter—it will automatically be connected in an efficient point-to-point way to the sentiment analysis job. Using `export` and `import` is a very powerful way to dynamically stream data between applications running under the same Streams instance.

MetricsSink

The `MetricsSink` adapter is a very interesting and useful sink adapter because it enables you to set up a *named meter*, which is incremented whenever a tuple arrives at the sink. You can think of these meters as a gauge that you can monitor using Streams Studio or other tools. If you've ever driven over one of those traffic counters (those black rubber hoses that lie across an inter- section or road), you've got the right idea. Although a traffic counter mea- sures the flow of traffic through a point of interest, a `MetricsSink` can be used to monitor the volume and velocity of data flowing out of your data stream.

Operators

Operators are at the heart of the Streams analytical engine. They take data from upstream adapters or other operators, manipulate that data, and create a new stream and new tuples (possibly pass-through) to send to downstream operators. In addition to tuples from an input stream, operators have access to metrics that can be used to change the behavior of the operator, for example, during periods of high load. In this section, we discuss some of the more common Streams operators that can be strung together to build a Streams application.

Filter

The `filter` operator is similar to a filter in an actual water stream, or in your furnace or car: its purpose is to allow only some of the streaming contents to pass. A Streams `filter` operator removes tuples from a data stream based on a user-defined condition specified as a parameter to the operator. After you've programmatically specified a condition, the first output port defined in the operator will receive any tuples that satisfy that condition. You can optionally specify a second output port to receive any tuples that did not satisfy the specified condition. (If you're familiar with extract, transform, and load [ETL] flows, this is similar to a `match` and `discard` operation.)

Functor

The `functor` operator reads from an input stream, transforms tuples in flexible ways, and sends new tuples to an output stream. The transformations can manipulate any of the elements in the stream. For example, you could extract a data element out of a stream and output the running total of that element for every tuple that comes through a specific `functor` operator.

Punctor

The `punctor` operator adds punctuation into the stream, which can then be used downstream to separate the stream into multiple windows. For example, suppose a stream reads a contact directory listing and processes the data flowing through that stream. You can keep a running count of last names in the contact directory by using the `punctor` operator to add a punctuation mark into the stream any time your application observes a changed last name in the stream. You could then use this punctuation mark downstream in an aggregation `functor` operator to send out the running total for that name, later resetting the count back to 0 to start counting the next set of last names.

Sort

The `sort` operator outputs the tuples that it receives, but in a specified sorted order. This operator uses a stream window specification. Think about it for a moment: If a stream represents a constant flow of data, how can you sort that data? You don't know whether the next tuple to arrive will need to be sorted with the first tuple to be sent as output. To overcome this issue, Streams enables you to specify a window on which to operate. You can specify a window of tuples in the following ways:

- `count`   The number of tuples to include in the window
- `delta`   Wait until a given attribute of an element in the stream has changed by a specified delta amount
- `time`   The amount of time, in seconds, to allow the window to fill up
- `punctuation`   The punctuation that is used to delimit the window, as defined by the `punctor` operator

In addition to specifying the window, you must also specify an expression that defines how you want the data to be sorted (for example, sort by a given attribute in the stream). After the window fills up, the sort operator will sort the tuples based on the element that you specified, and then send those tuples to the output port in sorted order. Then the window fills up again. By default, Streams sorts in ascending order, but you can specify a sort in descending order.

Join

As you've likely guessed, the `join` operator takes two streams, matches the tuples on a specified condition, and then sends the matches to an output stream. When a row arrives on one input stream, the matching attribute is compared to the tuples that already exist in the operating window of the second input stream to try to find a match. Just as in a relational database, several types of joins can be used, including `inner joins` (in which only matches are passed on) and `outer  joins` (which can pass on one of the stream tuples even without a match, in addition to matching tuples from both streams). As with the `sort` operator, you must specify a window of tuples to store in each stream.

Aggregate

The `aggregate` operator can be used to sum up the values of a given attribute or set of attributes for the tuples in the window; this operator also relies on a windowing option to group together a set of tuples. An `aggregate` operator enables `groupBy` and `partitionBy` parameters to divide up the tuples in a window and perform aggregation on those subsets of tuples. You can use the `aggregate` operator to perform `count`, `sum`, `average`, `max`, `min`, `first`, `last`, `count distinct`, and other forms of aggregation.

Beacon

The beacon is a useful operator because it's used to create tuples on the fly. For example, you can set up a beacon to send tuples into a stream at various intervals that are defined either by a time period (send a tuple every n tenths of a second) or iteration (send out n tuples and then stop). The beacon operator can be useful for testing and debugging your Streams applications.

Throttle and Delay

Two other useful operators can help you to manipulate the timing and flow of a given stream: throttle and delay. The throttle operator helps you to set the "pace" of the data flowing through a stream. For example, tuples that are arriving sporadically can be sent to the output of the throttle operator at a specified rate (defined by tuples per second). Similarly, the delay operator can be used to change the timing of the stream. A delay operator can be set up to output tuples after a specific time interval; however, with delay, the tuples exit the operator with the same time interval that existed between the tuples when they arrived. That is, if tuple A arrives 10 seconds before tuple B, which arrives three seconds before tuple C, the delay operator maintains this timing between tuples on exit, after the tuples have been delayed by the specified amount of time.

Split and Union

The split operator takes one input stream and, as the name suggests, splits that stream into multiple output streams. This operator takes a parameterized list of values for a given attribute in the tuple and matches the tuple's attribute with this list to determine on which output stream the tuple will be sent. The union operator acts in reverse: it takes multiple input streams and combines all of the tuples that are found in those input streams into one output stream.

Streams Toolkits

In addition to the adapters and operators that are described in the previous sections, Streams ships with a number of toolkits that enable even faster application development. These toolkits enable you to connect to specific data sources and manipulate the data that is commonly found in databases or Hadoop; perform signal processing on time series data; extract information from text using advanced text analytics; score data mining models in real time; process financial markets data; and much more. Because the Streams toolkits can dramatically accelerate your time to analysis with Streams, we cover the Database, Big Data, Advanced Text Analytics, and Data Mining Toolkits in more detail here. There are many more toolkits available as part of the product, such as the Timeseries, GeoSpatial, Financial Markets, Messaging, CEP, Internet, IBM PureData System high speed adapters, DB2 parallel adapter, and DataStage toolkits. There are also toolkits freely downloadable from the *Streams Exchange* on developerWorks (http://tinyurl.com/7sc6p8m) such as the OpenCV toolkit for image processing and the HTTP connectivity toolkit.

The Database Toolkit: Operators for Relational Databases

The Database Toolkit enables a stream to read from or write to an ODBC database or read from a SolidDB database. Moreover, it provides high-performance parallel operators to write to DB2 or IBM PureData System databases. This toolkit enables a stream to query an external database to add data or to verify data in the stream for further analysis. This Streams toolkit includes the following operators, among others:

- **ODBCAppend**   Inserts data from a stream into a table using SQL INSERT statements

- **ODBCSource**   Reads data from a table and puts each row into the stream as a tuple

- **DB2PartitionedAppend**   Inserts data into a specific DB2 partition, and can be used in parallel for high-performance loading

- **NetezzaLoad**   Inserts data into an IBM PureData System for Analytics (Netezza) using its high-speed loader

- **SolidDBEnrich**   Reads data from a SolidDB table and adds that information to tuples in the stream

The Big Data Toolkit: Operators for Integration with BigInsights

The Big Data toolkit has operators for connecting to the Hadoop Distributed File System (HDFS). This toolkit is essential for applications where Streams and BigInsights work together. It enables high-speed parallel writing to the HDFS for the fastest possible data exchange. This Streams toolkit includes the operators shown in the following list, among others.

- **HDFSFileSink**   Writes data from a stream to HDFS

- **HDFSFileSource**   Reads data from HDFS and writes it to a stream

- **HDFSSplit**   Splits a stream into multiple streams so that HDFSParallelWriter can write data in parallel to the HDFS

- **HDFSDirectoryScan**   Scans an HDFS directory for new files and writes the file names to a stream for use with HDFSFileSource

The Advanced Text Analytics Toolkit: Operators for Text Analytics

The Advanced Text Analytics toolkit lets your applications take advantage of the same powerful text analytics functions that you use with BigInsights. The TextExtract operator uses an Annotated Query Language specification or an analytics operator graph (AOG) file and processes incoming text documents that arrive as tuples. It then sends the results as tuples to downstream operators. Many parameters, such as dictionaries, language, and tokenizers, can be set. This toolkit is essential for analysis of social media in real time and is a key part of the IBM Accelerator for Social Data Analytics discussed in Chapter 9. Besides social media, Advanced Text Analytics is important for use cases ranging from log analytics where log lines need to be parsed to extract meaning to cyber security where message contents are analyzed as part of deep packet inspection.

The Data Mining Toolkit: Operators for Scoring Data Mining Models

The Data Mining Toolkit has operators to score several different types of data mining models in real time. Although data mining software such as SPSS requires multiple passes over data to build models, scoring can often be done on a record-by-record basis. The Data Mining Toolkit can score data mining models that are defined by the Predictive Model Markup Language (PMML) standard. This toolkit includes the following operators:

- **Classification**   Supports Decision Trees, Naïve Bayes, and Logistic Regression algorithms that are used to classify tuples

- **Clustering**   Supports Demographic Clustering and Kohonen Clustering algorithms that are used to assign tuples to a related group

- **Regression**   Supports Linear Regression, Polynomial Regression, and Transform Regression algorithms that are used for predictive analytics
- **Associations**   Supports association rules for predicting cause-and-effect relationships

In addition to scoring PMML models, Streams can score a wide range of algorithms that are exported by the SPSS Modeler Solution Publisher.

Enterprise Class

Many real-time application and parallel processing environments built in the past have come and gone. What makes Streams so different is its enterprise class architecture and run-time environment, which are powerful and robust enough to handle the most demanding streaming workloads; the rich tools for building, managing, and deploying Streams applications; the hundreds of built-in analytic operators and functions; and its integration with enterprise systems. This is the value that IBM and its research and development arms bring to the Big Data problem. Although some companies have massive IT budgets and try to do this themselves, wouldn't it make sense to invest that money in core competencies and the business?

Large, massively parallel jobs have unique availability requirements because in a large cluster, there are bound to be failures. The good news is that Streams has built-in availability characteristics that take this into account. Coupled with the application monitoring that we describe elsewhere in this book, Streams enables you to keep management costs low and the reputation of your business high. Integration with the rest of your enterprise architecture is essential to building a holistic solution. It's a recurring theme of this book: *IBM offers a Big Data platform, not a Big Data product.* In this section, we cover some of the hardened enterprise aspects of Streams, including availability and integration.

High Availability

When you configure your Streams platform, you specify which hosts (servers) will be part of the Streams instance. You can specify three types of hosts, as listed next, for each server in your platform.

- **Application host**   Runs SPL jobs.

- **Management host**   Runs the management services that control the flow of SPL jobs (but doesn't explicitly run any SPL jobs directly), manages security within the instance, monitors any running jobs, and so on.

- **Mixed host**   Can run both SPL jobs and management tasks.

In a typical small environment, you would have one management host and the remainder of your servers would be used as application hosts, but for large deployments, management services can be distributed to more hosts.

When you build a streaming application, operators are compiled into one or more processing elements (PEs). PEs can contain one or more operators, which are often "fused" together inside a single PE for performance reasons. A PE can be considered to be a unit of physical deployment in the Streams product. PEs from the same application can run on multiple hosts in a network, as well as communicate tuples across the network. In the event of a PE failure, Streams automatically detects the failure and chooses from among a large number of possible remedial actions. For example, if the PE is restartable and relocatable, the Streams run-time engine automatically picks an available host on which to run the PE; starts the PE on that host; and automatically "rewires" inputs and outputs to other PEs, as appropriate. However, if the PE continues to fail over and over again and exceeds a retry threshold (perhaps due to a recurring underlying hardware issue), the PE is placed into a stopped state and requires manual intervention to resolve the issue. If the PE is restartable, but has been defined as not relocatable (for example, the PE is a sink that requires it to be run on a specific host), the Streams run-time engine automatically attempts to restart the PE on the same host, if it is available. Similarly, if a management host fails, you can have the management function restarted elsewhere, assuming that you have configured the system with RecoveryMode=ON. In this case, the recovery metadata has the necessary information to restart the management tasks on another server in the cluster.

Data processing is guaranteed in Streams when there are no host, network, or PE failures. You might be wondering what happens to the data in the event of one of these failures? When a PE (or its network or host) does fail, the data in the PE's buffers (and data that appears while a PE is being restarted) can be lost without special precautions. With the most sensitive applications requiring very high performance, it is appropriate to deploy two or more parallel instances of the streaming application on different hardware—that way, if a PE in one instance of a graph fails, the other parallel instance is already actively processing all of the data and can continue while the failed graph is being restored. There are other strategies that can be used, depending on the needs of the application. Streams is often deployed in production environments in which the processing of every single bit of data with high performance is essential, and these high-availability strategies and mechanisms have been critical to successful Streams deployments. The fact that Streams is hardened for enterprise deployments helped one customer recover from a serious business emergency that was caused by an electrical outage. (If only everything were as reliable as Streams!)

Integration Is the Apex of Enterprise Class Analysis

Another aspect of an enterprise class solution is how well it integrates into your existing enterprise architecture. As we've discussed previously, Big Data is not a replacement for your traditional systems; it's there to augment them. Coordinating your traditional and new age Big Data processes takes a vendor who understands both sides of the equation. Streams already has extensive high-speed connection capabilities into enterprise assets, such as relational databases, in-memory databases, application server queues (such as IBM WebSphere), and more. Although we delve into the details and nuances of integration in a Big Data world in Chapter 11, let's briefly touch on some Streams-specific integration points in this section.

Streams has sink adapters that enable the high-speed delivery of streaming data into BigInsights (through the BigInsights Toolkit for Streams) or directly into your data warehouse for data-at-rest analysis. A new enhancement is the ability to include Streams applications in ETL flows with IBM InfoSphere DataStage (DataStage), and for Streams applications to move data to and from DataStage. This integration enables DataStage to embed analytics in flows, and Streams to access the specialized data sources and sinks that are available through DataStage. Finally, Streams has the ability to incorporate virtually any analytic flow from SPSS Modeler Solution Publisher into a

Streams application, enabling rich analytics to be incorporated into real-time applications.

As we mention throughout this book, Big Data problems require the analysis of data at rest and data in motion. The integration of Streams and BigInsights offers a platform (not just products) for the analysis of data in real time, as well as the analysis of vast amounts of data at rest for complex analytical workloads. IBM gives you the best of both worlds, and it is brought together under one umbrella with considerations for security, enterprise service-level agreement expectations, nationalization of the product and support channels, enterprise performance expectations, and more.

Industry Use Cases for InfoSphere Streams

To give you some insight into how Streams technology can fit into your environment, in this section we provide some industry use case examples that expand on the examples in Chapter 2. Most of these examples are Big Data platform examples, because they incorporate other components of the Big Data platform along with Streams. Obviously, we can't cover every industry in such a short book, but we think this section will get you thinking and excited about the breadth of possibilities that Streams technology can offer your environment.

Telecommunications

The quantity of call detail records (CDRs) that telecommunications companies have to manage is staggering. This information is not only useful for providing accurate customer billing, but a wealth of information can be gleaned from CDR analysis performed in near-real time. For example, CDR analysis can help to prevent customer loss by analyzing the access patterns of "group leaders" in their social networks. These group leaders are people who might be in a position to affect the tendencies of their contacts to move from one service provider to another. Through a combination of traditional and social media analysis, Streams can help you to identify these individuals, the networks to which they belong, and on whom they have influence.

Streams can also be used to power up a real-time analytics processing (RTAP) campaign management solution to help boost campaign effectiveness, deliver a shorter time to market for new promotions and soft bundles, help to find new revenue streams, and enrich churn analysis. For example, Globe Telecom leverages information gathered from its handsets to identify the optimal service promotion for each customer and the best time to deliver it, which has had profound effects on its business. Globe Telecom reduced from 10 months to 40 days the time to market for new services, increased sales significantly through real-time promotional engines, and more.

What's good for CDRs can also be applied to Internet protocol detail records (IPDRs). IPDRs provide information about Internet Protocol (IP)-based service usage and other activities that can be used by operational support to determine the quality of the network and detect issues that might require maintenance before they lead to a breakdown in network equipment. (Of course, this same use case can be applied to CDRs.) Just how real-time and low-latency is Streams when it comes to CDR and IPDR processing? In one example requiring fewer than 10 servers, we have supported peak throughput rates of some detail records equal to 500,000 per second, with more than 8 billion detail records analyzed per day (yes, you read that rate right), or more than 5PB (5000TB) of data per year. And all this while de-duplicating incoming records against seven days of data (56 billion records) and reducing latency from 12 hours to a few seconds (yes, that's more than 10,000 times faster). Streams has sustained rates of 10GB per second for network monitoring, and 100MB per second for X-ray diffraction (XRD). One thing worth noting here, if these examples are too modest for your environment, is that Streams is grid-scalable, so you can add more capacity on the fly in an elastic manner. Truly, Streams is game-changing technology.

Enforcement, Defense, Surveillance, and Cyber Security

Streams provides a huge opportunity for improved law enforcement and increased security, and offers unlimited potential when it comes to the kinds of applications that can be built in this space, such as real-time situational awareness applications, multimodal surveillance, cyber security detection, legal wire taps, video surveillance, and face recognition. Corporations can also leverage streaming analytics to detect and prevent cyber attacks by streaming network logs and other system logs to stop intrusions or detect malicious activity anywhere in their networks.

TerraEchos uses Streams to provide covert sensor surveillance systems that enable companies with sensitive facilities to detect intruders before they even get near the buildings or other sensitive installations. They've been the recipients of a number of awards for their technology (the Frost and Sullivan Award for Innovative Product of the Year for their Fiber Optic Sensor System Boarder Application, among others).

Financial Services Sector

The financial services sector (FSS) and its suboperations are a prime example for which the analysis of streaming data can provide a competitive advantage (as well as regulatory oversight, depending on your business). The ability to analyze high volumes of trading and market data, at ultra-low latencies, across multiple markets and countries simultaneously, offers companies the microsecond reaction times that can make the difference between profit and loss through arbitrage trading and book of business risk analysis. For example, how does such a transaction occurring at this very moment add to the firm's risk position?

Streams is also used by FSS companies for real-time trade monitoring and fraud detection. For example, Algo Trading supports average throughput rates of about 12.7 million option market messages per second on a few servers and generates trade recommendations for its customers with a latency of 50 microseconds.

Streams provides direct connectivity through the ubiquitous Financial Information eXchange (FIX) gateways with a function-rich library to help calculate theoretical Put and Call option values. Streams can even leverage multiple types of inputs. For example, FSS firms can leverage social media to understand customers better when offering new services. Similarly, real-time fraud detection can also be used by credit card companies and retailers to deliver fraud detection and multiparty fraud detection (as well as to identify real-time up-sell or cross-sell opportunities).

Health and Life Sciences

Healthcare equipment is designed to produce diagnostic data at a rapid rate. From electrocardiograms, to devices that measure temperature and blood pressure, to blood oxygen sensors, and much more, medical diagnostic equipment produces a vast array of data. Harnessing this data and analyzing it in real time delivers benefits unlike any other industry. In addition to providing companies with a competitive advantage, Streams deployment in healthcare is helping to save lives.

For example, the University of Ontario Institute of Technology (UOIT) is building a smarter hospital in Toronto and leveraging Streams to deliver a neonatal critical care unit that monitors the health of what we affectionately call "data babies." These babies continuously generate data: every heartbeat, every breath, every anomaly helping to produce more than 1,000 pieces of unique diagnostic information per second. Streams is used as an early warning system that helps doctors find new ways to avoid life-threatening infections up to 24 hours sooner than previously possible. There is synergism at play here, too. It could be the case that a separately monitored stream falls within normal parameters (blood pressure, heart rate, and so on); however, the combination of several streams with some specific value ranges can turn out to be a predictor of impending illness. Because Streams is performing analytics on moving data instead of just looking for out-of-bound values, it not only has the potential to save lives, but it also helps to drive down the cost of healthcare.

And the Rest We Can't Fit in This Book ...

We can't possibly cover all of the use cases and industries that could benefit from a potent product such as Streams, so we'll cram in a couple more, with fewer details, here in this section.

Government agencies can leverage the broad real-time analytics capabilities of Streams to manage such things as wildfire risks through surveillance and weather prediction, as well as water quality and water consumption through real-time flow analysis. Several governments are also improving traffic flow in some of their most congested cities by leveraging GPS data from taxis, traffic flow cameras, and traffic sensors embedded in roadways. This real-time analysis can help them to predict traffic patterns and adjust the timing of traffic lights to improve traffic flow.

The amount of data being generated in the utilities industry is growing at an explosive rate. Smart meters and sensors throughout modern energy grids are sending real-time information back to the utility companies at a staggering rate. The massive parallelism built into Streams enables this data to be analyzed in real time, so that energy generators and distributors are able to modify the capacity of their electrical grids based on the changing demands of consumers. In addition, companies can include data on natural systems (such as weather or water management data) in the analytics stream to enable energy traders to predict consumption requirements and meet client demand. This approach can deliver competitive advantages and maximize company profits.

Manufacturers want more responsive, accurate, and data-rich quality records and quality process controls to better predict and avoid defined out-of-tolerance events. E-science domains, such as weather prediction, detection of transient events, and Synchrotron atomic research are other opportunities for Streams.

From smarter grids, to text analysis, to "Who's Talking to Whom?" analysis, and more, Streams use cases are nearly limitless.

Wrapping It Up

In this chapter, we introduced you to the technical underpinnings behind Streams. We talked about all the new enhancements in Streams 3.0 that make it more consumable than ever before. With an easier up-and-running experience, guided task completion assistants, and round-trip editing through a rich and agile IDE, building Streams applications is easier than ever. This is a key point, because the consumability of Big Data technologies represents a steep learning curve for most enterprise shops. The usability enhancements in Streams 3.0 should come as no surprise, considering the impact of the Streams Processing Language on Streams application development in the Version 2.0 release.

The key value proposition of Streams is the ability to get analytics to the frontier of the business—transforming the typical forecast into a nowcast. This is a value proposition that few are even talking about in today's Big Data conversations, and even fewer can deliver. Streams is proven technology with multiple applications (as detailed in this chapter) that can help transform your business to be a leader in the Big Data era, because you can get the right answers and make better decisions faster than others in your industry.

Part IV

Unlocking Big Data

7

If Data Is the New Oil—You Need Data Exploration and Discovery

Vivisimo! **Say** it with us—use an Italian inflection while waving your hands for emphasis—as though you just ate the best-tasting piece of authentic pizza in your life! In April, 2012, we were saying this with gusto when IBM announced the acquisition of Vivisimo, a software company specializing in the indexing, searching, and navigation of data from multiple data sources.

One of the biggest challenges in business analytics today is that organizations store their data in distinct silos. We do this because it makes sense: for example, we keep our transactional data in online transaction processing (OLTP) databases, our email in Lotus Domino or Microsoft Exchange servers, and our call center engagement logs in customer relationship management (CRM) repositories such as SugarCRM. Each repository has specific availability requirements, security settings, service-level agreements (SLAs), and associated applications. But when it comes to building a complete view of all the relevant data for a particular customer from every data source in your organization, you're out of luck. The infrastructure that makes your silos effective tools for their designed purposes also makes them difficult to integrate. After all, you don't look at a picture by zooming in to 250 percent and examining one spot—unless, of course, you are editing it. There's huge value in zooming out and seeing the full picture, which you can only do by pulling in data from many sources.

IBM InfoSphere Data Explorer (formerly known as Vivisimo Velocity Platform—for the remainder of this chapter, we'll call this Data Explorer for short) represents a critical component in the IBM Big Data platform. Data Explorer technology enables users to access all of the data that they need in a single *integrated* view, regardless of its format, how it's managed, or where it's stored. Being able to retrieve data from all available repositories in an organization is a key part of doing analysis involving Big Data, especially for exploratory analysis. (We talked about this in Chapter 3—search and discovery is listed as one of IBM's five strategic ways to get started with Big Data.) Data Explorer includes a framework to easily develop business applications, called Application Builder. The customizable web-based dashboards you can build with Application Builder provide user and context-specific interfaces into the many different data sources that Data Explorer can crawl and index.

Data Explorer makes searching across your Big Data assets more *accurate*. The underlying indexes are smaller (compressed), don't need to be maintained as often as other solutions, and you can request more granular index updates instead of having to update everything. The efficient index size, coupled with the ability to dynamically expand the number of index servers makes this a highly *scalable* index and search solution. Data Explorer also includes a powerful *security* framework that enables users to only view documents that they are authorized to view based on their security profiles in the data's originating content management systems.

Data Explorer is a productivity boost for your organization at a time when it needs it the most: the dawn of the Big Data era. This technology has helped a large number of our clients unlock the value of Big Data by providing a number of techniques to locate, secure, and personalize the retrieval of business data.

Consider today's jumbo jet airplanes—typically each plane has support staff that are dedicated to it for years—like it's one of their children. In the same manner you get calls from the principal's office when your kid is sick (or in trouble), if something goes wrong with a specific airplane, a call goes out to its "parents." Now think about the last time you sat in a plane sitting at the gate for an extended period of time because there was a mechanical problem (something the authors of this book can relate to all too often). The airline calls that specific plane's support team. The worst thing an airline can do is keep that plane at the gate—it amounts to thousands of dollars lost per minute. In this scenario, a call comes in from the bridge to the customer support team who has to scramble to resolve whatever the problem could be. Of course, that plane is like a customer—it has a profile, a past, and so on. Time is money—in this case, airport fees, waiting fees, customer satisfaction, and other costs mount while the clock is ticking, and it's all adding up. One large airplane manufacturer IBM worked with had information locked away in separate systems, making it nearly impossible for support teams to access all of their knowledge repositories, each with a different security schema (data was in SAP, FileNet, Content Manager, Siebel, file shares, and more). Using Data Explorer, this large airplane manufacturer was able to build a single point of access to all of their repositories with seamless and more granular security controls on the data. A common back-end infrastructure was used to service multiple front-end applications for data retrieval. The support teams got such an injection of productivity from being able to "zoom in" and "zoom out" on the scope of the problem at hand, that the number of personnel that were needed to support an aircraft decreased. This allowed the client to realize better revenue yields as new planes could be staffed with existing teams, as opposed to hiring new staff for new plane deliveries. In the end, they were able to reduce help-desk resolution latencies by 70 percent, which ultimately resulted in multimillion dollars in savings and downstream customer satisfaction, all with Data Explorer.

Indexing Data from Multiple Sources with InfoSphere Data Explorer

Data Explorer is a search platform that can index data from multiple data sources, and that provides a single search interface, giving users the ability to see all of the relevant data in their organization and beyond. Although Data Explorer handles the indexing and searching, the data itself remains in the original data sources. (This *ship function to data* paradigm is one of the principles behind Hadoop as well.) Figure 7-1 shows the architectural layout of the main components of Data Explorer.

Connector Framework

When developing your search strategy, you first determine which data sources you need to access. Data Explorer makes this easy by including a Connector Framework that supports over 30 commonly used data sources, including

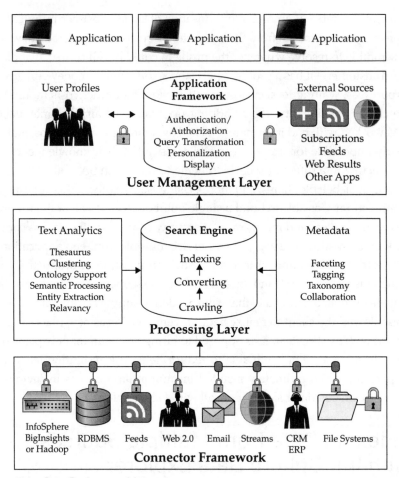

Figure 7-1 *Data Explorer architecture*

content management repositories, CRM systems, wikis, email archives, supply chain management stores, and more. There are also connectors to InfoSphere Streams and InfoSphere BigInsights, showing the deep integration of its components in the IBM Big Data platform. If you have a data source for which a connector doesn't exist, don't worry; Data Explorer also includes a mature framework for building additional connectors to proprietary data sources.

The Connector Framework taps into supported data sources to process data for indexing. We want to clearly state that Data Explorer doesn't *manage* information in the data sources; it just maintains an index of the available content for searching, navigation, and visualization.

There are many instances where people depend on data stores, such as web repositories, outside of their organization. You can use Data Explorer to add these remote sources to the unified search environment you've built for your internal sources as well. Data Explorer doesn't index these remote sites, but interfaces with the remote site's search engine to pass queries to them. It then receives result sets, interprets them, and presents them to end users alongside data from local sources.

A sophisticated security model enables Data Explorer to map the access permissions of each indexed data element according to the permissions maintained in the repository where it's managed, and to enforce these permissions when users access the data. This security model extends to the field level of individual documents, so that passages or fields within a document can be protected with their own permissions and updated without having to re-index the full document. As such, users only see data that would be visible to them if they were directly signed in to the target repository. For example, if a content management system's field-level security governs access to an Estimated Earnings report, it might grant a specific user access to the Executive Summary section, but not to the financial details such as pre-tax income (PTI), and so on. Quite simply, *if you can't see the data without Data Explorer, you won't be able to see the data with Data Explorer*.

Data Explorer connectors detect when data in the target data source is added or changed. Through these connectors, the Connector Framework ensures that the indexes reflect an up-to-date view of information in target systems.

The Data Explorer Processing Layer

The Data Explorer Processing Layer serves two purposes, each reflecting a distinct stage: indexing content as it becomes available and processing search queries from users and applications. At the beginning of this workflow, the Connector Framework makes data from each repository available to be crawled. As the data is parsed, it is transformed and processed using a number of different analytic tools, including entity extraction, tagging, and extraction of metadata for faceted navigation. Throughout this data-crunching stage, the processing layer maintains an index for the content from connected data sources. If your enterprise has existing information that describes your data sets, such as taxonomies, ontologies, and other knowledge representation standards, this information can also be factored into the index that Data Explorer builds.

Security information that is received from target data sources is ingested by the Processing Layer and also included in the indexes that Data Explorer builds for each target data source. This enables the granular role-based security capabilities that we described earlier, ensuring that users receive only the information that they are authorized to view, based on their security permissions with each target data source.

Like the other main components of the IBM Big Data platform, Data Explorer is designed to handle extremely high volumes of data by scaling out its footprint to large numbers of servers. It's been used in production settings to index trillions of records and petabytes of data.

From a high-availability perspective, the Data Explorer servers feature master-master replication, and failover capability. Whenever a server is taken offline, all search and ingestion traffic is redirected to the remaining live server. When the original server is put back online, each of its collections automatically synchronizes with a peer. If a collection has been corrupted, it is automatically restored. For planned outages, Data Explorer servers can be upgraded, replaced, or taken out of the configuration without any interruption of service (indexing or searching).

The Secret Sauce: Positional Indexes

An index is at the core of any search system and is a leading factor in query performance. In Big Data implementations, differences in index structure, size, management, and other characteristics are magnified because of the higher scale and increased data complexity. Data Explorer has a distinct advantage because it features a unique *positional index* structure that is more compact and versatile than other search solutions on the market today.

To truly appreciate why a positional index makes Data Explorer a superior enterprise search platform, you need to understand the limitations of conventional indexes, known as *vector space indexes* (see Figure 7-2).

When text is indexed using the vector space approach, all of the extracted terms are weighted according to their frequency within the document (weight is positively correlated with frequency). At query time, this weighting is also influenced by the uniqueness of the search term in relation to the full set of documents (weight is negatively correlated with the number of occurrences across the full set of documents—quite simply, if a word doesn't occur often, it's "special.") This balance between frequency and uniqueness

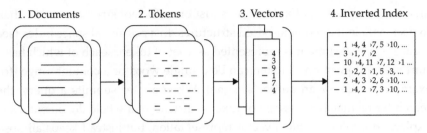

Figure 7-2   *A vector space index*

is important, so that frequently used terms like "the," which can occur often in individual documents—but also occur often in a whole set of documents—don't skew search results. Results from a complete set of documents are used to build an inverted index, which maps each term and its weight to locations of the term in the documents. When queries are issued against a search engine using a vector space index, a similar vector is calculated using just the terms in the search query. The documents whose vectors most closely match the search term's vectors are included in the top-ranked search results.

There are a number of limitations with the vector space approach, most of which stem from the fact that after a document has been reduced to a vector, it's impossible to reconstruct the full document flow. For example, it's impossible to consider portions of a document as separate units, and the only clues provided about such documents are the frequency and uniqueness of their indexed terms.

Big Data and modern search applications require more than just information about term frequency and uniqueness. Positioning information is required to efficiently perform phrase or proximity searches, to use proximity as a ranking factor, or to generate dynamic summaries. So, when keeping track of document positions (for example, the proximity of multiple search terms within a document), it's necessary for conventional index solutions to create a structure in addition to their vector space index—usually a document-specific positional space index. Of course, as with most things in life, nothing is free: this additional index comes at a cost as it takes more time to index documents, and the resulting index requires a significantly larger volume footprint.

As we mentioned earlier, Data Explorer also uses a positional space index—but the difference here is that there is no underlying vector space index. The positional space index is more compact than the traditional vector space indexes, because Data Explorer uses just one efficient structure rather than two less efficient document-based structures. In a positional space index (see Figure 7-3), a document is represented as a set of tokens, each of which has a start and end position. A token can be a single word or a content range (for example, a title, or an author's name). When a user submits a query, the search terms match a passage of tokens, instead of a whole document. Data Explorer doesn't compute a vector representation, but instead keeps all positioning information directly in its index. This representation enables a complete rebuilding of the source documents, as well as the manipulation of any subparts.

In Big Data deployments, index size can be a major concern because of the volume of the data being indexed. Many search platforms, especially those with vector space indexing schemes, produce indexes that can be 1.5 times the original data size. Data Explorer's efficient positional index structure produces a compact index, which is compressed, resulting in index sizes that are among the smallest in the industry. In addition, unlike vector space indexes, the positional space indexes don't grow when data changes; they only increase in size when new data is added.

Another benefit of positional space indexes is field-level updating, in which modifications to a single field or record in a document cause only the modified text to be re-indexed. With vector space indexes, the entire document needs to be re-indexed. This removes excessive indexing loads in systems with frequent updates, and makes small, but often important, changes available to users and applications in near-real time.

The concept of field-level security, which is related to field-level updates, is particularly useful for intelligence applications, because it enables a single classified document to contain different levels of classification. Data Explorer

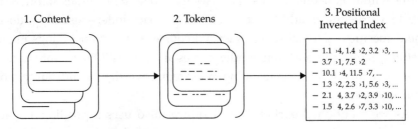

Figure 7-3   *A positional space index*

can apply security to segments of text within a document, including fields. A given document, although indexed only once, can appear differently to different groups of users based on their security settings (think back to the business plan example earlier in this chapter). Such security settings are not possible with vector space indexing, because users either have access to the whole document or to none at all, limiting an organization's flexibility in sharing information across the enterprise.

Index Auditing

For Big Data applications that require detailed auditing and accounting, the ingestion of data into indexes can be fully audited through Data Explorer's audit-log function. Data Explorer generates an audit-log entry for each piece of content being sent for indexing. The log entry is guaranteed to contain all of the errors and warnings that were encountered during crawling and indexing. Using the audit log, Data Explorer deployments can ensure that 100 percent of the content is always accounted for: each item is either indexed or has triggered an error that was reported to the administrator. Such content-completeness audits are a key requirement for many legal and compliance discovery applications.

User Management Layer

The User Management Layer includes all of the resources that users and applications need in order to interact with data that's indexed by Data Explorer. Most importantly, this includes an interface to the Data Explorer search engine, which handles all of the data requests from connected sources. Before querying any data, users must authenticate. The user's identity and group affiliations for each repository that has been indexed are stored in user profiles or accessed at login time from a directory service. (We'll note that if you are using LDAP or Active Directory services, this information is automatically retrieved.) After they are logged in, users can have a personalized interface that reflects their profile.

This layer also contains Data Explorer's ability to federate queries to external sources that are not natively indexed by Data Explorer, such as premium subscription-based information services on the Internet. The results can be merged with native Data Explorer results to create an enriched and expanded view of relevant information.

Data Explorer gives end users the ability to comment, tag, and rate content, as well as to create shared folders for content that they want to share with other users. All of this user feedback and social content is then fed back into Data Explorer's relevance analytics to ensure that the most valuable content is presented to users. Users can also comment on their search results. The comments are field-security protected, and can be created or viewed only if the user has the proper permissions. In addition, users with the appropriate permissions can save results into folders, and those folders can be personal, shared at the group level, or shared across the enterprise. This makes for a powerful collaboration environment, where users' profiles can be returned in search results, based on their activities. Suppose a user named Anna adds comments and tags including the word "Hadoop" to various documents. Any search queries including the term "Hadoop" will then return Anna's user profile, even if there is no mention of Hadoop in her profile data and job description.

Beefing Up InfoSphere BigInsights

Because Data Explorer is now an integrated component of the IBM Big Data platform, its enterprise-scale indexing and search capabilities also apply to InfoSphere BigInsights (BigInsights). While the Hadoop technologies upon which BigInsights is built have tremendous power to run complex workloads against large volumes of structured and unstructured data, there are use cases for which Hadoop is not a practical solution. The Hadoop Distributed File System (HDFS) is designed for large-scale batch operations that run against most or all of the information in a data set. However, queries involving small subsets of data in HDFS perform poorly. By indexing content stored in HDFS, Data Explorer offers a way to address the need for rapid response times without compromising the strengths of BigInsights.

Moreover, the ability to extract, recognize, and leverage metadata can greatly enhance search precision, usability, and relevance. In fact, search can add structure to unstructured content by recognizing entities and other important terms in natural language text. Data Explorer adds semantic capabilities, such as categorization, clustering, and faceted navigation, enabling you to browse search results by topic, or to navigate to a single result without ever typing a query.

An App with a View: Creating Information Dashboards with InfoSphere Data Explorer Application Builder

In any medium-to-large-sized organization, there are multiple repositories for business data, and employees invariably spend vast amounts of time searching for information. This is especially the case for many customer-facing roles, such as sales or product support, in which people depend heavily on many systems that contain critical business information, such as CRM data, product knowledge, and market data.

Data Explorer includes a compelling tool: the Application Builder application framework. Application Builder enables you to build a multifunction dashboard for the many relevant data sources that your employees need to access. While Data Explorer provides the raw power to index many disparate data sources and efficiently handle queries, you can use Application Builder to create front-end dashboards that can be an interface for presenting all this information. Figure 7-4 shows the architecture of Application Builder and Data Explorer working together. All of the powerful features of Data Explorer, such as its high-performing search and the preservation of user-specific access to data, are harnessed in Application Builder.

The options available for Application Builder applications are boundless. For example, you can federate Internet-based data sources to pull in news feeds, or stream financial data from securities markets or social media data sources like Twitter. The social capabilities from Data Explorer also work here: Users can collaborate through collective data tagging efforts, and share knowledge through comments and recommendations that are applied to data stored in sources aggregated by Application Builder.

Application Builder integrates with BigInsights and InfoSphere Streams (Streams). BigInsights and Streams can both feed data to Data Explorer, which can then syndicate it to Application Builder users. Alternatively, Application Builder can consume data directly from BigInsights or Streams. For example, a Streams feed can be surfaced as a live data source in Application Builder. In addition to hosting content that is customized for its users, Application Builder provides Data Explorer search interfaces. For example, the faceted search, clustered search, and recommendation engines can all be surfaced in Application Builder.

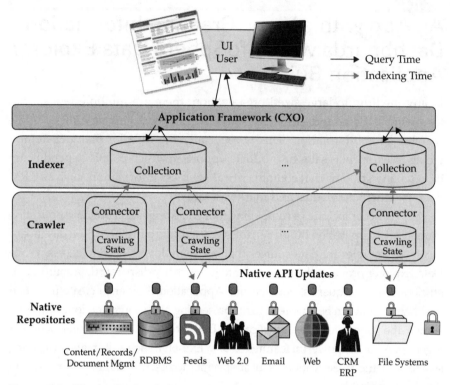

Figure 7-4 *The Application Builder architecture*

The dashboards you create with Application Builder aren't just about pulling in data from different sources. The real power comes from the definition of entity-relationship linkages between your users and the available data sets in Data Explorer. With this, your dashboards can provide information from all these data sources that are relevant to your users, without needing them to search for it. For example, your support personnel can have dashboards tailored to show data relevant to their own customers' accounts, such as their purchase history, open support tickets, and order status. This can also include data from external sources, such as news feeds relevant to the customer, or their stock price.

In short, Application Builder enables you to create custom mashups of content your employees need, where the search tools provide a mashup of content from multiple sources. The beauty of this architecture is that not only do users now have unified access to information across their business—in many cases they don't even need to search for it, as this technology "connects the dots" and brings relevant information to your users automatically.

Wrapping It Up:
Data Explorer Unlocks Big Data

Data Explorer helps organizations unlock and optimize the true business value of all their information, regardless of application or source. It provides industry-leading Big Data indexing and search techniques and includes a rich interface that enables you to easily build and expose personalized dashboards to end-user communities. Data Explorer was designed from the inside out for the Big Data era, with its positional indexing technology, granular security lockdown, and more. And with Data Explorer's connectivity framework, data can stay in the silos where it's managed, while data scientists, researchers, and business users can focus on asking the key questions.

In the Big Data world, it's even more important than ever to have powerful, accurate, agile, and flexible search across all of your data assets, because that data is in new shapes and sizes, in larger amounts than ever before, and arriving on your doorstep faster than ever. In our experiences, many large organizations are guilty of not knowing what they could already know—they have mountains of data assets, but they aren't holistically linked to users—leaving them to scramble and "get lucky" when searching. Data Explorer is an inflection point—it's great news for any organization needing to unlock information trapped in silos. You'll want to be saying it too! Vivisimo!

Part V

Big Data Analytic Accelerators

8

Differentiate Yourself with Text Analytics

Although Big Data classifications often fall into the structured, semistructured, and unstructured buckets, we want to put forward the notion that all data has some kind of structure (taking a picture with your smartphone is likely to tag it with location awareness, a timestamp, metadata as to its format and size, and so on. References to these varying degrees of structure speak to the relative ease with which the data can be analyzed and interpreted; the less structured it is, typically the more effort required to extract insights. For example, a Facebook posting is structured data—it's wrapped in the Java Script Object Notation (JSON) format. However, it's the free-form text within the structure's notation that's the unstructured part—and the hardest part of the data set to analyze. We've gotten very good at analyzing information in our databases, but that data has been cleansed and distilled into a highly structured form. Where businesses are finding enormous challenges today is in analyzing data that's not so nicely formatted, such as emails, legal documents, social media messages, and log files. As organizations increasingly rely on information that's locked in various forms of textual data, it's critical that they're provided with a framework that not only helps them make sense of what's in this text, but also helps them do it in a cost-effective (think non highly specialized skill sets) and relatively quick manner.

There are many problem domains characterized by unstructured and semistructured data. One area in which we think that text analysis can be a game changer is in fraud detection. To understand the complete story around transactions like securities trading, insurance claims, or mortgage applications, all of the data surrounding these transactions needs to be analyzed. In addition to relational data, this invariably includes raw text (from emails or text fields in forms) and semistructured data (from log files).

Data redaction is another area in which a text analytics platform greatly enhances the capability of the discipline. A great deal of data being stored today includes personally identifiable information (PII), which in many countries must be adequately governed to protect citizens' privacy. To ensure regulatory compliance, this data (for example, from forms, records, or legal documents) must be redacted to hide key elements, which would otherwise reveal people's identities. In fact, the IBM InfoSphere Guardium Data Redaction product uses the text analytics technology that's core to the IBM Big Data platform for this exact purpose.

For business-to-consumer–oriented companies, especially within the service industries, having a complete picture of an individual customer's account is essential—this is the domain of customer relationship management (CRM) analytics. Many valuable activities, such as targeted marketing and customer churn prediction, depend on understanding a customer's behavior, and because this involves not only their transactional history, but also transcriptions of their call center interactions, and even clickstream logs of their visits to the corporate web presence, text analytics are required to find "that next gear."

Text analytics can boost a Big Data project in a very obvious way in the area of social media analytics. With the advent of online communities such as Facebook, and micro-blogging services such as Twitter, people are publicly expressing their personal feelings on a scale we've never seen before. Businesses could gain a greater understanding of individual customers by understanding not just what they're saying in social media, but why they are saying it, too. In addition, knowing what groups of people are saying on social media can revolutionize how marketers assess the reach of and response to their campaigns.

While it's obvious that people quickly envision sentiment use cases when they hear the phrase "text analytics," we want to make very certain that you understand it's so much more; from piracy detection, sentiment analysis, investment research, and more, a Big Data platform requires a sound text analytics ecosystem.

What Is Text Analysis?

For each of the example scenarios we just mentioned, the challenge is to parse the text, find the elements that are being searched for, understand their meaning, and extract them in a structured form for use in other applications. IBM has a lot of experience in this area, and we've personally seen a lot of organizations try to get started on their own. Because of this, we can tell you that it's no easy task—you need a toolkit with accelerators, an integrated development environment (IDE), and preferably a declarative language to make this consumable and reachable for most organizations. After all, you can't democratize Big Data across your organization if the analysis solely depends on near impossible to find or learn skill sets. Beyond the fact that text data is unstructured, languages are complex—even when you don't factor in spelling mistakes, abbreviations, or advanced usage, such as sarcasm. As such, you need a system that is deep and flexible enough to handle complexity.

What follows is an example of this process, in which a text analysis application reads a paragraph of text and derives structured information based on various rules. These rules are defined in *extractors*, which can, for instance, identify an entity's name within a text field. Consider the following text:

In the 2012 UEFA European Football Championship, Spain continued their international success, beating Italy 4-0 in the Final. Spanish winger David Silva opened the scoring early in the game, beating Italian goalie Gianluigi Buffon. After a full 90 minutes of dominance, goalkeeper Iker Casillas accepted the championship trophy for Spain.

The product of these extractors is a set of annotated text, as shown in the underlined text in this passage. The following structured data is derived from this example text:

Name	Position	Country
David Silva	Winger	Spain
Gianluigi Buffon	Goalkeeper	Italy
Iker Casillas	Goalkeeper	Spain

The challenge is to ensure the *accuracy of results*. Accuracy has two components, precision and recall:

- **Precision**   A measure of exactness, the percentage of items in the result set that are relevant: "Are the results you're getting valid?" For example, if you wanted to extract all the play-by-play descriptions associated with goals scored from the UEFA Championships transcripts, and 30 of the 76 passages identified as goal commentaries weren't for goals at all, your precision would be just under 60 percent. In summary, precision describes how many passages identified are correctly identified.

- **Recall**   A measure of completeness, the percentage of relevant results that are retrieved from the text; in other words, are all the valid strings from the original text showing up? For example, if you wanted to extract all of the goals scored in the UEFA Championships from video, and got 60 out of 76 that would be found by a human expert, your recall would be about 79 percent, because your application missed 21 percent of goals scored. In summary, recall is how many matching passages are found out of the total number of matching passages.

As analysts develop their extractors and applications, they iteratively make refinements to tune their precision and recall rates. A great analogy is an avalanche. If the avalanche didn't pick up speed and more snow as it tumbles down a mountain slope, it wouldn't have much impact. The development of extractors is really about adding more rules and knowledge to the extractor itself; in short, it's about getting more powerful with each iteration.

We've found that most marketplace approaches to text analytics present challenges for analysts, because they tend to perform poorly (in terms of both accuracy and speed) and they are difficult to build or modify. These approaches flow the text forward through a system of extractors and filters, with no optimization. This technique is inflexible and inefficient, often resulting in redundant processing, because extractors applied later in the workflow might do work that had already been completed earlier. From what we can tell, today's text toolkits are not only inflexible and inefficient, they're also limited in their expressiveness (specifically, the degree of granularity that's possible with their queries), which results in analysts having to develop custom code. This, in turn, leads to more delays, complexity, and difficulty in refining the accuracy of your result set (precision and recall).

The Annotated Query Language to the Rescue!

To meet these challenges, the IBM Big Data platform provides the Advanced Text Analytics Toolkit, especially designed to deal with the challenges inherent in Big Data. This toolkit (originally code-named SystemT) has been under continual development since 2004, and its engine has shipped with many IBM products, including Lotus Notes, Cognos Consumer Insight, and more. IBM InfoSphere BigInsights (BigInsights) and IBM InfoSphere Streams (Streams) break new ground by including the SystemT technology in the Advanced Text Analytics Toolkit (and associated accelerators), which opens up this once "black box" technology for customization and more general purpose use than when it was delivered as function within a product. This toolkit includes a declarative language—Annotated Query Language (AQL)—with an associated cost-based optimizer, an IDE to write rules, a text analytics processing engine (ready for MapReduce and streaming data settings), and a number of built-in text extractors that include hundreds of rules pre-developed through IBM's customer engagements across a myriad of industries. The Advanced Text Analytics Toolkit also contains multilingual support, including support for double-byte character languages (through Unicode). By providing an optimizer, an AQL assistance framework, and debugging tools, you can see how the Advanced Text Analytics Toolkit is poised to democratize the ability to perform analysis on unstructured data in the same way that SQL has for database queries.

What's special about the Advanced Text Analytics Toolkit is its approach to text extraction: to ensure high accuracy (precision) and full coverage (recall), the solution builds many specific rules. This concept is built into AQL and its run-time engine, which form the heart of the Advanced Text Analytics Toolkit. AQL enables you to aggregate these many rules to represent an individual extractor. For example, an extractor for telephone numbers can contain literally hundreds of rules to match the many ways that people around the world express this concept. In addition, AQL is a fully declarative language, which means that all these overlapping rules get distilled and optimized into a highly efficient access path (similar to an SQL compiler for relational databases, where IBM researchers first developed this declarative concept), while the complexity of the underlying system is abstracted from the end user. Quite simply, when you write extraction logic in AQL, you tell the IBM Big Data platform *what* to extract, and the platform figures out *how* to extract it. This is an important differentiator of the IBM Big Data platform. The use of declarative languages (for example, AQL, the Streams Processing Language, and the machine learning statistical language) not only has significant performance benefits when this analytics code gets optimized, but it also hides the complexity of Hadoop from analysts. Notice that we referenced a number of Big Data declarative languages that are part of the IBM platform? While this chapter focuses on text analytics, it's important to realize that different Big Data projects require different kinds of optimizations. For example, text analytics is heavily dependent on CPU for processing. At the same time, crunching through trillions of key value pairs in Hadoop would tax a system's I/O capabilities (as you see in the Hadoop-respective `terasort` and `grep` benchmarks). By providing highly optimized optimization runtimes for specific tasks at hand, Big Data practitioners can focus on analysis and discovery as opposed to performance tuning.

To the best of our knowledge, there're no other fully declarative text analytics languages available in the market today. You'll find high-level and medium-level declarative languages, but they all make use of locked-up "black-box" modules that can't be customized, restricting flexibility and making it difficult to optimize for performance.

Being able to evolve text extractors is vitally important, because very few things ever remain the same when it comes to analysis. We see this often with social media analytics when popular slang terms or acronyms quickly become "tired" (for example, a few years ago, many people would say "that's sick!" if they liked something, but that's not used as often now—and we're happy about that for obvious reasons).

AQL is designed to be easily modifiable, and when you do make changes, your new code is optimized in tandem with existing code. In addition, AQL is designed for reuse, enabling you to share analytics across organizations. You can build discrete sets of extractors and use them as building blocks so that you don't have to "start from scratch" all the time.

The Advanced Text Analytics Toolkit includes sets of built-in extractors for elements that are commonly found in text collections. For example, `Person` (names), `PhoneNumber`, `Address`, and `URL` are just some of the many extractors that are shipped with BigInsights and Streams. In addition to a generic set of extractors, there are also extensive collections of extractors for social media text and for common types of log data. These built-in extractors really flatten the time to effective text analytics development curve. You can also build on these libraries with your own customizations, or use them in other extractors that you're building. We cover all of the IBM Big Data platform accelerators in Chapter 9.

If you need extractors beyond those provided out of the box, AQL is a SQL-like language for building new extractors. It's highly expressive and flexible, while providing familiar syntax. For example, the following AQL code extends the pre-existing extractors for telephone numbers and people's names to define a new extractor specifically for telephone numbers that are associated with a particular person.

```
create view PersonPhone as select P.name as person, N.number as phone
from Person P, Phone PN, Sentence S where Follows(P.name. PN.number, 0, 30)
    and Contains(S.sentence, P.name) and Contains(S.sentence, PN.number)
    and ContainsRegex(/\b(phone|at)\b/, SpanBetween(P.name, PN.number));
```

Figure 8-1 shows a visual representation of the extractor that is defined in the previous code block.

When coupled with the speed and enterprise stability of BigInsights and Streams, the Advanced Text Analytics Toolkit represents an unparalleled value proposition. The details of the integration with BigInsights and Streams (described in Figure 8-2) are transparent to the text analytics developer. After the finished AQL is compiled and automatically optimized for performance, the result is an analytics operator graph (AOG) file. For BigInsights, this AOG can be submitted as an analytics job through the BigInsights Web Console. After being submitted, this AOG is distributed with every mapper that is to be executed on the BigInsights cluster. When the job starts, each mapper executes code to instantiate its own Advanced Text Analytics Toolkit run-time and applies the AOG file. The text from each mapper's file split is run through the toolkit's run-time, and an annotated document stream is passed back as a result set.

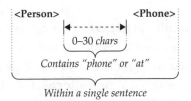

Figure 8-1 *A visual representation of the extractor rules from the code example*

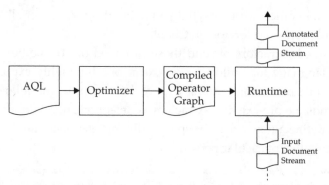

Figure 8-2 *The run-time process for analytics that are built with the Advanced Text Analytics Toolkit*

For Streams, the AOG is included in a Streams operator. During execution on a Streams node, the operator passes streaming text through the toolkit's run-time, which returns result sets back to the operator.

Productivity Tools That Make All the Difference

The Advanced Text Analytics Toolkit includes a set of Eclipse plug-ins to enhance your productivity. When writing AQL code, the editor features completion assistance, syntax highlighting, design-time validation (automatic detection of syntax errors), and more, as shown in Figure 8-3.

One of the most difficult aspects of text analysis is getting started. To make this easier, the Advanced Text Analytics Toolkit includes a workflow assistant that enables you to select elements of text that you know you're interested in, and it builds rules for you (see Figure 8-4). You can select additional variations of text for the extractors you're working on to continually refine these rules.

Also included is a facility to test extractors against a sample of the target data. Building text extractors is a highly iterative process, and the AQL tooling is not only designed to support analysts as they tweak rules and their result sets, but it's also designed to promote collaboration between the developer and the business user.

A major challenge for analysts is determining the lineage of changes that have been applied to text. It can be difficult to discern which extractors and

Content Assist

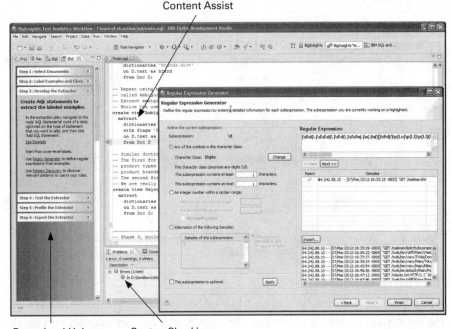

Procedural Help   Syntax Checking

Figure 8-3 *A plug-in provides a rapid application development platform for the creation, debugging, and execution of AQL.*

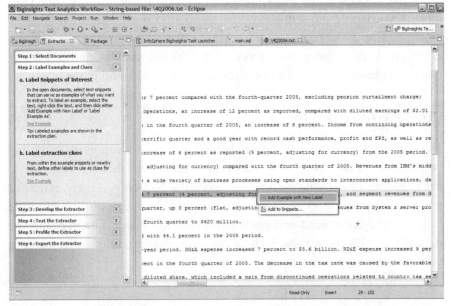

Figure 8-4 *An AQL work flow assistant: Guided help to get started with text analytics*

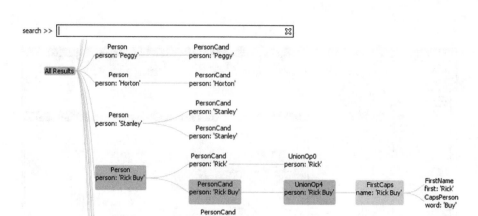

Figure 8-5   *The provenance viewer is one of the many development tools that are included in the AdvancedText Analytics Toolkit.*

which individual rules need to be adjusted to tweak the results. To aid in this, the provenance viewer, shown in Figure 8-5, features an interactive visualization capability that displays exactly which rules influence the resulting annotations.

Imagine manually building an extractor that contains 900 rules (like some of the extractors that are available out of the box in the IBM Big Data platform); if you have made a mistake, how do you figure out where that mistake is coming from? The provenance viewer is a necessity in this scenario. There are many other development accelerator features, such as the IBM Many Eyes visualization engine for upfront pattern detection, and more.

Wrapping It Up

The BigInsights Advanced Text Analytics Toolkit gives you everything that you need to quickly develop text analytics applications that will help you to get value out of extreme volumes of text data. Not only is there extensive tooling to support large-scale text analytics development, but the resulting code is highly optimized and easily deployable for either data in motion or data at rest. This toolkit also includes an extensive library of extractors that you can customize and extend.

9

The IBM Big Data
Analytic Accelerators

The IBM Big Data platform contains multiple general-purpose tools to analyze Big Data. Although these tools are rich in their capabilities, to monetize your Big Data assets, you inevitably need to write application logic that is suited to your business needs. This is no different than data you store in a relational database, where applications are needed to make databases applicable to specific use cases (for example, CRM software). Of course, we will note that the relational database industry is highly mature. Thousands of database applications can be bought, and development skills are ubiquitous. Today, out-of-the-box Big Data applications aren't easily found, leaving organizations to adopt a roll your own (RYO) approach. Now consider that Big Data development skills are priced at a premium due to scarcity, and we bet you're starting to see the challenge ... and the need.

To reduce the time it takes to extract business value from Big Data, IBM has developed a set of Big Data analytic accelerators—software modules that provide specific analytics functionality to the IBM Big Data platform. IBM's Big Data analytic accelerators are a culmination of expert patterns learned from countless customer engagements. You can use most of these accelerators across industries to extract true value from your Big Data. A number of these accelerators are available today, and more are in development for future releases. In this chapter, we describe three of the currently available accelerators: the Machine Data Accelerator, the Social Data Accelerator, and the Telco Data Accelerator.

The IBM Accelerator for Machine Data Analytics

Today's enterprises depend heavily on the uptime of their IT infrastructure. One of our clients makes money through a stock ticker-like application that conveys noteworthy news items—if it isn't running, they aren't making money. Another online retailer estimates that 17 kinds of logs are generated in the process of an online order. Web logs, application server logs, Hibernate logs, database logs, driver logs, and more, all contain discrete views into the transaction as a whole. These clients tell us they can't afford downtime, so they put a lot of investment and smarts into areas of concern. We think for as much thought and planning that goes into keeping systems highly available and recoverable from disaster, we still take too much for granted when it comes to the highly interconnected nature of our IT environments, where everyone's devices are networked, and a multitude of systems pump information through this maze of wires. Of course, when something goes wrong, our dependencies on these systems become painfully obvious. The activities of entire departments can be brought to a standstill without this lifeblood of connectivity. As such, when IT outages happen, there's an extreme sense of urgency around restoring connectivity. Here's the thing: if uptime is so critical, why are so few of us making a corpus of log information and finding trendline correlations between log events that seem harmless in isolation, but taken in context with other IT activities prove to be the root cause for a downstream outage? Big Data technologies give businesses an unprecedented opportunity to create insight into this myriad of log files that yields hints and clues on not just what went wrong in the past, but how to prevent things going sideways in the future.

As we alluded to in the previous paragraph, two main factors make IT outages challenging today: the high degree of interconnectedness and growing interdependencies between IT systems, and the high volume of usage against these systems. The key to diagnosing the root causes of failures involves system administrators combing through IT logs (also known as machine data) from their various servers and pinpointing the origin of the chain of events that led to an outage. And it's the nature of these logs that pose the biggest challenge. All these different systems store their logs in different locations, use different file formats, and use different presentation styles for elements such as date-time information. Extreme volumes make the variety of this information even more difficult to handle. It's not uncommon for organizations to rack up many terabytes—trillions of rows—of this machine data. Today, many organizations simply purge this data, almost as if it's a waste byproduct (which is why we often refer to it as data exhaust). Clearly, being able to find the hidden value in system logs is a Big Data challenge.

To meet this challenge, InfoSphere BigInsights (BigInsights) ships with the IBM Accelerator for Machine Data Analytics (known informally as the Machine Data Accelerator, or MDA for short)—a special module that's designed to handle the full lifecycle of log data analysis (shown in Figure 9-1).

Ingesting Machine Data

The first stage in the machine data analysis lifecycle is to ingest logs from IT systems into HDFS (for an explanation of HDFS, see Chapter 5). The MDA includes an ingest application, which handles this data movement operation, but also helps prepare the machine data for the subsequent data processing that will happen in BigInsights.

The MDA's data ingest function accepts logs in the form of batches, where each batch represents one type of log. In addition to the log data itself, each batch includes a metadata file, which describes key characteristics and inherent assumptions. This information is necessary for the MDA to properly parse and normalize the data. A common trait in machine data is for key metadata elements, such as the year or the server name, to be encoded in the name of the file where logs are stored. Clearly, when pulling together logs from different time periods and different systems, this information needs to be factored in.

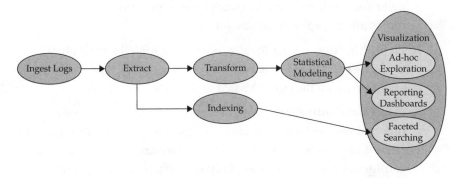

Figure 9-1   *The lifecycle of machine data analysis*

Extract

After your machine data is stored in HDFS, you can leverage the IBM Big Data platform's text analytics capabilities to parse it and extract items of interest. The objective of the MDA's extract function is to turn the log records from various sources into a consistent format. Without this, it's nearly impossible to do meaningful analysis, because so many log formats have significant differences.

The MDA includes out-of-the-box support for the following log types: Cisco syslog, WebSphere Application Server, Datapower, Webaccess, and CSVs with headers. The MDA also includes a base set of extractors that are common to all logs (for example, IP address and date-time) that can be used for other log types. For situations requiring more customization, you can use the Advanced Text Analytics Toolkit (covered in Chapter 8) and customize existing extractors, or build your own. For example, you can open up the MDA's Cisco weblog extractor and modify it to suit your log types. Really, you can think of the MDA components as a template, and you're free to customize it any way you want—and *that* lets you get to the value that's in your data faster.

The MDA's extract function parses all of a batch's log records (using the extractor that's suited to the applicable log type), and writes them in a form that can be analyzed alongside logs from other systems and time periods. This process involves the following steps:

1. **Record splitting**   This involves parsing the logs and identifying log record boundaries. Machine data from some sources (for example, Cisco syslogs) represents records as individual lines. Data from other sources (for example, WebSphere Application Server) represents records as multiple lines.

2. **Field extraction**   After the log records are split, the individual fields are extracted on the basis of rules for the log type that's associated with the current batch of log data.

3. **Event standardization**   When analyzing machine data from different devices, software, and applications, time stamps within the records need to be stored in a consistent manner, taking into consideration different time-stamp formats, time zones, or other time stamp–related information that's missing from the data itself.

This is required because information is often omitted from each record in the interest of reducing log sizes. For example, timestamps in each record might be missing the year or time zone, which is provided in the file name or known externally. The MDA uses values that are provided in the batch's metadata to fill in the missing fields. Without this standardization of time stamp data, apples-to-apples comparisons of log files are impossible.

4. **Event enrichment**   User-specified metadata—such as server name, data center name, or application name—can be associated with machine data batches during the ingestion process. For example, the server name is normally not included in batches of log records relating directly to the server itself, but it would be very useful when analyzing this information alongside batches of logs from other servers.

5. **Event generalization**   Machine data records usually contain varying values, such as time stamps, IP addresses, measurements, percentages, and messages. By replacing the varying values with constant values (*masking*), the events can be generalized. Generalized events are collected and given unique IDs, which are then used for downstream analysis. These generalized events can be used in *frequent sequence analysis* to identify which sequences of generalized events occur most frequently. They can also be used in *significance testing* to identify which generalized events are the most significant with respect to a specific error. The fields to be masked can vary with the log type. Event generalization is optional, so when users don't provide any fields, generalization is not performed.

6. **Extraction validation in BigSheets**   Before running the extraction operation, you can preview the results in BigSheets to ensure that the correct fields are being extracted, and that the standardization, enrichment, and generalization operations were applied correctly.

7. **Extracted log storage**   The resulting data is stored as compressed binary files in a hierarchy of directories where each directory contains the parsed log records from a batch of logs. The logs are formatted as JSON records; each record contains the original log record and the extracted fields for the log record.

Index

To facilitate the searching of machine data, the extracted logs must be indexed. The search interface also supports faceted browsing (where you can drill into a set of log records by selecting categories of interest). To enable this, you can customize which facets to use and what their labels should be.

Transform

The extracted machine data represents many individual log records in a format that can be analyzed with log records from other time periods and sources. One such analysis is based on the concept of *sessionization*, which is the grouping of log records that correspond to a single time period or underlying activity (this is commonly used in web-based shopping cart analysis, but it's also just as useful for network analytics). The ability to analyze machine data through the lens of sessions is useful for root cause analysis, pattern identification, and predictive modeling. The transform function in the MDA performs two kinds of sessionization: temporal and event-context relationships (where you can join two distinct sets of logs).

To leverage temporal sessionization, use the MDA to group log records into sessions based on slices of time. The MDA will divide the records based on a provided partition key (for example, a machine or process ID). Once the records are divided, you simply assign a time-gap threshold and the MDA will break the log records into sessions for each partition by combining log entries until the time-gap threshold is reached.

Event-context relationship sessionization enables you to define sessions around specific event types from one log collection and correlated information from another log collection. You start this processing by identifying the kind of event you need to analyze—this is known as a *seed* event around which the MDA will build sessions. Next, identify the kind of log information that you need to provide context for the originating event, and assign a partitioning key for the "event" log type and the "context" log type. (The partitioning key is a set of fields that are present in both event and context log records.) With this information, the MDA will break the log records into sessions defined by events you specify, such as a broken connection.

Statistical Modeling

Now that your large volumes and different formats of machine data have been normalized and transformed, you can start performing some meaningful analysis. Even without considering the different log types, volume can make statistical analysis prohibitive. In a Hadoop context, even though it's possible to deal with high data volumes and varieties efficiently, it's difficult to program statistical algorithms. BigInsights makes life easier here because it has a toolkit for machine learning and deep statistical analysis. The MDA leverages some of these statistical algorithms to help reveal valuable information that's locked in your machine data. There are currently two statistical models available for the MDA: Frequent Subsequence Identification and Significance Analysis. (Our lawyers don't like us hinting into the future, but imagine an MDA that has more statistical models at your disposal—sooner than later.) Both of these statistical models provide output that can easily be visualized and graphed using BigSheets.

The Frequent Subsequence Identification model shows which sequences of events happen most frequently across different sessions. A number of interesting patterns can be revealed with this analysis, which enables proactive administration to prevent future problems. For example, you can identify the series of events that frequently occur before failure conditions. Significance Analysis helps to identify which events, and patterns of events, are the most significant with respect to an error condition.

Visualization

The MDA includes tools that enable you to graphically drill into your machine data and visualize previously hidden trends. In fact, all extracted data and the sessionized records are available for processing by ad-hoc queries and visualization in BigSheets. In addition to refining reports and queries, you can explore your machine data using a powerful faceted search tool.

Faceted Search

After your machine data is in extracted form and has been indexed, you can browse it using the Data Explorer graphical faceted search interface included with BigInsights. This is a quick way to search machine data and expedite

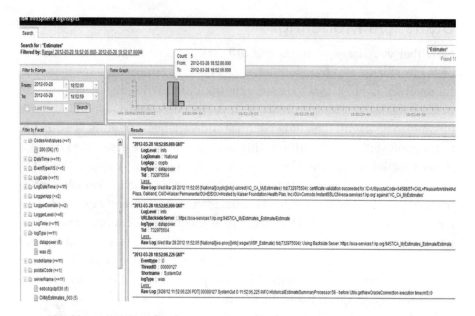

Figure 9-2 *Faceted search interface*

troubleshooting—you can focus on a small set of records within a very large set by defining a small window of time and performing a facet-based drill-down into your logs. Figure 9-2 shows the faceted search interface, in which search results are filtered by time range and a search term. On the left side of the interface, you can select other categories to further refine the search results.

The IBM Accelerator for Social Data Analytics

Of all the types of Big Data, none is as hyped and hotly debated as social media. Marketeers salivate at the prospect of understanding what's being said on Twitter about their brands. Because of this great demand, a cottage industry has sprung up around the interpretation of social media messages. We see this in the form of Twitter sentiment graphs during almost every significant cultural event. For example, during the 2012 Summer Olympics, the London Eye (the gigantic Ferris wheel on London's waterfront) was illuminated with lights whose color reflected people's overall sentiment around the games.

Almost invariably, these representations of sentiment from huge volumes of social media messages are very shallow. We found that most consist of a simple set of rules that assign positive weights for positive words, and negative weights for negative words. This might work for some tweets, but it can't be considered reliable. For example, consider this sentence:

"The <u>amazing</u> number of lip synched performances during the 2012 closing ceremonies <u>inspired</u> me to take a walk and have my own lip performance at the local pub with a pint."

Even though the two underlined words are considered positive, this tweet is overwhelmingly negative. What this sentence illustrates is that context is extremely important, and that any serious analysis of free-form text has to derive meaning through more sophisticated approaches, as opposed to a simple lexicon of classification. We've made this point in a couple of chapters throughout this book, and this is one of the differentiating pieces of the IBM Big Data platform.

Moreover, sentiment itself isn't enough. If you work in a car company's marketing department, you want to know if someone's interested in buying your company's product. Even better, you'd probably like to see market segmentation details so you can get a breakdown of how people are responding to your campaigns.

Building on the capabilities of BigInsights, Streams, and the Advanced Text Analytics Toolkit, IBM has developed a Social Data Accelerator (SDA for short, but officially known as the IBM Accelerator for Social Data Analytics), which provides a rich set of text analysis rules so that you can get an accurate and precise sense of what people are saying online.

The SDA includes extractors that are focused on lead generation and brand management for a number of industries. For lead generation, the focus is on discovering potential customers, while for brand management, how people feel about the brand and any competitors is the focus. In addition, each set of extractors for a particular use case is divided between rules that determine the meaning of a social media message, and rules that help to build profile information for a particular user. To pull the output of these extractors together, the SDA includes a workflow that helps you manage the flow of data through these extractors all the way from ingest to visualization.

Feedback Extractors: What Are People Saying?

As we've just seen, to get a sense of the meaning behind people's social media messages, it's not enough to score positive and negative words. Semantic understanding of raw text, such as tweets, is complicated and requires careful analysis. It's for this reason that IBM has built industry-specific extractors for the sentiment analysis tools in the SDA. These feedback extractors represent sets of industry-specific rules (for retail, finance, and entertainment) that apply to the brands, products, or services that you provide. Following are the kinds of feedback that the SDA rules are looking for.

- **Buzz** The amount of discussion
- **Sentiment** The degree of satisfaction or dissatisfaction. This can get quite granular. For example, if you were to tweet that you like the movie *Moneyball*, but dislike the lead actor (it's just an example; we think Brad Pitt is pretty cool), the SDA can isolate the sentiment for this movie.
- **Intent to buy** The level of commitment to spend money
- **CustomerOf** Whether someone is an existing customer (for example, someone said they bought a particular product)

Profile Extractors: Who Are These People?

For the context of what people are saying, it's extremely valuable to get a sense of who has been expressing sentiment. Profile extractors are typically applied over large sets of social media messages each time new batches are added. The first few times that you run these extractors, the profile data that you acquire will be sparse, but as your collection of social media messages grows, additional profile elements will be populated for more of the users that you are tracking. Profile extractors determine the following information from social media messages, in addition to the poster's online profile information (for example their user name, or Twitter profile):

- **Gender** The poster's sex, usually determined from the poster's online profile information
- **Location** Where the poster lives
- **Parental status** Whether the poster has children

- **Marital status**   Whether the poster is married
- **Employment status**   Whether the poster is employed

Workflow: Pulling It All Together

To successfully assess what people are saying about your brand or product, the SDA includes a workflow (see Figure 9-3) to coordinate all of the steps that are taken to analyze your social data.

Ingest

The first stage of social media analysis is ingesting social media messages. In the SDA, this stage is handled by Streams, which has source operators for the Gnip service (which provides messages from Twitter), and the BoardReader service (which provides messages from microblogs—blogs, newsgroups, forums, and so on). While Streams ingests the data into BigInsights, it also does some initial filtering of spam messages to address issues of veracity. Of course, it could be the case that you want to investigate this spam; perhaps some of it isn't spam and you can evolve the filtration process through customization—it's a learning environment, after all. Much like agile development, the more times you iterate, the better the solution becomes. Streams also provides real-time insights on the data as it's streaming into your organization.

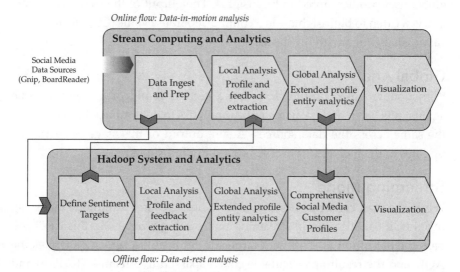

Figure 9-3   *The lifecycle of social data analysis*

The SDA is a result of thousands of iterations by IBM in this area, but as you know, the journey never ends.

Define Sentiment Targets

It seems pretty obvious when we write it, but you need to tell the SDA what you are looking for before your analysis can begin. When it comes to text extraction, you have to define the element to extract and discover from there. For example, you can provide the SDA a set of brands, products, and services that you're interested in tracking. You can make things more sophisticated by also defining product category information and aliases for the product. The SDA ingests the defined terms of interest and turns it into an AQL dictionary (see Chapter 8 for more information), which is factored into the feedback extractors that are executed in the SDA's downstream processing.

Local Analysis

This stage is the first of two text analytics passes against this batch of data. In this phase, each document is analyzed individually using both the feedback and profile extractors. Before analyzing the text itself, additional spam filtering is done, and mentions of the brand, products, or services are isolated. At this point, the feedback and profile extractors are run against the preprocessed social media messages. The output of the profile extractors is added to the global user profiles stored in BigInsights. The output of the feedback extractors is written to BigInsights—in a comma-separated value (CSV) format—for easy visualization with BigSheets.

Global Analysis

With updated user profiles in place, a second round of analysis is done against this batch of data, using entity analytics to determine which users are the same across the data sources. Again, output of this stage is written as updates to the global user profiles stored in BigInsights.

Streaming Mode

While the SDA can process social media messages in batch mode using Big Insights, it can also run in streaming mode using Streams. In this case, you pass the definition of sentiment targets to BigInsights, which generates the AQL, and the resulting executable code is passed to Streams. The local and global analysis happens on Streams in the same manner in which it is executed in batch mode, except that individual records are processed as they stream in from the social media source adapters.

Visualization

The SDA provides visualizations and reports on the results of its analysis. You can also publish these reports in the Data Extractor Application Builder dashboard. Figure 9-4 shows an example dashboard, where you can show overall sentiment, and at the same time highlight the sentiment for individual clients.

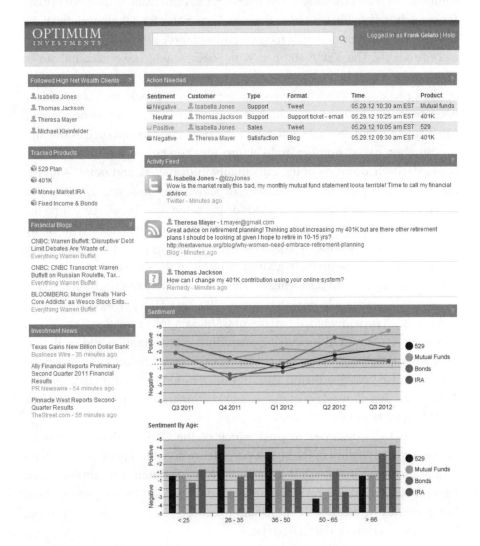

Figure 9-4   *Social data dashboard*

The IBM Accelerator for Telecommunications Event Data Analytics

The telecommunications (telco) industry has been an early and active adopter of the IBM Big Data platform, especially in dealing with data in motion. This is no surprise, given the data management challenges that telco companies face, especially in the area of high-velocity data. Based on experiences in providing solutions for telco businesses, IBM has built the Telco Data Accelerator (TEDA for short, but officially known as the IBM Accelerator for Telecommunications Event Data Analytics), which focuses on in-motion processing of call detail records (CDR). The TEDA shipped with Streams, which we talked about in Chapter 6.

CDR processing is an acute pain point for telco providers today, mainly because of high volumes and high velocities. Every time someone places a call, telco switches create a CDR, which includes information such as the calling number, called number, time stamp for the start of the call, call type (voice or SMS), duration of the call, quality information, and more. With the advent of cell phones, the number of CDR logs has greatly increased because additional CDRs are created for the same mobile call *every* time the call is transferred to a different cell tower. For telco providers with many customers, it's very difficult to process these CDR logs proactively, especially during peak usage periods. To give an example of the scale of these volumes, one of our large Asian telco clients has to deal with about six billion CDRs per day, where the daily peak rate is over 200,000 CDRs per second!

Most telco providers load batches of CDR data into a relational database, and then perform CDR processing, including transformation and analytics, used for applications like revenue assurance or fraud detection in real-time. There are also post-processing activities, such as removing duplicate entries. This means there are delays of many hours before the telco business can track billable activity or other issues.

The TEDA is designed to push much of the CDR analytics and post-processing activity out of the at-rest persistence layer and get the work done in-motion, using Streams, just after the CDR is generated. This approach not only provides the telco provider more immediate access to billing information, but a wealth of additional information can be harvested by performing in-motion analysis of the CDR data.

The technologies in the TEDA have been implemented successfully at the Asian telco client we just mentioned earlier, and others as well. The inflection point that the TEDA can deliver is astounding. Our Asian telco client previously took 12 hours to process its CDR data. Now, Streams-based ingest and transformation of CDRs is complete in less than one minute from the point the CDR is generated, enabling them to achieve real-time insights and offer new services such as usage-based offers. Another benefit is processing efficiency: Streams typically only needs one tenth of the amount of processing or storage required by typical batch applications used by telecommunications providers today.

The following sections explain the three main analytics functions that are included in the TEDA: CDR enrichment and de-duplication, network quality monitoring, and key customer experience indicators tracking.

Call Detail Record Enrichment

Using the TEDA, Streams can ingest CDRs and perform enrichment and de-duplication activities in near-real time. Figure 9-5 shows a high-level view of the TEDA architecture, including the flow graphs of TEDA logic and their

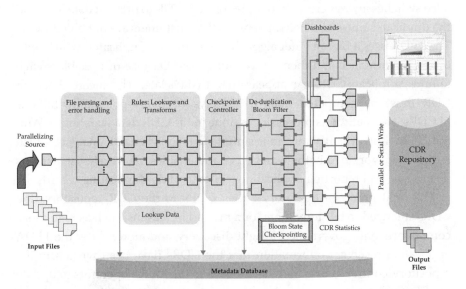

Figure 9-5 *The TEDA architecture*

interaction with the various data stores in a telco company's transaction processing system.

In many jurisdictions, there are a number of regulatory requirements surrounding CDR data. As such, transaction processing systems require detailed tracking of when a CDR has been successfully processed and written to the CDR data store. The Streams TEDA application continuously monitors its directories to detect new CDRs, and writes records to maintain the state of each file. A parallelizing operator splits the CDRs into multiple parallel branches (or paths) to expedite processing and apply full parallelization techniques to the stream.

TEDA supports the Abstract Syntax Notation One (ASN.1) CDR format, and other proprietary formats. For other CDR formats, the TEDA ingest rules that can easily be customized to accommodate variations in those formats.

The TEDA includes over 700 rules that represent expert patterns that were created by folks at IBM who live and breathe telco in order to facilitate the CDR analysis process. The TEDA also includes a series of in-memory and table look-ups to enrich the CDRs with information such as the customer's importance, the customer ID, and estimated revenue for the call.

Streams also performs de-duplication of CDRs during enrichment. The telco switches always create two copies of each CDR to prevent data loss, and the duplicates must be deleted to ensure that customers are not billed twice. The TEDA uses a Bloom Filter algorithm to eliminate duplicates, which optimizes performance and memory consumption. Because of possible switch failures, duplicate CDRs can appear up to 15 days later. This means that each CDR must be compared against 15 days of data—potentially billions of CDRs. Normally, this processing is done in the CDR data warehouse. With the TEDA, however, it's now done simultaneously with CDR analysis, which reduces the workload in the warehouse, and enables the warehouse to focus on analytic and reporting applications, instead of de-duplicating records.

The final group of operators writes CDRs to the CDR repository (the CDRs still need to be stored here for a myriad of reasons, such as regulatory compliance, data governance, insight discovery, and more). After the TEDA application receives confirmation that the CDRs have been written to the repository, control information is sent back to the source operators to update the CDR state information and to delete the relevant input files.

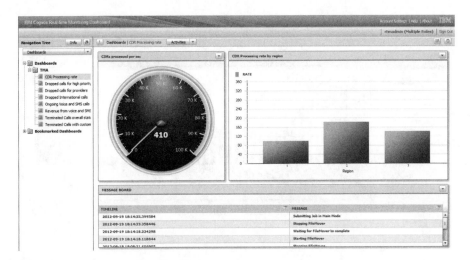

Figure 9-6   *The CDR metrics dashboard*

Network Quality Monitoring

The core capability of the TEDA lies in CDR enrichment and de-duplication, which are traditionally done with at-rest technologies through batch processing. But processing CDRs immediately upon ingest yields some interesting possibilities to gain additional value from the CDR data. Specifically, there is data in CDRs that can facilitate network quality monitoring. As CDRs flow through the graphs, the TEDA counts completed and dropped calls, along with contextual data, such as provider, country, region, cell ID, termination codes, and cell site. Using this data, the TEDA provides dashboards such as the one depicted in Figure 9-6, which shows the current throughput of CDRs ordered by region. Historical aggregations are stored in database tables for future visualization in Cognos.

Customer Experience Indicators

Another benefit of the TEDA is the ability to track key indicators of customer experience, most significantly, dropped calls. Using some of the enriched CDR data that is added by the TEDA, you can view summaries about your most important customers. Figure 9-7 shows a dashboard reporting on dropped calls that were experienced by high-priority customers.

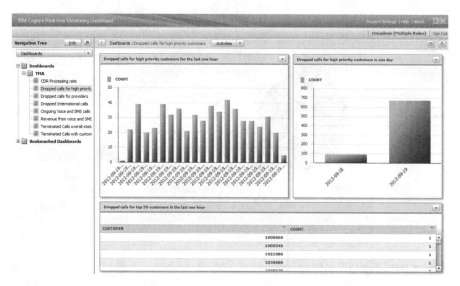

Figure 9-7   *Dashboard reporting dropped calls experienced by high-priority customers*

Similar to the network quality reports, historical aggregations for this customer experience data are stored in database tables for future visualization in Cognos.

Wrapping It Up: Accelerating Your Productivity

The common thread in all three accelerators is this: IBM provides tooling and a workflow that's optimized to reduce the time that it takes you to get actionable information out of your Big Data. With Streams and BigInsights, you have two powerful engines to deal with a broad scope of in-motion and at-rest data. When coupled with these analytic accelerators, you have processing power combined with out-of-the-box analytic capabilities that can greatly speed up your deployments. With the IBM Big Data platform, not only do you get smarter, you get faster too! With a set of accelerators, IBM has packaged together expertise and proven usage patterns in a form factor that makes it faster than ever to monetize and analyze your Big Data.

Part VI

Integration and Governance in a Big Data World

10

To Govern or Not to Govern: Governance in a Big Data World

The question of whether Big Data needs to be governed is poised to become a Big Data hot topic (we'd argue that it should have been so from the beginning). Big Data is a phenomenon and it's changing the data characteristics of *every* system; in order to make Big Data usable, it needs to be governed such that it's more certain, more trusted. Some believe that Big Data needs to be analyzed in a pristine form (maintaining fidelity), and that any form of governance or attempt to "clean it up" might actually throw away some valuable insight. Others believe that governance capabilities can simply be "built into" the Big Data ecosystem, if and when you need them. Both of those views are wrong. The answer to the question posed in this chapter's title is an unequivocal *"yes"*: Big Data needs to be governed.

It's pretty obvious when you think about it. If data that's stored in traditional repositories is subjected to governance, the fact that you're bringing in more of it, or different types of complementary data, or alternative persistence engines, doesn't change anything. Suppose that your client signs up on your Facebook page as a friend and agrees to share their information with you; if they later unfriend your business, according to Facebook's terms and conditions, you are no longer allowed to use that information. Is this built into your social sentiment governance process? If you're using a test environment, whose data contains personally identifiable information (PII), it's still

PII data whether it's packed into a nice and neat relational schema enforced with referential integrity rules, or sitting on a file system with a consistency mechanism that's akin to the wild wild west. The point is that data is data, and if you're subject to governance today, why would that change if you enhance your insights with different kinds of data or more fidelity?

We always remind our clients just how important governance is to an information management platform. There's no question that the choice of a Big Data platform should include some discussion of governance and that's the focus of this chapter.

Why Should Big Data Be Governed?

Let's level-set and start this section with a broad definition of governance. *Governance* is a set of policies that define how you will manage your data. The policy may or may not involve actively governing the data (cleansing it, securing it, and so on); but all data should have a policy that manifests the decision of whether or not to govern it. No one would advocate making un-informed decisions about how to treat their data, but the sad reality is that many do adopt that approach. This places them in the unfortunate predica-ment of "reactive governance," fixing problems (or worse yet, violations) as they arise, which is more costly and complex. Therefore, organizations must track all of their data and define policies for how it's managed. Let's look at some examples.

Consider your data's lifecycle and the management practices that sur-round it. The moment a piece of data is born into the enterprise, it has an expiry date. Although the data might never expire in some cases, it will cer-tainly cool off with time and be accessed less frequently, if at all. But here's the question: Do you actually know the expiry date and aging policy that's attached to your data, and do you explicitly manage it? Do you know when data can be archived or legally deleted? For example, pharmaceutical clinical trials require retention periods that span more than a decade after the death of a subject, and most financial records must be retained for seven years; Facebook has agreed to keep 20 years of your Facebook musings for federal privacy audits.

Now consider how the retention problem can magnify in a Big Data world. Big Data often has a short shelf life and it can accumulate quickly.

If you don't define lifecycle policies and enforce them with automated technology, you'll either become overwhelmed with Big Data accumulation, or your administrators will expend a lot of manual effort determining how and when to delete or retire this data. Consider social media data—how long do you need to keep it? What about the insights derived from it—how long are they relevant? At the same time, some of the Big Data promise is to keep a corpus (complete history) of information, so while you may never delete this data, it still has a temperature associated with it.

Many use cases for Big Data involve analyzing sensitive information. Organizations must define security policies to safeguard such information, and those policies must be monitored and enforced.

The integrity aspect of Big Data is such a hot topic that it ended up with a sexy term, *veracity*, which we introduced in Chapter 1. You need to determine whether your Big Data should be cleansed with the same approach that you would apply to your traditional data, or whether you risk losing potentially valuable insights by cleansing it. The answer depends entirely on what you're planning to do with this data. Some use cases, such as customer analysis, require or would at least benefit from higher-quality data. Other use cases, such as fraudulent identity analysis, which might require analyzing data exactly as entered to discover false identity patterns, would not depend on higher-quality data.

Many Big Data use cases center on key master data management (MDM) concepts, such as customers, products, locations, and suppliers. But many organizations haven't established a single version of the truth for those domains before the onset of the Big Data craze. Consider a social media–based customer profiling application. One of its key starting points is knowing your customers. The linkage is that many MDM projects have the goal of providing a single view of your customers. The linkage between MDM and Big Data centers on the most valuable business entities that an organization concerns itself with, including: customers, products, and households. That's the linkage between MDM and Big Data. MDM is a good starting point for many Big Data use cases, and it also provides a logical hub to store insights gleaned from Big Data analytics. For example, if you consider a master data project that centers around a person, then extracting life events over Twitter or Facebook, such as a change in relationship status, a birth announcement, and so on, enriches that master information and acts as a kind of feeder to such a system. MDM can play a pivotal role in the governance of Big Data initiatives, providing a governed, single version of the truth that's annotated by valuable insights from Big Data initiatives.

We noted earlier that many organizations don't acknowledge the need to govern a lot of the new data that their Big Data initiatives bring into the enterprise, and therefore don't properly account for it in the planning phase of their Big Data projects. We thought that it would be interesting to share with you the two reasons for this that we hear over and over again.

The first one is: "Big Data started as a research initiative. The concept of governance wasn't required—we used a small data set and operated within a trusted environment. When the business approved the project and we started to work on it, that's when we realized this was no different than any other enterprise IT project—it needed to be governed." That's an example of not thinking about your new data in the same way as your old data, and then trying to retrofit a governance plan that's going to end up being more costly and complex than it needed to be.

The second most common answer we get is: "We were building a lot of new capabilities into our Big Data project—analytics, models, and so on—so we just figured we could build governance if we needed it. Write some code to enforce security here, write some other code to match data there, and in the end, it crept up on us that governance isn't a tactical issue, and that addressing it in a one-off manner was very costly."

Are you starting to see a theme here? Those organizations that don't plan for the governance of their Big Data systems from the start end up falling behind and must face significant additional costs to retrofit governance into their ecosystems.

But those that leverage their existing information integration processes and governance technologies are the ones who will derive the most benefit from new Big Data analytics technologies in a secure, trusted, and compliant fashion.

Competing on Information and Analytics

Many organizations pursue Big Data analytics to find breakthrough insights that give them a competitive advantage. They are competing on analytics. But can you really compete on analytics alone? After all, what does analytics analyze? The reality is organizations are competing on information *and* analytics—and in order for the information to be acted upon, it must be trusted. While we all want data to be trusted, there are classes of data where this may not be entirely possible. For example, do you trust a random tweet? It depends—think about the Mexican presidential election we talked about in Chapter 1. In essence, enterprises acquire and create data they trust, but they will undoubtedly have some data they can't entirely trust. For this data, a risk estimate and assessment is required. This is a key point that's all too often overlooked. That risk estimate has to be attached to the data and decision-making processes that come in contact with this data need to know about it. In fact, processes should be forced to look at the assessment before acting on the class of data. The end goal of the work that you perform on the integration and governance of your data is *trusted information*. That said, studies have shown that in most organizations, business users don't trust the information that they use in their day-to-day jobs. In a Big Data world, as shown in Figure 10-1, there are more sources that dilute our ability to

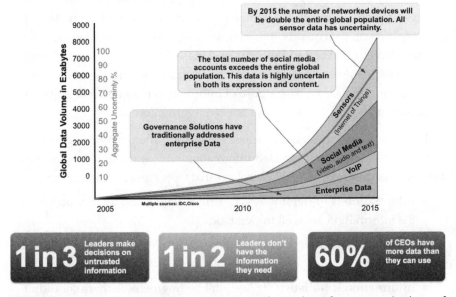

Figure 10-1 *Trust in data decreases as the increasing variety of sources and volume of data makes data more uncertain.*

trust the data, and the more data sources around which you cast your analytics "net," the more trust issues you are going to have.

A decline in trusted data represents a serious impediment to the adoption of new applications and technologies that are intended to enrich an analytics ecosystem. Information integration and governance technologies address the quality issues that compound in a Big Data world by proactively managing information governance, thereby establishing trust in information and fostering the adoption of Big Data analytics applications. Trust, combined with risk assessment, is essential before action can be taken.

The Definition of Information Integration and Governance

The marketplace has amassed many definitions for information integration and governance. Although resolving the nuances among these definitions is outside this chapter's scope, we offer the following working definition for the discussion that takes place in the remainder of this chapter.

> *Information integration and governance (IIG)* is a business strategy for how an organization treats information. At its heart, it defines the policies for how information is used, shared, and proactively monitored within an organization. It involves technology for policy definition, metadata management, data quality, information integration, information lifecycle management, privacy and security, and master data management. It also involves people and processes, which ultimately determine and enforce governance policies. The purpose of information integration and governance is to establish and deliver trusted information.

Let's examine the essence of the last statement: "The purpose of governance is to establish and deliver trusted information." What makes an organization and its users trust information? We believe that there are six key factors involved.

- **Information is understood**   The origin, value, and quality profile of the information are well understood.

- **Information is correct**   It's standardized, validated, verified, and matched.

- **Information is holistic**   It shouldn't be fragmented; there shouldn't be competing versions of the same information.

- **Information is current**   Only the most recent and relevant data is stored, and old data is either archived or deleted. Big Data often presents new challenges for lifecycle management, as Big Data is often very time sensitive and loses its value quickly; it may be the case that the lifecycle of the entire group of Big Data (such as social media data) isn't actively governed, the entire dataset is analyzed, and then deleted once the analysis is complete. That said, there are also considerations in a Big Data world where you want to store a corpus of data to build better predictive models.

- **Information is secure**   The level of protection from data breaches (encryption, redaction, security, and monitoring) matches the governance requirements of the data.

- **Information is documented**   The information's source system, and all of the governance rules and transformations that were applied to it, must be tracked, explainable, and made visible to end users. Sometimes folks refer to this factor as *end-user transparency*, because every governance rule and process should be documented and surfaced to the end user to assist in establishing trust.

Do all six factors of governance need to be applied to Big Data? It depends on the use case: we'll talk about two of them that illustrate entirely two different governance approaches. For example, analyzing Big Data to detect fraud patterns may certainly require documentation of the origin of the data: perhaps it may involve standardization and matching to cleanse duplicate records, understanding holistic master customer data to match to fraud records, security to mask sensitive data, and even lifecycle management to archive or retire individual records at different intervals. At the same time, using Big Data to investigate customer sentiment through social media requires an entirely different treatment of governance. It's likely to involve integrating master customer data with Big Data to identify customers, but the social media data may not require cleansing, documentation, or individual record lifecycle management—the entire dataset might even be deleted at the conclusion of the analysis.

An Information Governance Process

Information governance is a business strategy, not an IT project—you can't just buy it, you have to live and breathe it, making it part of your business processes and a core expectation that's put on the organization as a whole. As such, it requires changes to both organizational processes and how people treat information. In order to achieve the objective of trusted information, an organization must embrace both technology and changes to process and the way people work and are incented. It's impossible to achieve this objective with change to just one. What's more, each ensures the success of the other. A fully functional governance platform makes it possible to change processes to proactively govern information, and a people-oriented focus will encourage them to embrace and adopt the new technology.

For the most part, the information governance process that was established for traditional relational data works equally well for new sources of Big Data, so we thought we'd briefly outline the key process steps for information governance that you can use as a kind of roadmap for Big Data governance.

1. *Identify the business problem to be solved.* It's imperative that a tactical business problem be identified to drive adoption. The approach of building technology first and driving business adoption second never works. While this point isn't directly related to Big Data governance, it's an "any" project imperative and it naturally pulls in governance as a project-scoped topic.

2. *Obtain vocal executive sponsorship early on for the governance of any Big Data project, thereby reaffirming the importance of governance for Big Data projects across the organization.* This sponsor will typically be closely related to the business problem. Because governance is truly an enterprise-wide initiative, you'll want to evaluate whether the sponsor has the political clout to push the importance of governance into other projects across the enterprise. You'll also want to establish an executive steering committee, to which you'll report your progress on governing Big Data on a periodic basis.

3. *Determine what parts of the Big Data stream needs to be governed and to what extent.* A critical first step of governance planning is determining whether the data needs to be governed. Questions to

ask include: Is this data sensitive, and does it need to be protected? Is this data governed by regulation? Does this data need to be standardized? Depending on the use case, some Big Data might require only certain aspects of governance, and some data might require none at all. But we want to emphasize that it's crucial that an organization *make a conscious* choice of whether that data should be governed, and at what level. For example, governance treatments may be applied to an entire body of data (delete all Facebook data from last month) or to individual files or records (delete John Doe's record from last month). In fact, explicitly evaluating a Big Data source and choosing not to govern it is a form of governance itself.

4. *Build a roadmap.* A roadmap involves several Big Data projects, which require governance. It's important to map out at least the first three phases of your implementation project for a governance initiative. In order to sustain momentum from Phase 1 to Phase 2, an organization must plan out Phase 2 at the onset. We can't stress enough how important momentum is—it's crucial—especially between that first and second phase, because this is the point at which an enterprise initiative can truly take hold, or fizzle out and become a one-phase wonder. A good second phase leverages some aspect of Phase 1—so that you can go faster in Phase 2. If you utilize security capabilities in Phase 1, perhaps you leverage them in Phase 2 for a different Big Data source; or perhaps Phase 2 focuses on the same source of Big Data, but adds new data quality elements. The point is to keep one thing the same—either the governance capability or the Big Data source—this creates leverage.

5. *Establish an organizational blueprint.* A blueprint is a matrix-style structure of both business and IT participants, at different levels of the organization. The working team includes business participants to determine governance policies, and IT participants for implementation. It also includes an executive steering committee to which the action team reports. The executive sponsor chairs the steering committee.

6. *Define metrics and targets.* It's essential to define metrics and set targets to track success. It isn't necessary to track every possible metric for a governance business case; start by focusing on no more

than a dozen key metrics that are accurate predictors of success and achievement for the overall business case. The metrics tracked and reported on should be closely tied to the business value or trustworthiness of the information.

7. *Establish governance policies.* The action team determines governance policies for the project and drives business adoption of the new processes for governing data.

8. *Implement governance technology.* While the IT team implements and integrates governance technologies for redaction, activity monitoring, rights usage, and so on, the business representatives of the action team help to drive adoption of the data as a trusted source.

9. *Measure metrics and evangelize.* As with an ignored New Year's resolution, we all acknowledge that this step is *very* important, but most of us never follow through. Why? Often it's because of an exhaustive list of metrics or difficulty gathering the information after the fact. Pick only a handful of metrics that are easy to collect. Evangelization is crucial, because that's when success, and therefore momentum, is created.

Information governance is a business strategy that drives change to processes and the people implementing those processes. Big Data certainly has implications for governance technology, but the governance strategy and structure that you are accustomed to laying down for relational data are almost completely transferable to the Big Data era.

The IBM Information Integration and Governance Technology Platform

Information integration and governance (IIG) in the IBM Information Management portfolio is represented by a number of industry-leading technologies that IBM has unified into a trusted information delivery platform under the brand name InfoSphere. IBM has also invested in a well-defined Information Governance process to help organizations plan their governance initiatives and how it will impact people and processes. Although these technologies work in concert as a single platform, organizations that require different components,

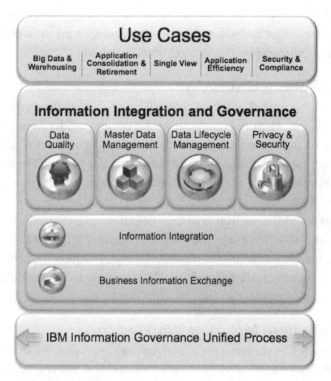

Figure 10-2 *The IBM unified information integration and governance platform helps you deliver trusted information to the business.*

depending on their use cases, can leverage specific access points into the platform. The key capabilities of the IBM IIG technology are shown in Figure 10-2.

In the remainder of this section, we briefly talk about these core platform capabilities, the associated IBM products that deliver these capabilities, and their applicability to the Big Data world.

IBM InfoSphere Business Information Exchange

InfoSphere Business Information Exchange (BIE) is a core component for all aspects of IIG—whether you're improving data quality, mastering data, securing a database, or managing the lifecycle of data, you must first begin by understanding the data and defining governance policies. BIE contains several components that help organizations to understand and profile data sources—it contains unique services to blueprint information governance projects, discover data in its source systems, manage enterprise metadata, and to represent that metadata in business-friendly terms via a glossary, and to define governance policies, among other capabilities.

IBM InfoSphere Discovery

InfoSphere Discovery (Discovery) is a BIE component that automatically creates a profile for structured data sources. Discovery can determine the logical model of a source system (for example, inferring a customer object by looking at the physical data and tables). It can also infer some of the transformation or validation rules for that data source by examining the relationships of data across fields; it can determine cross-field validation rules, allowable values, and so on. This greatly aids in the integration process by short-circuiting the labor-intensive process of profiling and documenting existing sources of data. IBM also has capabilities for discovering, profiling, indexing, searching, and navigating unstructured Big Data, using InfoSphere Data Explorer (formerly known as the Vivisimo Velocity Platform).

IBM InfoSphere Metadata Workbench

Shared metadata is the basis for effective data integration. By sharing a common definition of terms and data transformations at the enterprise level, an organization can quickly translate data from one system to another. Metadata also documents data lineage (where the data comes from), where it's heading, and what happened to it along the way. Data lineage metadata is one of the most powerful forces of trust because when it's exposed to a business user, it quickly establishes trust. InfoSphere Metadata Workbench has capabilities for managing and sharing enterprise metadata in a structured format. IBM InfoSphere Information Server also contains capabilities for parsing unstructured Big Data sources and storing metadata on all sources of Big Data with more features coming to address some of the new challenges associated with Big Data.

IBM Business Glossary

Effective sharing of metadata relies upon a common vocabulary, one that business and IT can agree upon. That's how Business Glossary can help. It manages the business definition of the metadata—putting IT terms into common ones that business users can understand. This function becomes even more important in the era of Big Data. As data comes from many new sources, it also comes in many new terms and formats. The need for a common vocabulary has never been greater.

One of the greatest challenges in information governance is developing policies—you literally have to develop them in every system that manages and governs data. But what if you could develop governance policies at the same time that you define metadata? Business Glossary allows you to do that, to define governance policies in plain language at the same time as you define metadata. Business Glossary provides business-driven governance by allowing business analysts and users to define governance policies.

IBM InfoSphere Information Analyzer

This component profiles the quality of data from source systems, and thereby profiles the systems themselves. For example, is the billing system a reliable source for residential addresses and email addresses? This is a crucial step for establishing trust. The number one question that business users ask when trying to establish trust is "What system did this data come from?" Being able to answer that question, and being able to gather statistics on whether a system is truly trustworthy, are key steps to establishing trust. IBM InfoSphere Information Analyzer profiles source systems, and analyzes the quality of data within those systems. For example, completeness of records, whether data stored in a field actually conforms to a standard (for example, an SSN is nine digits), and reports and visualizes aggregate data quality profiles (percentage of accurate and complete records, and so on.). This capability may be utilized on enterprise structured Big Data sources; in larger data sets, representative data sets may be profiled. The concept of information analysis applies more to structured data, where a set structure may be expected and subsequently analyzed. In the future, semistructured data sources may also be analyzed and key words/values may be examined utilizing text analytics. The concept of information analysis applies more to structured data.

IBM InfoSphere Blueprint Director

InfoSphere Blueprint Director (Blueprint Director) maps and manages active integration architecture diagrams. It's a visual tool for designing integration architectures, which also allows you to dive into specific integration steps and launch various other integration tools—for example, a user interface for developing quality rules. Blueprint Director may also be used for mapping out Big Data integration architectures, and can help you actively manage your Big Data integration architecture.

IBM InfoSphere Information Server

There are three styles of data integration: bulk (or batch movement), real-time, and federation. Specific projects, such as Big Data analytics, often require a combination of all of these styles to satisfy varying requirements.

Information integration is a key requirement of a Big Data platform, because it enables you to leverage economies of scale from existing investments, yet discovers new economies of scale as you expand the analytics paradigm. For example, consider the case where you have a heavy SQL investment in a next best offer (NBO) application. If this application were SQL warehouse-based, it could be enhanced with the ability to call a Hadoop job that would look at the trending sentiment associated with a feature item stock-out condition. This could help to determine the acceptability of such an offer before it's made. Having the ability to leverage familiar SQL to call a function that spawns a MapReduce job in a Hadoop cluster to perform this sentiment analysis is not only a powerful concept; it's crucial from an investment enhance perspective.

Perhaps it's the case that you have a machine data analysis job running on a Hadoop cluster and want to draw customer information from a system that manages rebates, hoping to find a strong correlation between certain log events and eventual credits. This goes back to the baseball analogy we talked about in Chapter 1. The Big Data era is characterized by various fit-for-purpose engines, and it's the coordination of these engines (like the baseball player who is better at throwing with one hand and catching with the other) that's key: information integration makes this all happen.

Information is often structured or semistructured, and to achieve high-volume throughput requires a powerful processing engine. Your Big Data integration platform should provide balanced optimization for different integration and transformation needs, ranging from ETL (extract, transform, and load), to ELT (leveraging the target system to process the transformations while providing the transformation logic), to TELT (transform, extract, load, and transform).

Some developers believe that new technologies, such as Hadoop, can be used for a multitude of tasks. From a batch and integration perspective, the Big Data world is characterized by various approaches and disciplines with Big Data technologies. This leads to a "build mentality," which assumes that everything can be built around the new technology. If you think back to when the data warehouse industry was in its infancy, many IT professionals attempted to build in-house integration capabilities. Few would do that today, because mature information integration technologies exist. The same pattern is playing out in Hadoop, with some believing that it should be the sole component for integration or transformation workloads.

For example, some folks propose that they should only use Hadoop to prepare data for a data warehouse; this is generally referred to as ETL. But there's a huge gap between a general-purpose tool and a purpose-built one, and integration involves many aspects other than the transformation of data, such as extraction, discovery, profiling, metadata, data quality, and delivery. Organizations shouldn't utilize Hadoop solely for integration; rather they should leverage mature data integration technologies to help speed their deployments of Big Data. New technologies such as Hadoop will be adopted into data integration; for example, during an ELT-style integration (where the T may be performed by stored procedures in a data warehouse), organizations may look to utilize Hadoop for transformation processing. We think you'll find the need to use Hadoop engines as part of an ETL/ELT strategy, but you will also greatly benefit from the flexibility of a fit-for-purpose transformation engine, massively parallel integration engine to support multiple transformation and load requirements, integration into common run-time environments, and a common design palette that's provided by a product such as InfoSphere Information Server (IIS). In fact, this product's parallel processing engine and end-to-end integration and quality capabilities yield a significant total cost of ownership advantage over alternative approaches.

For example, if the transformation is full of SQL operations, IIS can push down those operations into an IBM PureData System for Analytics appliance (formerly known as Netezza). Your integration platform should be able to not just automatically generate jobs to run on an Hadoop infrastructure or ETL parallel engine as required, but manage them with a common job sequencer. IIS includes connectors into Hadoop and a Big Data file stage

(BDFS) container for data persistence and retrieval. A single data integration platform, such as the one provided by IIS, gives you both capability and flexibility. IIS includes a multitude of prebuilt transformation objects and hundreds of functions, all atop a parallel execution environment that gives you the flexibility to use a myriad of technologies (including Hadoop) that are best suited for the task at hand. IIS integrates with HDFS as both a source and a target system for data delivery. IIS can also model certain integration tasks within an integration stage and specify the process to be performed on Hadoop, which would take advantage of Hadoop's MapReduce processing and low-cost infrastructure. This may be often used in ELT-style integration, where instead of the T being performed by data warehouse stored procedures, transformations are performed by a Hadoop system. IIS also integrates with InfoSphere Streams (Streams), and it may accumulate insights or data filtered by Streams into a staged data file, which is then loaded to a target system (say a data warehouse for further analysis).

High-speed integration into data warehouses is going to be key, and IIS delivers this capability as well. An example of an IIS Big Data transformation flow is shown in Figure 10-3. You can see that this job analyzes high-fidelity emails (stored in Hadoop) for customer sentiment, and the results of that analysis are used to update the warehouse (for example, the Customer dimension); this is an example of risk classification based on email analytics.

Other integration technologies that are commonplace in today's IT environments (and remain key in a Big Data world) include real-time replication and federation. Real-time replication, utilizing a product such as IBM InfoSphere Data Replication (Data Replication), involves monitoring a source system and triggering a replication or change to the target system. This is often used for

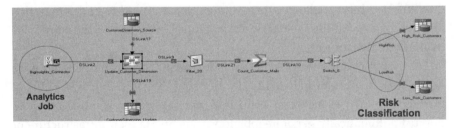

Figure 10-3 *A data-flow job that utilizes a combination of Big Data assets, including source data in Hadoop joined with DB2 relational data, and various transformations to classify risk*

low-latency integration requirements. Data Replication has sophisticated functionality for high-speed data movement, conflict detection, system monitoring, and a graphical development environment for designing integration tasks. Furthermore, it's integrated with the set of IBM PureData Systems for high-speed data loading/synchronization, and also with Information Server to accumulate changes and move data in bulk to a target system.

Federation involves accessing data that's stored in federated repositories through a federated query. This is often used to retrieve data from multiple systems or to augment data that's stored in one system with information from another system. IBM InfoSphere Federation Server (Federation Server) accesses and integrates data from a diverse set of structured data sources, regardless of where they reside. It enables hybrid data warehousing by joining data from multiple repositories, and also exposing information as a service (IaaS) via InfoSphere Information Services Director. From a federation perspective, it's important to be able to federate search (as the Data Explorer technology we outlined in Chapter 7) across your enterprise assets, as well as with a query API such as SQL. In the future, Federation Server may integrate with Data Explorer to provide structured data source search and query within an overall Big Data (structured and unstructured) federated search and discovery.

We believe that organizations shouldn't try to solely deliver enterprise integration with Hadoop; rather they should leverage mature data integration technologies to help speed their deployments of Big Data, whenever that makes sense. There's a huge gap between a general-purpose tool and a purpose-built one, not to mention that integration involves many aspects other than the delivery of data, such as discovery, profiling, metadata, and data quality. We recommend that you consider using IBM Information Server with your Big Data projects to optimize the loading (via bulk load or replication) of high-volume structured data into a data warehouse, and extending it with federation when required; the loading of structured or semistructured data into Hadoop; and the collecting of information that's filtered and analyzed by stream analytics. You can then load the data into a relational system (such as a data warehouse), federate queries across relational databases as part of Big Data federation and navigation, and replicate data sources to a Hadoop cluster or other data warehouse.

Data Quality

Data quality components can be used to ensure the cleanliness and accuracy of information. IBM InfoSphere Information Server for Data Quality (IIS for DQ) is a market-leading data quality product. It contains innovative features such as information profiling and quality analysis, address standardization and validation, and it's fully integrated into the InfoSphere Information Server platform for quality rule development, execution of quality jobs on Information Server's parallel processing platform, and sharing metadata with enterprise metadata component. Data quality discussions typically involve the following services:

- **Parsing**   Separating data and parsing it into a structured format.

- **Standardization**   Determining what data to place in which field and ensuring that it's stored in a standard format (for example, a nine-digit zip code).

- **Validation**   Ensuring that data is consistent; for example, a phone number contains an area code and the correct number of digits for its locale. It might also include cross-field validation, such as checking the telephone area code against a city to ensure that it's valid (for example, area code 416 is valid for Toronto, 415 is not).

- **Verification**   Checking data against a source of verified information to ensure that the data is valid; for example, checking that an address value is indeed a real and valid address.

- **Matching**   Identifying duplicate records and merging those records correctly.

Organizations should determine whether their Big Data sources require quality checking before analysis, and then apply the appropriate data quality components. A Big Data project is likely going to require you to focus on data quality when loading a data warehouse to ensure accuracy and completeness; when loading and analyzing new sources of Big Data that will be integrated with a data warehouse; and when Big Data analysis depends on a more accurate view (for example, reflecting customer insight), even if the data is managed within Hadoop.

Master Data Management

Master data management (MDM) creates and maintains a single version of the truth for key business entities such as customers, patients, products, parts, suppliers, accounts, and assets, among others. MDM is an operational system of record, and it plays an important role in a Big Data ecosystem. IBM's InfoSphere Master Data Management is the most comprehensive MDM solution in the market.

We think that MDM can provide a compelling starting point for Big Data analysis, as MDM by definition focuses on the highest value entities within an organization. Many organizations imagine that they would like to analyze social media to determine customer sentiment, but do they know who their customers are? Do they know their best customers? When embarking on Big Data analysis of a precise subject, it often makes sense to leverage the knowledge of an MDM system within a Big Data analytic application; for example, understanding the sentiment and next best action for a particular group of profitable customers instead of analyzing broad sentiment toward your company.

Integration points between MDM and Big Data include ingesting and analyzing unstructured data, creating master data entities, loading new profile information into the MDM system, sharing master data records or entities with the Big Data platform as the basis for Big Data analysis, and reusing the MDM matching capabilities in the Big Data platform (such as customer matching). You'll find that IBM is a leader in this space, and although we can't comment on some of the integration points coming to this problem domain, IBM plans to continue and build integration points between MDM and Big Data based on real-world customer use cases.

You should consider using MDM solutions with Big Data when the target of your analysis is precise versus broad (aggregate)—an individual customer or group of customers, a particular product or group of products, and so on. In addition, consider integrating your Big Data into MDM systems when the output of Big Data analytics should be "operationalized"; specifically, when acquired insights are to be acted upon in operational systems. For example, consider the case in which the next best action for customer retention should be consistently acted upon across multiple channels; the action flag (or insight) should be stored in a MDM system.

Data Lifecycle Management

Don't think of Big Data as "a new technology" (for example, Hadoop). Think of it as a phenomenon. And the primary characteristic of the Big Data phenomenon is the fact that data is growing, in every one of your systems. Unchecked data growth has a huge impact on your existing systems—data warehouses, transactional systems, and applications. Data growth can lead to high costs and poor performance of those applications. The growth of data to "Big Data levels" also impacts test data management. Think about it. Every time you deploy a system you need to generate test data systems from production, for development to test, and so on. Often that data is copied from production environments, and as the total data volume grows, so too does the exponential growth of your test data environments. A second major issue with test data is ensuring security and privacy—masking sensitive data before it's used in non-production environments. In short, the growth of data in existing systems is crippling them, and the problem will only get worse in the era of "Big Data," unless it is proactively addressed.

Data lifecycle management controls the growth and therefore the cost of data. It manages data lifecycle in two primary ways. First, it helps with data growth management, providing a framework to profile and manage the lifecycle of data and to proactively archive data in a highly compressed and efficient manner. Second, data lifecycle management is critical for proper test data management; specifically, for creating right-sized, governed, test data environments to optimize data storage and costs. The IBM InfoSphere Optim (Optim) family of products is the market leader in data lifecycle management. Optim contains market-leading capabilities for data growth management and archiving of complete business objects across heterogeneous environments, while also enabling easy retrieval of archived information via queries. InfoSphere Optim Test Data Management (Optim TDM) contains sophisticated test data management capabilities to generate right-size test data sets, masking to ensure that sensitive data is protected, and automation to enable self-service for generating test data sets.

You're already thinking about data lifecycle management when you archive relational data warehouses to ensure that only current information is stored, thereby improving performance and reducing cost as data volumes grow.

Lifecycle management is also essential to ensure legal compliance with data retention and protection regulations, and to be able to audit compliance with data retention policies. In the Big Data world, low-cost engines like Hadoop offer the opportunity of a low-cost alternative for storing online archives to host colder data. While transferability between platforms is improving, the business process of lifecycle management and archiving is a separate challenge (in other words, Hadoop may be a low-cost platform, but there are many more capabilities required to truly manage data growth). That's where Optim comes in. It manages the lifecycle and the archiving process—discovering and profiling Big Data and tracking lifecycle milestones (when to archive), automatically archiving Big Data from data warehouses and transactional databases, providing visibility and the ability to retrieve and restore data if required, ensuring the immutability of archived data to prevent data errors, and complying with legal requirements for data retention and auditability. Optim can store archived data in a highly compressed relational database, an archive file on a file system, and that file may be loaded onto a Hadoop file system. And that latter integration point between Optim and Hadoop is a key one, by placing an archive file onto a Hadoop system it provides low-cost storage, while also allowing data to be analyzed for different purposes, thus deriving insight from the archived files. It's not wonder why some of us refer to Hadoop as the new tape!

Test data management should be a definite consideration when implementing a Big Data project, in order to control test data costs and improve overall implementation time. Optim TDM automatically generates and refreshes test data for Big Data systems such as data warehouses, and it has an optimized integration with the IBM PureData System for Analytics. Optim generates right-sized test data sets, for example, a 100 TB production system may require only 1 TB for user acceptance testing. InfoSphere Optim also ensures that sensitive data is masked for testing environments. It will generate realistic data for testing purposes (for example, changing Jerome Smith at 123 Oak Street to Kevin Brown at 231 Pine Avenue), but will protect the real data from potential loss or misuse. The possibility of data loss becomes even more real in the new era of Big Data. More systems and more data lead to more test environments and more potential for data loss. Optim TDM also has a tremendous cost advantage with self-service data generation through to right-sized environments, Optim TDM streamlines the test data process.

Big Data is associated with data growth and there's not question that data is growing in every one of your enterprise systems. Data Lifecycle Management should be a top priority to help curb unchecked Big Data growth, reducing the cost of data while making your applications more efficient.

Privacy and Security

There are multiple privacy and security notations within an information integration and governance discussion, most of which can be applied to Big Data. You need to protect and block unauthorized access to sensitive data no matter where it resides. If you have to apply governance to a certain class of data that you collect, there are privacy and security concerns whether you store this data in a file system (such as the HDFS) or in a relational database management system (RDBMS). For example, your security mantra (separation of duties, separation of concern, principle of least privilege, and defense in depth) applies to data stored anywhere. You'll want to consider role-based security, multitenancy, and reduced surface area configurations through reverse proxies (among other security services), all of which BigInsights can provide to Hadoop.

Of course, it's worth noting that if IBM InfoSphere Guardium (Guardium) is an industry leader in auditing and alerts via its heterogeneous data activity monitoring (DAM) services, based on activities at the data management level, why couldn't it do so for the HDFS? In 3Q 2012, IBM announced Guardium's initial support for providing DAM services to a Hadoop environment (NameNode, JobTracker, and DataNodes) and its subsystem projects (for example, Oozie), giving administrators the ability to clearly understand who did what, who touched what, and so on. As of this writing, most BigInsights components that currently have audit logs can be monitored; for example, HDFS name space operations, MapReduce (job queue and job operations, refresh configuration), HBase Region Server (database activity), Hive, and Avro. Because Guardium works with open source components, it can integrate with BigInsights and/or other open source distributions of Hadoop. Guardium also recognizes the Thrift and MySQL protocols (used by Hive). These components all send existing BigInsights audit logs to Guardium and can leverage it to meet compliance requirements such as persisting, processing, alerting, and reporting on audit logs. Future areas of interest could include capturing audit logs for HBase, the BigInsights Web Console, among others.

Database activity monitoring is a key capability that's needed for an effective governed Big Data environment. In fact, we'd argue that such capabilities are needed even more than in a traditional database environment, because currently, Hadoop governance controls are typically weaker.

Big Data, as is the case with traditional data, might require data masking for both test and production environments. Masking data is one of the biggest concerns with new Big Data technology, as many customers realize they might accidentally expose very sensitive information in test and production Big Data environments. You need to create realistic versions of real data, but at the same time protect sensitive data values from being compromised. Masking sensitive data that's delivered to HDFS or to a data warehouse will become (and should already be) a pressing concern for Big Data environments. IBM InfoSphere Optim Masking Solution addresses this concern by masking data in a Hadoop system. In fact, Optim's API-based approach to masking means that any system can take advantage of its advanced masking capabilities, and incorporate masking within its processing. The benefit is clear—the ability to define masking rules centrally and apply them in multiple Big Data systems.

The obfuscation and blacking out of specific sensitive content within documents will also be key; after all, if you are storing email with sensitive data in HDFS, that email could be subject to redaction requirements. It's worth noting here that the Text Analytics Toolkit that's part of BigInsights and Streams is used in InfoSphere Guardium Data Redaction.

Wrapping It Up: Trust Is About Turning Big Data into Trusted Information

Information integration and governance is a critical component that should be considered during the design phase of any Big Data platform because of the eventual mass injection of unwieldy data from a volume, velocity, variety, and veracity perspective. It's fair to note that IBM is a leader in information integration and governance; and as you've likely noticed, a number of products that make up the IBM InfoSphere Information Integration and Governance platform are being extended to support the IBM Big Data platform; some are there today, and some are well on their way (although our lawyers want us to keep it a surprise, we're sure that we've given you a crystal ball look into the future with the topics that we detail in this chapter).

Although information integration and governance creates trusted information, we really want you to remember that information integration and governance is more than technology; it's also a business strategy and associated trickle-down change processes to meet corporate-wide governance objectives. As you design your first Big Data project, it's critical to ascertain what parts of your project need to be governed, and to what extent.

The first and most critical step of the governance process is the decision of *whether* Big Data needs to be governed, and *to what extent* it needs to be governed. This should be mandatory for any Big Data project. Not making a conscious decision can be a recipe for disaster...as in poor adoption, or worse still, being a one-phase wonder. That is the true value of information integration and governance technology—it can ensure the success and drive adoption of your Big Data initiatives. *Success with Big Data analytics depends on a supply of trusted information.*

11

Integrating Big Data in the Enterprise

One thing is certain—Big Data technology should not be a silo. It must be integrated within the enterprise to fully realize its value. Let's think about that for a moment. Organizations need a technology platform for developing Big Data analytic applications. And those applications must be able to interact with that Big Data platform to exploit certain Big Data capabilities. Therein lies the first integration point: analytic applications built on the Big Data platform.

A Big Data platform has within it many capabilities. To fully address requirements, multiple Big Data components are often required. That's the second point of integration: Big Data platform components and products must be integrated with one another.

After all, is there any point to a Big Data initiative if you don't plan to act upon the insights that you've gleaned from it?

Well, in our experience, in order to act upon insight, you typically have to share the insight with some other application that makes use of it. So there's the third point of integration: enterprise applications and repositories.

Platforms should be open so that partner technologies across the broader ecosystem can extend the solution. That's your final integration point: plug-in components for the Big Data platform. So the four types of integration that we explore in this chapter are analytic applications, intraplatform integration, enterprise integration with other repositories, and platform plug-ins.

A lot of clients are on the right track when they ask us about integration points from their existing technology investments and their new Big Data projects; indeed, that's always encouraging to hear, because it means that the client is thinking beyond the "science experiment" phase that rarely produces value. Note that there are many more integration points than we can possibly cover in this chapter, so we encourage you to use this chapter as a jumping-off point, rather than a definitive discussion of integration options and patterns.

Analytic Application Integration

The IBM Big Data platform is designed from the ground up to simplify the process of developing applications that run on top of it and to deliver analytical benefits through an underlying set of optimized Big Data technologies. This section describes some of the IBM Business Analytics software and other applications that are integrated with the IBM Big Data platform. With a Big Data ecosystem that spans well over 200 business partners, there are many more applications than we could cover, of course, and the list grows longer every day.

IBM Cognos Software

IBM Cognos BI, a component of IBM Cognos Enterprise, is widely deployed business intelligence software that's been extended for use with Big Data through its integration with the IBM Big Data platform. As of this writing, Cognos can access data that is stored in Hive and use it for reporting (there is more coming, so stay tuned). Cognos BI is integrated and certified with InfoSphere BigInsights (BigInsights), InfoSphere Streams (Streams), DB2, the IBM PureData System for Analytics (formerly known as Netezza), and the IBM PureData System for Operational Analytics (formerly known as the IBM Smart Analytics System).

IBM Cognos Real Time Monitoring (Cognos RTM), a component of IBM Cognos Enterprise, is software that provides visualization and analysis on real-time streaming analytics from Streams. Visualization is one of the major challenges that Big Data brings to business analysts; in fact, some universities today actually offer degrees in Big Data visualization. Throughout this book we've emphasized how data in motion is a differentiator for the IBM Big Data platform, because velocity (one of the four Big Data characteristics) isn't being addressed by vendors in this space with the same degree of focus that IBM brings to the problem domain. If velocity is such an important aspect of Big Data, it stands to reason that data in motion needs to be integrated with business intelligence for users to gain insight into the past, present, and future.

IBM Cognos Consumer Insights (CCI) is a rich social media analytic application. It allows users to analyze, visualize, and report on consumer sentiment and evolving market topics from social media sources. IBM CCI is integrated with IBM's Big Data platform and in particular BigInsights. BigInsights provides CCI the power and flexibility to process large volumes of raw social media data.

IBM Content Analytics with Enterprise Search

IBM Content Analytics (ICA) provides leading capabilities for analyzing unstructured content. But what happens when data sets grow too quickly to process, as we know that they often do? BigInsights is integrated with ICA and the two work together to ensure ballooning data volumes are not a problem. IBM Content Analytics is also integrated with the analytics-based IBM PureData Systems so that they can share insights and information. Along with IBM InfoSphere Data Explorer (the technology that was obtained through the Vivisimo acquisition, and which we cover in Chapter 7), ICA provides broad and extremely capable unstructured information processing, discovery, and consumption options.

SPSS

IBM SPSS software is a broadly deployed and sophisticated predictive analytics portfolio. It's no surprise that customers want to leverage SPSS to interact with the IBM Big Data platform. At-rest modeling is reasonably well understood, but what if you want to take predictive analytics to the extreme—to make predictions as the data comes into being, be it at a point of sale, a hedge fund trader's Bloomberg terminal, or even emergency room monitoring equipment? After all, the whole point of predictive modeling is to improve outcomes. The combination of SPSS and Streams is the answer, as it gives you the ability to build predictive models at rest which are then scored using the data in motion. To support this powerful usage pattern, SPSS predictive models can be directly exported to the Streams run-time environment. Additionally, Streams supports models defined by the

Predictive Model Markup Language (PMML)—which is also supported by SPSS. Streams provides the power to run both predictive models on a massive scale and scope in real time. Almost the entire IBM Big Data platform is integrated with PMML. For example, you can build models in SPSS and then run them within IBM PureData System for Analytics appliance to perform deep analytics with very fast performance.

SAS

SAS business analytics applications are integrated with the IBM Big Data platform. In particular, SAS is integrated with the IBM PureData System for Analytics. This integration allows SAS scoring and modelling to be run inside this PureData System, which is more efficient in terms of bringing analytics to the data, and of course it also benefits from the tremendous advantages an analytics-based PureData System provides for deep analytic queries on large data sets.

Unica

Unica is an advanced solution for cross-channel campaign management and marketing performance optimization. It's fully integrated with both the IBM PureData System for Operational Analytics and the IBM PureData System for Analytics, and can be used to perform campaign analytics and reporting on these platforms. The benefits that IBM PureData Systems bring are clear— the ability to perform deep analytics on large data volumes and to get the answers that you need lightening fast, or to support operational analytic workloads. Utilizing the power of the Big Data platform, the Unica solution can analyze more data more quickly to produce more targeted campaigns.

Q1 Labs: Security Solutions

The topic of security and Big Data is white hot. The most pressing question is, "How can existing securities solutions be extended with Big Data technologies?" In 2011, IBM acquired Q1 Labs and their QRadar Security Intelligence Platform (QRadar), which provides a unified architecture for collecting, storing, analyzing, and querying log, threat, vulnerability, and risk-related data. In response to customer demand, IBM security and Big Data teams have worked on integration points to pass insights and analysis between the two platforms, leading to scale-out options and expanded situational awareness. QRadar was very compelling as a stand-alone technology, but when combined with Big Data, we're doing never-before-possible things to help lock down our enterprise customers' domains.

IBM i2 Intelligence Analysis Platform

IBM i2 provides an extensible, service-oriented environment that is designed to integrate with your existing enterprise infrastructure. This platform facilitates and supports operational analysis, improves situational awareness, and delivers faster, more informed decision making across and within organizations. Since the acquisition, IBM has been busy integrating the i2 platform with the IBM Big Data platform, and extending the data that i2 end users can discover and explore. i2's highly visual and intuitive end-user analytics help you to identify and explore patterns, and then take action in rapidly evolving environments.

Platform Symphony MapReduce

In 2011, IBM acquired Platform Computing, including their Platform Symphony MapReduce technology: a Hadoop-inspired run time specifically designed for applications that require low-latency or sophisticated scheduling logic across many simultaneous short-running jobs. BigInsights is the lead IBM product offering for Hadoop, and Platform Symphony is considered to be a complementary component of that offering.

What's interesting is the integration work that's been done for these products. For example, BigInsights can leverage Platform Symphony MapReduce as the low-latency distributed run-time component running on its own cluster. This enables customers who have specific low-latency or heavy computational workloads to leverage this technology as part of a BigInsights deployment. BigInsights may be deployed on one or more instances within a Platform Computing grid, thereby leveraging its technical computing capabilities that support heterogeneous applications. Existing Platform Symphony customers (of which there are many) can add BigInsights to their existing grid and manage multiple types of workloads across a common pool of resources. This eliminates the need to set up a separate grid environment for BigInsights, and supports the sharing of resources across both compute- and data-intensive applications.

Component Integration Within the IBM Big Data Platform

All of the components of the IBM Big Data platform are well integrated. In this section, we briefly highlight some of this integration, and provide pointers to the chapters where you can find more detailed information.

InfoSphere BigInsights

BigInsights is deeply integrated throughout the IBM Big Data platform. BigInsights can accept real-time input from Streams, such as insights or decisions made by analytic algorithms deployed to the Streams run time, and then perform additional analysis on a deeper data set (for example, to test and remodel the algorithm for promotion back to Streams).

BigInsights is also integrated with the analytics-based IBM PureData Systems and other IBM data warehouse solutions, such as InfoSphere Warehouse. This enables BigInsights to write data to a warehouse and to accept input from it too. It's also possible to access data in BigInsights by using SQL. In-database functions that present SQL-wrapped user-defined functions enable you to call a BigInsights job from within the database. (Note, however, that the laws of physics apply here: You're not going to leverage these functions to pull trillions of rows across the network into your warehouse, you more likely want to invoke a job and retrieve a scored result.) This integration point is helpful when BigInsights is used to analyze raw data or to perform experimental analysis, and then share insight with the data warehouse.

There's integration between BigInsights and InfoSphere Information Server (Information Server). Information Server can provide information to Hadoop or take data from Hadoop and integrate it to any number of other systems. BigInsights is also integrated with Guardium to provide real-time system monitoring and security. InfoSphere Optim Masking Solution can mask BigInsights data to ensure that it's protected and secure. And InfoSphere Optim can store archived data in BigInsights, making it available for analysis. IBM Research has also developed integration points between MDM and BigInsights, including the ability to analyze raw data and to determine which master entities are to be loaded into MDM. You can find more details about this integration in Chapters 5 through 8.

InfoSphere Streams

Streams can provide real-time updates to BigInsights, which could be the result of a Streams operation or a scored SPSS model. BigInsights is often used in conjunction with Streams to provide deeper analysis of models, which can be subsequently promoted and scored in Streams (a similar usage pattern is discussed in Chapter 2).

Streams is integrated with various data warehouse solutions through a set of database adapters that enable it to write insights to or filter data in a target warehouse system. We often see Streams integrated with a warehouse for deeper analysis, modeling, and discovery on structured data. In fact, Streams has set load-optimized high-speed connectors that are deeply integrated with the analytics-based IBM PureData Systems. These details are discussed in Chapter 6.

Finally, Streams can share data with or supply input to Information Server, from which it can be integrated with any number of systems, as required.

Data Warehouse Solutions

Data warehousing solutions are well integrated with the Information Integration and Governance (IIG) aspects of the IBM Big Data platform: information integration for high-speed data loading and unloading; data quality to standardize and improve data; data lifecycle management for archiving and controlling data growth, and for generating right-sized test data environments; MDM systems to provide a single view of business entities; and privacy and security monitoring to mask data and monitor database activity. Both the IBM PureData System for Analytics and the IBM PureData System for Operational Analytics have optimized integration points to many of the IIG solutions (we cover these later in this chapter). Of course, as previously mentioned, the IBM Big Data platform warehousing solutions also have integration points to both BigInsights and Streams.

The Advanced Text Analytics Toolkit

IBM ships the Advanced Text Analytics Toolkit as part of its Big Data platform. This toolkit includes samples, built-in extractors that can be used in production right away, an integrated development environment, a text-extraction declarative language called Annotated Query Language (AQL), a text analytics engine and associated cost-based optimizer, and more. The Advanced Text Analytics Toolkit is shipped with BigInsights and Streams, and enables you to develop text analytics models on data at rest, and then transparently deploy them on data in motion. You'll find more details about this toolkit in Chapter 8.

InfoSphere Data Explorer

IBM InfoSphere Data Explorer (Data Explorer) is the new name for the product set that was acquired when IBM bought Vivisimo in early 2012. Data Explorer provides secure and highly accurate federated search and navigation of Big Data assets throughout the enterprise. It can be integrated with BigInsights and Streams under two scenarios: data from BigInsights or Streams can be accessed and shared with Data Explorer and its visualization interface, or Data Explorer can consume data directly from BigInsights. Data Explorer can also be integrated with InfoSphere Federation Server and become part of its federated index of structured data repositories. You'll find more details about this Big Data technology in Chapter 7.

InfoSphere Information Server

IBM InfoSphere Information Server (Information Server) is one of the components of the IBM Big Data platform. Information Server provides a gateway to the enterprise through its ability to integrate with multiple enterprise systems. BigInsights is integrated with Information Server, which can load data into BigInsights, or move data from BigInsights to other enterprise systems. Streams is also integrated with Information Server, enabling organizations to acquire real-time insights and load that data into a target system at specified intervals.

Information Server is deeply integrated with the IBM PureData System for Analytics; it has the "smarts" to push SQL-based transformations into its field programmable gate array (FPGA)-assisted processing architecture (see Chapter 4 for more information). Information Server is also integrated with the IBM PureData System for Operational Analytics. Many clients are attracted to the IBM PureData Systems because of the sheer simplicity of its approach. The Information Server integration work that's gone into the IBM Big Data platform ensures that clients realize the benefits of a trusted information infrastructure as quickly as possible. In Chapter 10, we provide an example that illustrates the Information Server design canvas, using drag-and-drop gestures to create a flow that involves a Hadoop data source.

InfoSphere Data Replication integrates with the analytics-based IBM Pure-Data Systems through its low-impact, low-latency database monitoring that provides real-time replicated data to either repository. IBM's Information Integration satisfies the batch and real-time integration requirements of Big Data projects, because it captures rich design and operational metadata to support data lineage and data governance analysis. This enables business and IT users to understand how enterprise data is being used within the Big Data platform. And because the Big Data platform can leverage Information Integration in this way, Big Data projects can leverage just about any data source that matters.

InfoSphere Master Data Management

IBM has demonstrated BigInsights working with the IBM InfoSphere Master Data Management (MDM) suite of products. This work was done by the IBM Research team in conjunction with a number of clients who wanted to draw on events and entity resolution from Big Data sources to populate master profiles in the enterprise. BigInsights is used to analyze raw data and to extract entities, such as customers and suppliers, for entity analysis algorithms. The data is then further refined (identifying relationships between entities, for example) before being loaded into the MDM system.

The MDM probabilistic matching engine has also been integrated with BigInsights, enabling matching on Big Data sets. Raw data is refined and structured, and then matched against other records. Many customers ask about the use of Big Data with MDM. The link is a natural one. Think of MDM as "bookending" the process; it can provide clean master data entities to a Big Data system for further analysis, and the insight gleaned from the Big Data system can be fed back to MDM for action.

InfoSphere Guardium

InfoSphere Guardium Database Security (Guardium) is IBM's leading data activity monitoring (DAM) solution, whose benefits were recently extended to Hadoop. Guardium integrates with BigInsights as well as open source Hadoop, to monitor Hadoop systems and to ensure the security of your enterprise's

Big Data. Of course, Guardium has been integrated with relational systems for a long time, enabling it to monitor and protect structured Big Data. As we've said before: if governance is needed for an important warehouse environment, it's needed in Big Data land as well. We cover some of the details of how Guardium can be used to secure Hadoop and more in Chapter 10.

InfoSphere Optim

The InfoSphere Optim (Optim) suite of products offers industry-leading data growth management, test data management, and security capabilities. It has long helped data warehouse systems control Big Data growth through archiving. It's also ensured efficient test data management by generating right-sized test data sets. Moreover, it has ensured the security of sensitive test data through masking, the practice of using realistic (but not real) data in test environments.

All of these capabilities can be extended to new Big Data technologies. For example, Optim works with Hadoop; it can mask data within a Hadoop system. Big Data systems have sensitive data too, sometimes more so than other systems. Masking ensures that sensitive Big Data isn't compromised. Optim can also take archived data from other target systems (operational applications, data warehouses, and so on) and store that data in Hadoop, where it can be analyzed.

Optim is also deeply integrated with the various flavors of the pattern-built IBM PureData Systems, offering an optimized connector to archive data and to generate right-sized test data deployments for these systems. We discuss many of these integration points in Chapter 10.

WebSphere Front Office

IBM WebSphere Front Office (Front Office) is made up of integrated components for receiving, consolidating, and distributing market data to front, middle, and back-office applications within financial organizations. This robust product offers flexibility and reliability in virtually any customer environment. Streams is integrated with Front Office, which provides Streams with real-time insights and data feeds.

WebSphere Decision Server: iLog Rules

Big Data processing often requires complex rules for data analysis, and rules deployment has rightfully received significant enterprise focus in the last few years. Your Big Data environments can leverage WebSphere Decision Server (iLog Rules) to build smarter application flows. Our research teams have shown how to use iLog Rules with Streams to analyze a data stream based on conditions and vectors that are passed by iLog Rules (we expect to say a lot more in this space after the book is published—our lawyers won't let us detail it just yet).

Rational

Job and application development lifecycle management is often overlooked in Big Data environments, which is a costly mistake. Eclipse is a pluggable integrated development environment (IDE) that was invented and donated to the open source community by IBM. Eclipse is used extensively in the open source Big Data technologies, as well as the IBM Big Data platform.

The IBM Big Data platform provides plug-ins for the development of Streams Processing Language (SPL) flows, SQL, Java MapReduce, Hive, Pig, Jaql, AQL-based text analytics, and more. These plug-ins are installable either from an open source Eclipse installation or from Eclipse-based value-add offerings such as Rational Application Developer (RAD). The IBM Big Data platform extends the Eclipse IDE with out-of-the-box plugs-ins for Streams and BigInsights that can leverage underlying Eclipse project artifacts. These artifacts, in turn, can be managed by extended Rational tool sets for version control (such as Rational ClearCase or Rational ClearQuest), collaboration (such as Rational JAZZ), or for enterprise-class lifecycle management.

Data Repository-Level Integration

If the Big Data platform is to work effectively, data must be shared among the various repositories within the platform. The many integration points are described in this chapter and throughout this book (see Chapter 5 and Chapter 6). Remember, the business process doesn't start and stop within the Big Data platform—data must be shared with other repositories and platforms.

Enterprise Platform Plug-ins

A platform must be an open system into which third-party products can be plugged. IBM's Big Data platform is exactly that. At the time of writing, IBM has well over 100 Big Data partners! Rather than attempt to detail specifics, in the remainder of this section, we describe some of the partnership categories of integration.

Development Tooling

IBM has several partners who have development tools for specific processes and components. There are a few partners with specialized development tools for BigInsights. IBM has partners, such as Datameer, which provides Big Data visualization capabilities, and Karmasphere, which provides data analysts with a development and visualization tool for data analysis on top of Hadoop.

Analytics

As described earlier in this chapter, there are several analytic applications and engines within IBM that are integrated with the Big Data platform. There are also analytic engines that can be integrated with the Big Data platform as components. Several open source analytic components have been integrated with the Big Data platform for client engagements: video analytics, audio analytics, and statistical analytics, among many others.

Visualization

Several IBM partners specialize in visualization of Big Data. Some focus on visualization of Hadoop-system data, others on visualization of structured data in warehouse appliances, and some others on visualization of data in motion. We've covered some examples in the previous section on analytic applications, such as Cognos Consumer Insights (CCI), which visualizes social media data for consumer sentiment and trend analysis. In fact, a famous food and beverage company ended up detecting negative sentiment about their recent environmentally friendly packaging change, which was met with a backlash of sentiment, manifesting itself in thousands of YouTube videos and

Facebook pages complaining about how noisy the new packaging was with over 50,000 followers! They used CCI to discover *what* was being said. CCI runs on top of BigInsights, which is used to discover and analyze *why* they are saying it.

Wrapping It Up

A Big Data platform and the applications that are built upon it aren't meant to be a silo. To be actionable, the insights that are derived from Big Data must be shared, and the platform that's most capable of integration is the one that delivers the most value. IBM's Big Data platform has numerous integration points with analytical applications, enterprise applications, enterprise repositories, and platform plug-ins, making it the most comprehensive Big Data platform in terms of functionality *and* integration capabilities.

Figure 11-1 illustrates the effectiveness of integration, and showcases what IBM has accomplished with its Big Data platform.

In this example, multiple sources of customer interaction data are being analyzed. Web site logs and social media feeds are being analyzed in

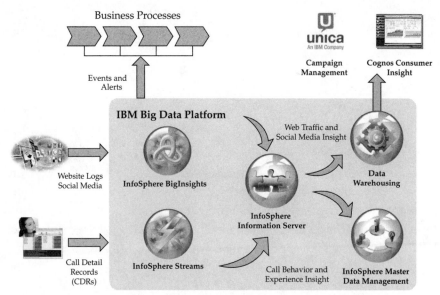

Figure 11-1 *The value of integration in a 360-degree multichannel customer sentiment analysis project*

BigInsights. Business users can visualize that analysis by using Cognos Consumer Insights. Information Server feeds any resulting insights to the data warehouse for further modeling and analysis. In parallel, real-time call detail reports (CDRs) are being analyzed by Streams, and Information Server feeds any resulting insights to the data warehouse. MDM technologies provide a single view of the customer as the starting point for analysis in BigInsights, Streams, and the data warehouse, and it can also be the place to operationalize any insights. Finally, campaign management systems, such as Unica, are integrated with data warehouse solutions to perform deep analysis (for example, a customer retention campaign offer) and to execute the campaigns.

Additional Resources for Big Data Skills

BigInsights Wiki
Rely on the wide range of IBM experts, programs, and services that are available to help you take your Big Data skills to the next level. Participate in our online community through the BigInsights wiki. Find white papers, videos, demos, downloads of BigInsights, links to social media sites, all the latest news, and more.

Visit **ibm.com/**developerworks/wiki/biginsights

Information Management Bookstore
Find the electronic version of this book and links to the most informative Information Management books on the market, along with valuable links and offers to save you money and enhance your skills.

Visit **ibm.com/**software/data/education/bookstore

BigData University
Learn about Hadoop and other technologies at your pace and at your place. BigData University offers helpful online courses with instructional videos and exercises to help you master new concepts. Course completion is marked with a final exam and a certificate.

Visit **bigdatauniversity.com**

IBM Data Management Magazine
IBM Data Management magazine delivers new kinds of interactive, highly dynamic content, such as webinars and videos. It also provides a platform on which to create a strong community of the world's top information management professionals and a broader range of voices from across the industry.

Visit **ibmdatamag.com**

IBM Certification and Mastery Exams
Find industry-leading professional certification and mastery exams. Mastery exams are available for BigInsights (M97) and InfoSphere Streams (N08).

Visit **ibm.com/**certify/mastery_tests

IBM Training Services

Find cost-effective and green online learning options, such as private onsite training, as well as traditional classroom, all taught by our experienced, world-class instructors.

- InfoSphere BigInsights Analytics for Business Analysts (DW640, 2 days)

- InfoSphere BigInsights Analytics for Programmers (DW651, 2 days)

- InfoSphere BigInsights Foundation (DW611, 2 days)

- Administration of InfoSphere Streams v2 (DW730, 2 days)

- Programming for InfoSphere Streams (DW722, 4 days)

For a summary of Big Data training services, visit
  ibm.com/software/data/education/bigdata.html
For information on the broad range of software services that we have to support Big Data, visit
  ibm.com/software/data/services/offerings.html

Information Management Subscription and Support

Access the award-winning IBM Support Portal to find technical support information for Information Management products, including downloads, notifications, technical documents, flashes, alerts, and more.

Visit **ibm.com**/support